ERICH MARIA
REMARQUE

ERICH MARIA REMARQUE

THE LAST ROMANTIC

HILTON TIMS

CARROLL & GRAF PUBLISHERS
New York

Carroll & Graf Publishers
An imprint of Avalon Publishing Group, Inc.
161 William Street
NY 10038-2607
www.carrollandgraf.com

First published in the UK by Constable,
an imprint of Constable & Robinson Ltd 2003

First Carroll & Graf edition 2003

Disclaimer
The publisher has made every effort to obtain permission for use
of copyrighted material from the relevant copyright holders.
The publisher apologises in advance for any errors or omissions made.
Queries regarding the use of material should be addressed to the author,
c/o the publishers.

ISBN 0-7867-1155-8

Printed and bound in the EU

For my granddaughter Eleanor Margaret
(born September 2002)
whose arrival was the perfect celebration
for finishing this book

The last of the romantics. Besides the great writer that he was, he had a capacity few men have. The capacity to understand the emotions of all living creatures.

Marlene Dietrich

He's the last of the old romantic school, and if the school were opened again, he'd be the first.

Paulette Goddard Remarque

CONTENTS

CONTENTS

Illustrations

Erich Maria Remarque in German army uniform
Photo: Fales Library, New York University

Die Traumbude, 1915
Photo: Fales Library, New York University

Film still from All Quiet on the Western Front

Dolores Del Rio

Lupe Velez

Maureen O' Sullivan

Luise Rainer

Jutta Ilse Zambona
Photo: Fales Library, New York University

Paulette Goddard

Marlene Dietrich

Greta Garbo

Erich Maria Remarque, portrait, 1935
Photo: AKG London

Nazi Book Burning in Berlin
Photo: AKG London

Erich Maria Remarque, portrait, 1940
Photo: AKG London

Film still from A Time to Love and a Time to Die
Courtesy of the Cinema Bookshop, London

Erich Maria Remarque – sitting on a chair
Courtesy of the Cinema Bookshop, London

Acknowledgements

The initial impulse to write the first comprehensive British biography of Erich Maria Remarque nearly foundered when I began to realize the challenges it would entail. It was a chance encounter with Terry Charman, a near neighbour but, more important, the Research and Information Officer at the Imperial War Museum in London and an expert on the First World War, who set me on course. His enthusiasm and resourcefulness in guiding me to the necessary sources proved an invaluable spur to the project. I am greatly indebted to him.

Luise Rainer responded with no less enthusiasm to my enquiries about her memories of Remarque. Listening to her reminiscences not only of Remarque but equally of Hollywood in its golden years proved to be one of the most fascinating phases of my research. A remarkable and gracious lady, she went to considerable trouble to provide me with mementoes as well as memories of their friendship, including the poem published in the Appendix for the first time with her kind permission. My thanks go to Iris Fräulin Sampson for making an idiomatic translation of the verses.

Dr Heinz Nawratil, a lawyer in Bavaria and a valued friend for nearly fifty years, has been supportive throughout the gestation of this book, particularly in locating German source material and obtaining for me, and interpreting legal aspects of, the transcripts of the Nazi trial of Elfriede Remark Scholz. My daughter Anna Tims Dowler whose German is far superior to my own nobly translated the daunting pages of indictments, witness statements, counsel submissions and personal letters.

My thanks to Margaret Mitchell of Kingston upon Thames Central Library whose help in tracking down source books has been invaluable, the staff of the Goethe Institut in London, the staff of the newspaper library at Colindale, London, the staff of the Imperial War Museum Library and Reading Room, Ethelda Potts and Ellen Woodward Potts who located material for me in the United States, John Prescott, Patricia Roc Reif and Oliver Tims.

I cannot express my gratitude warmly enough to my agent Carolyn Whitaker and to Carol O'Brien, my editor at Constable & Robinson, for their patience, understanding and unfailing support during a difficult period while writing the book, and above all to my wife June who endured the stresses and temperaments of writing with unstinting support and encouragement.

H.T.

Preface

As a protest against the literary betrayal of the soldiers of the Great War and on behalf of the education of our people in the spirit of truth, I consign to the flames the writings of Erich Maria Remarque.[1]

On the night of 10 May 1933, four months after the National Socialists had come to power in Germany, the students of Berlin ritually hurled the books of 160 authors on to a flaming pyre of petrol-soaked logs in the Opernplatz.

Against a backcloth of leaping shadows on the walls of their university, they howled and pranced, identifying and condemning each writer with an incantation of hate. Around 20,000 books were incinerated that night.

Newspaper photographs and reports of the Nazi book-burning shocked the civilized world. It was the first widely disseminated portent of the horrors to come, an act of barbarism that reflected in its flames an image of pagan-like savagery at the heart of one of the most cultured societies on earth.

Many of the proscribed names were internationally renowned, by no means all of them Jewish: the brothers Thomas and Heinrich Mann, Lion Feuchtwanger, the unrelated Arnold Zweig and Stefan Zweig, Albert Einstein, Walther Rathenau.

Erich Maria Remarque was arguably, at that moment, the most famous of them all. His novel of the First World War *All Quiet on the Western Front,* published four years earlier, had become a worldwide literary sensation, setting unprecedented best-selling standards for twentieth-century publishing. It remains the most famous anti-war novel of all time.

The new Nazi oligarchy despised it, as did a vociferous minority of Prussian military traditionalists. The war weariness it articulated, the futility and disillusionment of the conflict on the western front, were anathema to their rigid code of honour and heroism under arms. But to a younger generation of conscripts, barely out of their teens, who had endured and survived the carnage of the trenches, it spoke of their sacrifice and the nihilism of so much of their shell-shocked post-war experience.

Erich Maria Remarque was neither a Jew nor a Communist, the twin butts of Nazi hatred. He had never been known to voice an opinion for or against the Party. Indeed, physically, genetically and in the pride he took in his German heritage, he was the quintessential Aryan so prized by the Nazis. His novel and its ground-breaking success were enough to condemn him.

On that night of the burning books he was beyond their reach, safe in the luxurious home his sudden wealth had bought him in Switzerland eighteen months before. A few weeks earlier, on one of his frequent return visits to Berlin, he had been warned that the Nazis had plans for him. He had driven through the night to the border. From that moment he was a hounded man. It would be twenty years before he returned to his beloved Germany, never again in his lifetime to be fully accepted by his countrymen.

For the rest of his life he would keep a suitcase, ready packed, to hand. As he explained in his old age: 'It's a case that's always kept ready if sometime I should suddenly have to take off.'[2]

1

Schooldays in Osnabrück

Osnabrück, an ancient Hanseatic city in Lower Saxony founded by Charlemagne, was as propitious a birthplace as any for an author and self-proclaimed pacifist whose most celebrated book would become a testament to the scourge of war. At the time of his birth its burghers were celebrating the 250th anniversary of the signing in the city's Rathaus of the Peace of Westphalia, the treaty which ended the Thirty Years' War in 1648.

Erich Paul Remark was born in the Provincial Midwifery and Delivery Institution on Knollstrasse on 22 June 1898. His distant forebears had been French, the family name Remarque until his grandfather had 'Germanized' its spelling early in the nineteenth-century. There is no record of when or why the French Remarques had crossed the border from Alsace into Germany but they had been established in the western region of the country for at least a century before Erich's birth.

His great-great-great-grandfather with the uncompromisingly French name of Toussaint Remarque is recorded as living in Aachen – capital of Charlemagne's empire and his final resting place, and a Belgian and later French possession, known as Aix-la-Chapelle. Here too the two succeeding generations of Remarque scions were born, first another Toussaint who married the equally Francophone Catherine Courteaux, then Erich's great-grandfather, the first to be tentatively 'Germanized' with the name Johannes Adam, though still Remarque, in 1789, the year of the French Revolution.

The Remarques were a humble, staunchly Catholic family, reconciled to their modest circumstances until Erich broke the mould. His father Peter Franz Remark, born at Kaiserswerth am Rhein near Dusseldorf in 1867, had settled, newly wed, with his bride Anna Maria in Osnabrück three years before Erich's birth, in 1895. Exotic trails of legend, never confirmed, veiled his early working life. Some said he had been a cabin-boy who had sailed the world and been shipwrecked off the coast of Samoa and had served with German colonial troops in Africa before being pensioned off.[1]

If true, these years must have encapsulated a hyperactive period of employment and incident. He was still only twenty-eight years old when he arrived in Osnabrück. By the time Erich was born he had lapsed back into the conventional artisan pattern of his antecedents, employed prosaically as a poorly paid bookbinder for Prelle, a firm of printers.

The earlier swashbuckling image seems to have been at odds with surviving descriptions of Peter Remark by his contemporaries. A man of medium height, thin, with a luxuriant moustache, he was taciturn to a degree of gruffness. His workmates found him 'unfriendly' and his absorbing interest in the occult and 'magical things' unsettling.

Erich the celebrity writer would later depict his childhood as arid, bereft of stimulus and unfulfilling. The publisher and diplomat Count Harry Kessler, recounting a conversation with him soon after the publication of *All Quiet on the Western Front*, noted in his diary: 'As a boy from a lower middle-class family in Osnabrück, he was very unhappy at the lack of an intellectual mentor . . . it always seemed to him extraordinary that he should exist at all. He spent a disconsolate youth interspersed with thoughts of suicide.'[2]

Certainly, he could not look to his father for encouragement. Peter Remark, stern, insular and unimaginative, showed little interest in establishing a rapport with his son. Even allowing for the difficulties – indeed, the dangers – of communicating during the Third Reich, there was no contact between them for almost two decades after Erich's final flight from Berlin, though he helped his father financially and bought him a house in later years. After Peter Remark's death in 1954 Erich would be stricken with remorse at not having been a more sympathetic and attentive son.

Anna Maria Remark contributed good looks to the family genes but her health had been far from robust since childhood and was further undermined by childbearing and the tragedy of losing her first-born. A son born in the early months of their marriage died at the age of six in 1901 when Erich was three years old. His mother's mourning rooted a vague feeling of 'second best' in the boy's sensibilities, not wholly expiated by the compensation of two sisters, Erna born in 1900 and, completing the family unit in 1903, Elfriede whose fate under the Nazis would be a searing injustice on Erich's conscience in later years.

The shadow of solitariness over his boyhood years, disconsolate as they may have seemed in later memory, framed the identity he would develop as a writer. Left to his own devices, he had recourse to little other imperatives than his imagination. Like most families of that time, the Remarks had a piano and Erich discovered a love and talent for music. He gave it serious study, in time becoming accomplished enough to consider taking it up professionally, and at least earning money as a pianist and organist in periods of financial hardship. 'I wanted a musical career at one time,' he told an early interviewer in 1929, 'but a wound in the hand during the war put an end to that hope.'[3]

Compounding any nascent sense of rootlessness, a recurring theme through his life and novels, was the Remark household's chronic impermanence. Financial constraints were constantly forcing the family to move home, frequently between neighbouring houses in the same Osnabrück street. In Erich's first four years they lived at no fewer than five different addresses in Jahnstrasse, twice at intervals in the same apartment. When he left home for the first time as an army conscript in 1916 the Remarks had occupied eleven different dwellings within a small central area of the city.

One likely explanation for such an intensive migratory existence was that new houses and apartments were cheaper to rent while the wall plaster was still damp and settling. As soon as they had been 'lived in' the tenants would move on to avoid increased charges.

Erich would later recall the Jahnstrasse addresses with nostalgia. The street backed on to Am Pappelgraben – ditch, or trench, of poplars – and this open space with its vegetation and wildlife became as much a 'secret garden' as a playground for him – 'a child's paradise' his closest Osnabrück friend Hanns-Gerd Rabe recalled.

In *All Quiet on the Western Front* the eighteen-year-old soldier narrator Paul Bäumer, a thinly disguised Erich, on lonely sentry duty, consoles himself with a wistful memory:

> Between the meadows behind our town there stands a line of old poplars by a stream. They were visible from a great distance, and although they grew on one bank only, we called them the poplar avenue. Even as children we had a great love for them, they drew us vaguely thither, we played truant the whole day by them and listened to their rustling. We sat beneath them on the bank of the stream and let our feet hang in the bright, swift waters. The pure fragrance of the water and the melody of the wind in the poplars held our fancies. We loved them dearly, and the image of those days still makes my heart pause in its beating.

Here he discovered his interest in butterflies and small fish. At home he rigged up an aquarium – there would always be one in his subsequent homes – and accumulated a prized collection of butterflies. He also collected stamps and stones and developed an interest in painting, prefiguring a lifelong appreciation of art.

These were solitary occupations, driven by the restrictive glumness of the atmosphere in the Remark home but, virtually as a rebellion against it, nurturing inchoate powers of imagination that the young Erich was scarcely conscious of himself. 'I found little enough sympathy for my dreams, either at home or at school,' he would say.[4]

Erich was to find a degree of release from the intellectual inhibitions of his home life at school. The scholastic atmosphere was hardly less austere than that of the Remark household but here at least there were learning disciplines and motivation to channel his interests. He was a bright boy. A later classmate, Josef Witt, recalled: 'Remarque found learning easy. He had a very good power of comprehension and studied little at home.'[5]

Attending just two schools in his formative years was a welcome constant and a steadying Catholic influence in comparison with the domestic upheaval of incessantly changing addresses. In 1904, when he was six, he was enrolled at the Domschule (cathedral school). Four years later he moved to the Johannisschule. The environments of the cathedral and the Church of St Johannis, both monumental early Gothic buildings dating from the thirteenth century, no doubt stimulated the imaginative corners of Erich's nature. Their Catholic ambience did not. Despite his parents' efforts, he would successfully resist the rigours of Catholicism. Any incipient spirit of religion he may have acquired during his schooldays was to be tested and found wanting by his experiences on the western front, evolving instead into a brand of humanism he worked out for himself. At the Johannisschule, however, he joined the church choir, a decision that consolidated his lifelong love of music.

His closest school friend of this period Kristen Kranzbühler, immortalized as Kemmerich in *All Quiet on the Western Front*, would remember him as 'always the best in class'. Far from being the quiet, submissive dreamer his family knew at home, he could be opinionated, questioning, even argumentative in the classroom. Whether he realized it or not, Erich was striving to hone his intellect.

By the time he moved on from the Jobannisschule he had developed a passion for literature. At the age of fourteen he was reading Dostoevsky, Goethe, Jack London and Thomas Mann. He particularly admired Herman Hesse, newly fashionable, whose first successful novel *Peter Camenzind* must have struck a plangent chord with him. It dealt with the inner conflicts of an artist-dreamer struggling for a deeper understanding of the forces within himself stifled by the conventions of the times. Before long Erich would be emulating the protagonist's ideals himself in a club of like-minded young people.

'We were really romantic in those days,' he would recall, adding wryly, 'One was intended for the post office, the school house or the chemist's shop.'[6]

Erich's destiny was to be the school-house, determined by his mother's ambitions for him. In his 1956 novel *The Black Obelisk* (*Der schwarze Obelisk*), as near to a *roman à clef* of his post-First World War years as any he would write, the autobiographical narrator comments: 'I finally became a school master as my sick mother had wished and as I had promised her before she died.'

At the age of fourteen in 1912 he entered the Catholic *Präparande*, a preparatory school for student-teachers behind the Marienkirche in the Altmarkt, the market square in the heart of the old city, where he remained for three years. According to Josef Witt, Erich's classroom manner was lively, sometimes rebellious, often controversial. He enjoyed challenging and arguing with the school's head, Rektor Kortahus, who went by the nickname *'Schlächter'* (Butcher), and he exacted sly revenge on another teacher in *All Quiet on the Western Front* by reincarnating him as Kantorek, the sanctimonious little master whose paeans to the glories of war 'preached us into enlisting'. Meeting him again at the front, Bäumer/Remark's reaction to his schooldays' tormentor is contemptuous:

> Nothing could look more ludicrous than his forage-cap and his uniform. And this is the object before whom we used to stand in anguish as he sat up there enthroned at his desk, spearing us with his pencil for our mistakes in those irregular French verbs with which afterwards we made so little headway in France . . . an impossible soldier, I cannot reconcile this with the menacing figure at the school master's desk. I wonder what I, the old soldier, would do if this skinful of woe ever dared to say to me again: 'Bäumer, give the imperfect of "aller"'.

At the *Präparande* Erich, too, acquired a nickname, *'Schmieren'* (Smudge), with which he would later sometimes sign letters to old school mates from the front. He worked diligently if unexceptionably,

6

in easy familiarity with his fellow students and cultivating, they noted, a touch of adolescent vanity in appearance and mannerism. He was always well turned out, already aware of the good impression smart clothes and a few judicious accessories could make, especially on the opposite sex. 'I can never imagine a life without women,' he said half a century later.[7] With his blond hair, eyes that were a 'sea-clear blue' beneath fair brows and innately romantic approach, he would never need to.

There was little enough spare money in the Remark household for frivolous indulgences so, resourcefully, he began at this time to earn his own by giving piano lessons. He had several pupils, including girls who, according to a classmate, Ernst Däuber, 'often left the room blushing. He gave cheerful lessons and was a lively, happy chap.'

The money he earned was spent on books. He had a magpie impulse to collect them. They were his pride and pleasure. In *All Quiet on the Western Front* Bäumer/Remark, on home leave, contemplates the collection in his room:

> The books I bought gradually with the money I earned by coaching. Many of them are second-hand, all the classics for example, one volume in blue cloth boards cost one mark twenty pfennig. I did not trust the editors of selections to choose all the best. So I purchased only 'collected works'. I read most of them with laudable zeal, but few of them really appealed to me. I preferred the other books, the modernists, which were of course much dearer. A few I came by not quite honestly, I borrowed and did not return them because I did not want to part with them.

In August 1914, less than two months after Erich's sixteenth birthday, Europe went to war. Germany, no less than Britain and France, was swept along on a surge of patriotic fervour.

'At that time I was brimming over with enthusiasm and animated, as all young Germans were, by a great feeling of patriotism,' he told an interviewer in 1930, 'We were fighting for the salvation of the world and the salvation of civilization. But afterwards . . . afterwards! The war was too terrible and too long for me not to learn to think otherwise. After it was all over I saw all its hideousness.'[8]

Flights of emotional patriotism did not, however, inspire him to enlist immediately, as three of his class compatriots did. 'How can anyone enlist voluntarily?' he wondered.

Instead he joined the Osnabrück Youth Corps, a militaristic cadet movement which practised war games. The mood of the moment may have spurred him but it was no more voluntary an impulse than the one he decried; all German youths at this time were required to enrol in one of several such organizations.

All the same he seemed to enjoy the activities membership involved – the parade-ground drills, the make-believe battleground tactics that served as a surrogate for patriotic action. And if he derived nothing more positive from the experience, at least it gave him a first glimmer of his future as a writer.

He had been writing extra-curricular essays and verses for some time, driven by his passion for literature which by now had expanded to the more rarefied purlieus of Schopenhauer, Nietzsche and Stendhal. Rainer Maria Rilke was a particular favourite, the dream-like lyricism of the poet's interpretation of human emotions a potent mirror to Erich's own nature. He would quote Rilke throughout his life.

The sixteen-year-old Erich seemed to be recognizing and defining the seam of romanticism so firmly embedded in his character. Count Harry Kessler was impressed to learn that at that age he had 'swotted his way . . . though without much appreciation' through the *Critique of Pure Reason* by the eighteenth-century German philosopher Immanuel Kant, whose works had been influential in identifying the role of art in ideal-istic thought and left their mark on the writings of such Romantic poets and dramatists as Friedrich Schiller.

An essay Erich wrote for the Youth Corps' magazine was his first appearance in print and brought him the first payment he would receive for writing. It won him a small cash prize.

In 1915 the die was cast for the career his mother so ardently desired for him. He graduated from the *Präparande* to the *Lehrerseminar*, a training college for elementary school teachers. At the same time he became involved with a small group of like-minded friends who had formed an aesthetic cell to celebrate and discuss the principles and forms of the *Jugendstil* (art nouveau) movement. Idealistically, they were seeking to formulate structures for bettering a chaotic world through art and nature. Notwithstanding the lack of enthusiasm with which he had ploughed through Kant's heavy-weather philosophies, the exercise would enable Erich to hold his own amid the crossfire of opinion.

They called themselves the *Traumbude* (den of dreams) and the long evenings of readings, argument, polemic and analytical thought in the *Traumbude* itself – the attic rooms in Liebigstrasse of their leader Fritz Hörstemeier – would have a profound influence on Erich's philosophical and creative development, not least as the incubus for his first apprentice novel.

So would Hörstemeier himself. He became, for the impressionable young student eager for aesthetic challenge, a mentor of iconic significance, a father-figure who would show him the encouragement, the vitalizing motivation and respect for his qualities that his own father could not. Hörstemeier was thirty-three, twice Erich's age, when they first met. Tall, thin as a garret poet, with an ascetically high forehead, an unruly mass of dark hair and a straggling beard, he was a prototype bohemian, a man of charm and firm, quiet principles who eked out a living by painting. His love of nature and gentle humanism – he was a lapsed Catholic – accorded powerfully with Erich's own evolving credo.

There were six in the group; apart from Erich and Hörstemeier, another struggling artist Friedrich Vordemberge, Rudolf Kottman, Paula Spenker and Erika Haase with whom Erich fell in unrequited puppy love, the first of countless women who would snare his passing fancy. Virtually every evening they would adjourn to Hörstemeier's *Traumbude* to shape their illusionary world over wine and cigarettes. These were exultant days for Erich, days to be remembered with a wistful nostalgia in the long months of disillusion after his ordered world shattered.

On 26 November 1916 Erich Paul Remark was conscripted into the army.

2

Action on the Western Front

Erich was an unwilling recruit, one of the fast-growing corpus of conscription-age German teenagers disenchanted by the duration of the war and the horror stories filtering back from the front line. For Erich's intake it was a circumstance and attitude realistically summarized by Carl Zuckmayer, two years older than Erich and later to become one of Germany's leading dramatists. He recalled in his memoirs:

> It is remarkable how swiftly in such times a difference between generations develops and how deep a gulf between groups only a year or two apart in age. Everything that I am relating here applies to that first contingent who became soldiers and went to the front in 1914. It is no longer applicable to those who were a year and a half or two years younger, so that at the outbreak of war they were below military age, exposed to the jingoism of their schoolmasters and the freezing of the battlefronts, the degeneration of the initial advance into a war of attrition, into a universal, systematic mass slaughter.
>
> Erich Maria Remarque and his age group belonged to that generation. The heroic gesture of the volunteers was barred to them; they had to sweat out their normal time in school and then be unwillingly drafted, drilled and harassed, and they went into the field without illusions, for they had some inkling of the horrors that awaited them there.[1]

Ernst Jünger, another future literary figure, whose blood-and-guts espousal of militarism and the glory of war was the antithesis of Remarque's perspective, and who subsequently won favour with the Nazi regime, would write:

> I had set out to the war gaily enough, thinking we were to hold a festival on which all the pride of youth was lavished, and I had thought little, once I was in the thick of it, about the ideal I had to stand for. Now I looked back: four years of development in the midst of a generation predestined to death, spent in caves, smoke-filled trenches and shell-illumined wastes.[2]

Erich and several of his classmates from the *Lehrerseminar* went to war at a time of concentrated, almost panicked effort by the German high command to break the deadlock on the western front. Between June and December 1916 thirty-four new army divisions were frantically raised in Germany. On the plains of Flanders the armies confronted each other in a stalemate of carnage.

He reported to the Caprivi Barracks in Osnabrück, named after Bismarck's successor as imperial chancellor who had re-organized and enlarged the Kaiser's army to its eve-of-war strength, and was posted to Lüneburg Heath, some 200 kilometres to the north-east, for basic training. At this stage of the war, despite the urgent need for front-line replacements, the induction period for enlisted men had been extended to between four and five months in order to harden them in the newly evolving techniques and rigours of trench warfare.

The comparative stability of this period and the relative ease of travel back home were significant factors for Erich in those first months of service. His mother, who had been in frail health since girlhood, was critically ill with cancer and had been given only a few months to live. Erich was frequently granted compassionate leave to visit her.

The family, too, had finally stabilized. Their peripatetic odyssey between homes had brought them in 1917 to what would become a permanent address in Hakenstrasse, a second-floor apartment in a property owned by Prelle, Peter Remark's employers, in the same street as the printing works. It was to be Erich's home until he left Osnabrück in 1922, and his father's until 1935.

On 12 June 1917 his troop set out for France. It was initially attached to a company of the Guards Reserve Division for a toughening-up course of 'front line polish' training on the banks of the Canal de la Sensée at the village of Hem-Lenglet near Cambrai. Soon he was moved north into Belgium to be quartered near Houthulst Forest, twenty-five kilometres north-west of Ypres.

Erich's duties involved trench maintenance, constructing dug-outs and laying barbed wire in rear positions, working day and night: hard manual and potentially dangerous labour for which he had neither experience nor aptitude, but he pitched in cheerfully enough. Georg Middendorf, a school friend serving alongside him, recalled: 'He never lost his calm. We laid a lot of barbed wire together'.

Though constantly under long-range artillery fire, Erich had only a brief experience of the horrors of battle and hand-to-hand combat he described so harrowingly in his novel. Fate, in fact, ensured he narrowly missed out on them. After the armistice, back in Osnabrück, he was tempted to imply a more heroic record at the front than his service warranted, but the tales he spun had little more substance than youthful braggadocio, and even that, such as it was, inhibited – and rebutted – by the evidence of friends who had served alongside him with whom any boastfulness on his part cut no ice.

As well as Middendorf, there were others from his student days – some destined to become characters in *All Quiet on the Western Front* – Wilhelm Katchinsky, Seppel Oelfke, and Theo Troske who, as we shall see, had a briefly dramatic and poignant role in Erich's real-life action at the front – as Kat, in the novel of that name.

It was one of the subtle strengths of German military morale that territorial bonds were recognized and consciously encouraged – a cement of team spirit and committed loyalty among troops from a shared locality. Enlisted men from a given city or country district invariably served as an integrated unit, a practice which, though not necessarily the prime purpose, had the bonus of easing the transition from civilian life to the hardships of military routine. Even more intensely than the British army's corresponding system of county or Highland regiments, it engendered a sense of common purpose and group bonding.

It was a proven practice in German military organization that even extended into the Second World War. The American war historian Stephen E. Ambrose in his book *Citizen Soldiers* observes: 'One reason [for the intensity of comradeship among German troops] is that generally German squads were made up of men from the same town or region, so the men had known each other as children,' and he quotes a Wehrmacht corporal:

> The worst thing that could happen to a soldier was to be thrown into some group in which he knew no one. In our unit we would never abandon each other. We had fought in Russia together. We were comrades and always came to the rescue. We protected our comrades so they could go home to their wives, children and parents. That was our motivation.[3]

It is a binding relationship that Remarque reflects movingly throughout *All Quiet on the Western Front*.

The area of Houthulst Forest was a strategic defensive point in the Ypres salient and a prime objective for an advancing army. One of history's great British commanders, John Churchill, 1st Duke of Marlborough, who had led his army to victory in the battles of Ramillies and Oudenaarde in the Belgian campaign during the eighteenth-century War of the Spanish Succession, had avowed: 'He who holds Houthulst commands Flanders'.

The Germans had held the forest since the early months of the war and turned it into an impregnable fortress, honeycombed with trenches and studded with pill-boxes and machine-gun nests. Even today the public is barred from entering the forest's depths because of its First World War legacy. It is the base and collection point for the permanent bomb disposal unit responsible for disarming the explosives from that war which still surface during ploughing, road building and other excavation work in the old battlefields of Flanders. Shells and bombs, still primed, are taken into the depths of the forest to be destroyed by controlled explosion. Occasionally they still claim victims among the Sappers dealing with them.[4]

Erich's squad was stationed in open country on the north-eastern side of the forest between Houthulst village and the hamlet of Handzame. On the same front, further down the German lines at Fromelles, south of Ypres, another soldier, the antithesis of Erich in his militarist zeal and fanaticism for the war, was serving as a dispatch runner with the First Bavarian Infantry Regiment. His rank was corporal, his name Adolf Hitler.[5]

Throughout the summer weeks the opposing armies had been dead-locked, facing each other across flat, desolate vistas moonscaped by the murderous artillery barrages from both sides. The distant thrump of the guns was an endless threnody of doom in the background of day-to-day life. It was a checkmate that couldn't last.

By mid June when Erich arrived at Houthulst German intelligence was anticipating a major allied offensive. Preparations intensified. As we have seen, Erich and his comrades were out in the field, day and night, strengthening the defences. There were times of relaxation, nevertheless, and it may have been in one of them that the nineteen-year-old Erich had his first sexual experience.

He was scrupulously careful not to identify specific locations when he was writing *All Quiet on the Western Front*, but thirty years later, in *The Black Obelisk*, he was less inhibited. Referring to his front-line experience, the autobiographical narrator Ludwig Bodmer austerely comments: 'So it came about that we marched into the field as virgins and seventeen of us fell without ever knowing what a woman is. Willy and I lost our virginity half a year later in an estaminet in Houthulst in Flanders.'

The reference chimes with an interlude in *All Quiet on the Western Front* in which Paul Bäumer and some of his mates flirt with three French girls who watch them swimming naked in a river and agree to meet them that evening. The house they go to, though not described as such, could be construed as a bordello, and sexual activity is implied.

If Erich did indeed lose his virginity in Houthulst, it was an occasion that set in train a conflict, for his libido would alternately visit both pleasure and torment on him throughout his life . . . a conflict of need and shame between romantic love and anonymous whoring. 'I can never imagine a life without women. I've tried to reproduce encounters in my books. Changed, naturally.' He was in his sixties when he shared that confidence with an interviewer.[6]

At this time, too, a time of physical and psychological stress, an addiction to alcohol that would bedevil the rest of his life and ultimately ruin his health probably began. Bodmer/Remarque, again in *The Black Obelisk:* 'I make coffee . . . and pour a little kirsch into it. That's something I learned in France and despite the inflation I always manage to have schnapps.'

In mid July, barely a month after Erich's arrival at Houthulst, the allied guns began their softening-up bombardment for the great battle, to be known in history as Third Ypres or Passchendaele. The impact was hellish. A dispatch from a *Times'* correspondent vividly caught the grandeur and horror of it:

> A thousand guns broke on the stillness all at once, and, above all the deafening roar of gunfire and bursting shells, the air shrieked and whistled as it was torn by the projectiles overhead. As far as the eye could see to right and left the whole earth flickered and twink-led with the firefly flashes of our guns. The fumes of bursting shells rose almost like a solid bank in which the stab of bursting shrapnel grew redder as the cloud thickened, and here and there dazzling white flares and signal lights rose out of the murk to hang in incandescent points against the sky above. Far out to the left rose fountains of golden rain.
>
> And then began the rain. Such rain! Slowly at first, then in sheets, and then in a tropical downpour, slashing and pitiless, through which the twin thunders of gun and sky went on and lightning flashes and shell bursts flickered strangely and inextricably through the veil of rain.[7]

The battle front extended some thirty kilometres with Houthulst six kilometres behind the German's front line on its northernmost flank where French infantry was supported by British artillery to the rear.

With the allied bombardment intensifying during the second half of July, troops on both sides knew the great offensive was imminent. *The Times* reported:

> The cannonade at present raging in Flanders has, during the last forty-eight hours, attained an unprecedented violence . . . Veritable masses of artillery, such as never before have been gathered together, are crashing out, one against the other, in titanic combat which yesterday evening seemed to have reached its greatest intensity.

Erich's detail did not escape the horror of it. On one of those days in the last week of the month, Theo Troske (in his novel Kat) was hit in the leg by shrapnel. Erich, slightly built but strong, lifted him on to his shoulders and carried him under a hail of shellfire to the dressing-station, an act of heroism later vouched for by his Osnabrück comrades.

> The wound begins to bleed fast. Kat cannot be left by himself while I try to find a stretcher. Anyway, I don't know of a stretcher-bearer's post in the neighbourhood. Kat is not very heavy; so I take him up on my back and start off to the dressing-station with him.
>
> Twice we rest. He suffers acutely on the way. We do not speak much. I have opened the collar of my tunic and breathe heavily, I sweat and my face is swollen with the strain of carrying. All the same I urge him to let us go on, for the place is dangerous.[8]

By the time they reach the dressing-station Kat has died, as Troske was to die from a head wound Erich had failed to notice. The knowledge that his friend had died across his shoulders even as they were in sight of medical aid left a wounding scar on his sensibilities.

Zero hour for the allied assault was 0350 hours on 31 July 1917. The weather had broken the day before. Thunderstorms heralded the coming Armageddon. Rain fell continuously. The moment was recorded by *The Times* correspondent:

> There was just a visible paling of the sky in the east, and against it the bombardment was a weird and terrible spectacle . . . As usual there had been a comparative lull before the moment arrived. Then, on the instant, the air and earth shook and the whole horizon blazed as all our literally thousands of guns broke out at once.[9]

In the first hours of that awesome barrage Erich, according to Hanns–Gerd Rabe, his Osnabrück friend and chronicler of his war experiences, had again gone to the aid of a wounded comrade and carried him to comparative safety. His own nemesis soon followed. Shrapnel from a British shell felled him.

He was hit in five places, in the neck, left leg and right arm. His wounds were serious enough to keep him *hors de combat* and in hospital for the next fifteen months, though like many of the wounded he exploited the system to be classified as a convalescent and so avoid being returned to the front for as long as possible. He was taken first to a nearby field hospital at Tourout, then transferred home to Germany, spending the rest of the war in St Vincenz Hospital at Duisburg.

His active service was over.

3

The Peacock and the German Shepherd

The process of re-shaping Erich Paul Remark into Erich Maria Remarque began in hospital. As he recovered he bided his time, savouring the first prolonged respite he had had from the depredations of active army life. Clean clothing . . . fresh bed linen . . . adequate food . . . nurses to chat up . . . time to himself. He was enjoying an environment that was evidently a contradiction of the harsh conditions of the military hospital he was to depict in *All Quiet on the Western Front*.

'It will take some time with my wounds, they do not heal so well,' he wrote to Middendorf. 'It doesn't matter. I am not sorry.'[1]

But he had other, emotional wounds to contend with. Just over a month after his arrival at Duisburg his mother died at the age of forty-two after a long struggle against cancer. Though clearly affected by her death, Erich's feelings towards her remained ambiguous. In guarded statements later, he would indicate a resentment that neither parent encouraged or sympathized with his childhood interests and dreams but he made scant public reference to filial or emotional bonds with either of them. Instead he left clues in his books.

In *All Quiet on the Western Front* the soldier on leave muses:

Ah! Mother, Mother! You still think I am a child – why can I not put my head in your lap and weep? Why have I always to be strong and self-controlled? I would like to weep and be comforted too, indeed I am little more than a child; in the wardrobe still hang short, boy's trousers — it is such a little time ago. Why is it over? . . . Ah, Mother, Mother! Why do I not take you in my arms and die with you? What poor wretches we are!

And in *The Black Obelisk*, debating the ethos of mortality with the priest Bodendiek:

'I knew a woman who had cancer for ten years, who survived six frightful operations, who was never without pain, and who finally doubted God . . . She gave up going to mass, to confession, and to communion, and according to the Church she died in a state of mortal sin. According to those same rules she is now burning in the hell which the God of love created. Is that justice?'

Bodendiek looks for a while into his wine. 'Was it your mother?' he asks then.

I stare at him. 'What has that to do with it?'

'It was your mother, wasn't it?'

I swallow. 'Suppose it was my mother — '

Erich was granted extended leave to attend her funeral on 26 September 1917. Judging from letters he wrote at the time, behind the obligatory pall of mourning he enjoyed being back in Osnabrück, meeting old friends in cafés and bars, catching up on news of front-line comrades.

Six months later he suffered another bereavement, in its way probably more grievous than the death of his mother. News reached him in March 1918 that his idol Fritz Hörstemeier had died at the age of thirty-six; Fritz of the *Traumbude*, the father-figure who, more than any other person, had recognized and nurtured Erich's unformed intellectual aspirations and enthusiasms. Again he was given leave to attend a funeral, this time travelling to Bremen where he played the organ for the service.

Underlying the immediate grief of these losses was the ongoing inner conflict of coming to terms with the psychological scars inflicted by the horrors of the battlefields. Haunted by the prospect of returning to the front, he connived to prolong his stay in the Duisburg hospital, even after his wounds had healed. He made himself useful in the administration office where his literacy gave him an edge over other clerks. He played the piano at hospital concerts, though the wound to his right wrist now forced him to abandon any thought of becoming a professional pianist, and he gave lessons to the children of staff members. His outwardly high humour and good looks made him popular. He flirted with the nurses and reportedly formed a relationship with the daughter of one of the hospital's managers.

Most significant, during this period of relative calm and relaxation his creative instincts crystallized. He began to write. He tried his hand at composing, setting to music verses by a fellow patient, the poet Ludwig Bate. He painted. Moved and inspired by Hörstemeier's death, he also started a novel. He called it *Die Traumbude*.

Its sub-title *Ein Künstlerroman* (*an artist novel*) signalled its theme, the rite of passage of a struggling young musician, already a well-trodden literary genre in Germany at that time. It was a florid romantic confection – 'dreadful' he admitted later – loosely based on the aesthetic Osnabrück circle and their ideals. Yet it was some measure of his embryonic if still amateurish skills as a writer that it would find a publisher.

A Dresden-based monthly arts magazine *Die Schönheit* (*Beauty*) agreed to publish it in book form in 1920, albeit with a little help from Erich who would pawn his piano to subsidize the printing costs. Nearly a decade later when the Berlin publishers of *All Quiet on the Western Front* realized the magnitude of the success they had on their hands and launched a massive promotion campaign for it, they attempted to obliterate all evidence of *Die Traumbude* by buying in surviving copies and pulping them. The future Erich Maria Remarque, already the author of two published novels, was to be hyped as an overnight first-book sensation.

He had paved his way to *Die Schönheit* by submitting several short prose pieces and poems during his period in hospital, some of which were accepted. Unwittingly he was laying up problems for himself in years to come. The magazine was part of the vast Hugenberg publishing empire which controlled two-thirds of the total German press at that time as well as UFA, the country's biggest film studio and producer of classic silent movies. Hugenberg's various magazine titles espoused racial and nationalist doctrines, glorifying German cultural purity – it was no accident that it would become one of the Nazis' official propaganda outlets – and Erich's naïve early association with the firm would be unfairly cited by some of his detractors as evidence of fascist sympathies when he became a household name. The credibility of such a charge was somewhat voided by the fact that Bertolt Brecht, the arch Leftist, had also graced the columns of *Die Schönheit* around the same time.

Erich was unaware of such political undertones, still less concerned about them. It was enough that he had found a publisher willing to print his apprentice works. They were conventional enough exercises, very gushing in language and sentiment. One poem, *Ich und Du (Me and You)*, his earliest to appear in print, nevertheless hinted at the world-weariness and cynicism, the *Weltschmerz*, with which the experience of war had scarred his generation and which he would express so intensely in *All Quiet on the Western Front*.

His time at the hospital was running out. In October 1918 he was ordered to report for assessment and pronounced fit for a return to active service. But fate was smiling on him. Time was also running out for Germany and its allies. On 31 October Erich was discharged from hospital and posted back to Osnabrück for remedial training with the 1st Guards Reserve Battalion. But morale in the armed forces was collapsing. Two days earlier a naval mutiny at Kiel had signalled the beginning of the end. Erich had been back in his home town less than a week when riots broke out in Berlin and other major cities and a Communist uprising in Munich proclaimed Bavaria a republic. On 9 November Kaiser Wilhelm II abdicated and fled to exile in Holland. The war was over.

'After it was all over I saw all its hideousness, but there was one thing I could not accept,' he told an interviewer in 1930. 'I saw my best friend lying in the mud, his abdomen torn open. That is what was really insupportable and incomprehensible, and what is no less comprehensible is that it required so many post-war years and so much reflection for me to realize the full atrocity of these occurrences.'[2]

Bitterness ran deep in the *Heimkehrer*, the young 'homecomer' serviceman returning to a defeated, sullen homeland which felt betrayed by the armistice and in its frustration regarded the innocent soldier as a symbol of the betrayal. There was scant welcome and little sympathy from an older generation of civilians who, apart from food shortages, had not had to face the brutalities of war and in many cases vented its humiliation on the battle-scarred soldier.

Erich resumed civilian life in January 1919; back to the cramped Hakenstrasse apartment, presided over by his father's new wife, back to the *Lehrerseminar*, as though nothing had changed. But Erich himself had changed. A superficial self-assertiveness Erich had acquired at the front and in hospital now overrode his innate sense of inferiority.

His anger and resentment were concealed behind a carapace of flamboyance in dress and attitude. Even before his discharge, Erich, who had never risen above the rank of private, was to be seen strutting round Osnabrück outrageously wearing the uniform of a lieutenant. In November 1918, mere days after the war had ended, a photograph of him, thus attired, appeared in the *Osnabrücker Tageblatt* with an accompanying report that he had been awarded the Iron Cross First Class. In the picture he was wearing not only the First Class but also the Second Class medal as well as the *Verwundetenabzeichen*, a decoration awarded to the troops who had been wounded. He had no official entitlement to display any of them.[3]

It was a foolhardy act of bravado which he must have known would be immediately spotted not only by his army comrades but also by the army authorities. Military police patrols were reported to have orders to arrest him. When Middendorf taxed him about this provocative demonstration, Erich produced a document from the *Arbeiter- und Soldatenrat* (the Council for Workers and Soldiers) purporting to verify his right to them. There was no confirmation that it had been issued to him and after months of investigation by the Osnabrück authorities he was obliged to answer charges of 'deception' by admitting in writing:

> I have worn the officer's uniform without being an officer. For approximately two months I have also worn the Oldenburg Cross without being entitled to it. I consider I wore the Iron Cross First Class legally, since it was conferred on me by the Soldiers' Council with a provisional certificate. I applied to obtain a permanent one but received no reply.

This *fracas*, set in train so trivially and thoughtlessly, dragged on for more than a year, until in January 1920 Erich was formally advised: 'We severely censure his deportment during the time he attended the seminary and after his return from army duty, and we expect in future he will endeavour to comport himself immaculately in every respect.'

In that respect at least he gave no grounds for reproof. The sartorial Erich who emerged from army uniform attracted both admiration and ridicule. It was as though he were trying to redress the bleakness of his war memories with a peacock display of plumage as he promenaded with his German shepherd dog Wolf, which he liked to claim had saved his life at the front.[4]

The dog was a coded statement in itself, although Erich's love of animals was genuine. The shepherd dog had become a token of German superiority since Max von Stephanitz, a Prussian cavalry officer, had founded the Shepherd Dog Association in 1899 and decreed that members should only give their dogs German food and names, on pain of a fine. The breed had become working mascots for army units during the war and had served honourably on the front line. Wolf, then, was the perfect fashion accessory for a veteran of the trenches cutting a dash on the streets of Osnabrück and in the concert garden of the smart Hotel Germania where Josef Witt recorded meeting him.

Witt recalled that the twenty-year-old boulevardier 'now placed special value on civilian elegance. He dressed conspicuously well, wore on his walks a panama hat and caused a stir with his beautiful dog. Occasionally he wore great fluttering artist's ties.' He also took to sporting a monocle.

Once, when Witt complimented him on his appearance, Erich told him: 'If you wish to get on in life, you must set great store by your clothes.' He would remain true to that dictum all his life. *The Black Obelisk* begins with the narrator agonizing over the difficulty of raising enough money to buy a new suit in the inflationary Weimar Republic of 1923!

4

A New Sense of Identity

In January 1919 Erich resumed his studies at the Seminary. The old stultifying regime still prevailed in the classroom. The teaching staff made no allowance for the sensibilities of the returning war-hardened students, continuing to treat and discipline them as the callow adolescents they had been three years before. No sympathy was shown for their war service or its seismic impact on their lives. The teachers were condescending, if not altogether contemptuous of them, reflecting the attitude of the public in general.

Erich recalled this atmosphere in *The Road Back* (*Der Weg zurück*), the sequel to *All Quiet on the Western Front* which would closely chart his return to civilian life:

> There they stand now and propose to teach us again. But we expect them to set aside some of their dignity. For, after all, what can they teach us? We know life now better than they; we have gained another knowledge – harsh, bloody, cruel, inexorable.

The *Hehmkehrer* assemble for a welcoming address by the Principal who extols the glory of the cause and the heroism of the German soldiers, then:

> We at home here have done our duty, too; we have thieved and

gone hungry for our soldiers; we have agonized; we have trembled.
It was hard. Sometimes perhaps it has been almost harder for us than
for our brave lads in field-grey out yonder . . .

But especially we would remember those fallen sons of our
foundation who hastened joyfully to the defence of their homeland
and who remained upon the field of honour. Twenty-one comrades
are with us no more; twenty-one warriors have met the glorious
death of arms; twenty-one heroes have found rest from the clamour
of battle under foreign soil and sleep the long sleep beneath the
green grasses . . .

The assembly erupts in derisive laughter and one angry young veteran
harangues the platform:

Hero's death! And what sort of thing do you suppose that was, I wonder?
Would you like to know how young Hoyer died? All day long he lay
out in the wire screaming, and his guts hanging out of his belly like
macaroni. Then a bit of shell took off his fingers and a couple of hours
later another chunk off his leg; and still he lived; and with his other
hand he would keep trying to pack back his intestines, and when night
fell at last he was done. And when it was dark we went out to get him
and he was as full of holes as a nutmeg grater. Now you go and tell his
mother how he died – if you have so much courage.

With civil unrest sweeping Germany – though Osnabrück was barely
touched by it – Erich and the other ex-soldiers rebelled. Student
councils were formed to demand recognition of their special status
and separate classes for the *Hehmkehrer* who would not be subjected to
the outdated disciplines and regulations. Erich was appointed leader of
the Catholic group; Hanns-Gerd Rabe, who had been an officer in
the war, headed the Protestant equivalent. Co-ordinating their tactics
was the first contact between the pair and the foundation of a friendship
that would last for the rest of their lives.

Together they worked hard for their cause – even at the cost of
their studies – lobbying the higher schools' authority in Hanover, the

state capital, and making representations to the Prussian ministry of education in Berlin.

Their campaign was successful in as much as the Seminary was required to create a separate class for the ex-servicemen and a new system was instituted for teaching and treating veterans with the respect they felt they deserved. Erich, for his pains, was duly elected president of the servicemen's student union for the whole Hanover region. But his activities gained him a reputation in official records as an agitator and potential 'leftist' troublemaker which, allied to the episode of the lieutenant's uniform and war decorations, would cause problems for him in the months to come.

Rabe, close as he became to Erich, had no illusions about his character and motivations. He recalled his:

> rather nonchalant attitude towards the pursuit of the required studies. He was more concerned with the development of his own interests, especially through reading, theatre and concerts. He dressed well . . . After he had donated his household keep to his father, the money he earned giving piano lessons and selling his poetry and essays went mainly towards personal finery.[1]

Male friends may have scoffed at his debonair image but it made a desired impression on women. Erich was already involved in his first serious love affair. Lotte Preuss – he nicknamed her Lolott – was an actress, the first of many in his romantic life. She had a moderately successful career touring German theatres when they first met in Osnabrück. A surviving letter to her, dated November 1918 and written from barracks, is typical of the romantic flights of eloquence edged with self-mockery with which he would woo his women: 'O Lolott, I often miss your hands . . . many a time in the nights you were there with me, you sat on my bed and said: Dearly beloved – and it was a dream of you . . . you are spellbinding! I love you.'[2]

The affair didn't last but a nebulous contact did – it was a characteristic that endeared Erich to all his lovers that he rarely bore grudges after a romance had faded and kept in touch with them. In Lolott's case three decades and another world war would pass before they met again. During his first return visit to Germany in 1952 he called on her at her home in ruined Berlin. The literary ardour of his youth failed him this time. She was, he recorded in his diary, 'too fat, smelled bad, bad breath. Kissed me. Had to hold my breath. She has no hot water in the house. Horrible attempt to make clear to her that there was no longer anything between us; that it had been a youthful episode.'

Erich left the Seminary – with average grades – in July 1919 and was recommended, albeit grudgingly, by the Osnabrück schools board for his first teaching post. It was almost as though he were being banished to the furthermost outpost of the board's empire. Lohne at that time was a cheerless town set in a landscape of bogs and mosses sixty kilometres to the north of Osnabrück – 'one of the poorest, saddest areas of Prussia' was how one observer described it.

It must have been some consolation for Erich to know that his job as a temporary assistant teacher for the elementary classes would be short lived. He buckled down and made the best of it, nevertheless, even enjoying a dalliance with a local girl, a certain Fräulein Diederichs. The son of the headmaster, a Dr Wöste, later reported: 'He visited our house daily, to our great pleasure, for he brought life. His piano playing delighted us. In school he had no difficulties, either with his colleagues or the children, he was throughout correct.'[3]

He had barely settled in before his recent past caught up with him. Four months after arriving in Lohne he received a summons from Osnabrück city council charging him with 'having taken part in Spartacist subversions' at the Seminary. Spartacists were members of a German socialist revolutionary movement founded in 1916 which had fomented much of the unrest following the armistice and had just reconstituted itself as the German Communist Party.

That Erich should be deemed one for his role in demanding fairer conditions for his student comrades was unjust but indicative of the edgy state of mind of officialdom at that period. 'I have taken part in no Spartacist subversion whatsoever,' he replied curtly. But his card had been marked. The authorities were not minded to let the matter drop, asserting in his personal file that 'During the Seminary period after returning from army service, his proven behaviour was to be extremely disapproved of.' Erich hardly helped his case with his somewhat lofty, condescending attitude.

He left Lohne after nearly nine months and enjoyed the comparatively sophisticated social whirl of Osnabrück for several weeks before accepting another appointment. Again a backwoods village posting: again a lowly temporary post at a one-class church school of fifty pupils where he was the sole teacher, substituting for the incumbent, a Herr Nieberg who was on sick leave, and lodging with the Nieberg family in their rooms above the classroom.

Klein-Berssen was even further from Osnabrück, a strictly Catholic community in the middle of a bogland nowhere. The schools board seemed determined to make him suffer for his perceived follies. But he needed the money. Almost immediately he crossed swords with Father Brand, the elderly priest who ruled the village and its school from his church next door. The two men were at loggerheads from the start, the priest closely monitoring, disapproving and openly criticizing Erich's methods and character, and withholding his salary. It was little consolation to learn that Herr Nieberg, too, was a victim of the priest's spleenish authoritarianism. Indeed, Erich attributed Nieberg's ill-health to it. Soon he and the priest were no longer on speaking terms and reduced to communicating with notes.

'You have your church; I have my school,' Erich wrote 'I don't interfere with your duties, so may I expect that you don't disrupt mine.'

He complained to the local education office at nearby Sögel: 'He tells me off in the highest tones as if I'm a schoolboy. "You must go to church more . . . you are a bad model for the children . . . you do nothing at all in religion."'

The situation had not been resolved by the time school broke up in June for the summer holidays, nor would it be. The priest was a revered institution; the teacher was a young upstart – and a temporary one at that. When school re-assembled on 31 July there was still no response to his complaints from Sögel. Erich resigned the same day, leaving Klein-Berssen without a teacher.

He requested a posting nearer home and the Osnabrück education department acquiesced, notwithstanding his growing reputation as a troublesome candidate. Three weeks later he was allocated his third school, considerably more civilized this time, at Nahne on the southern outskirts of the city. His complaints to Sögel had been forwarded to Osnabrück and he had been in his new job barely a month before he was being interrogated about his disputes with Father Brand.

It was the final straw. Erich decided teaching was not his forte. When his Nahne contract expired in November 1920 he left the schoolroom for good. The career that had been his mother's dying wish for him was ended.

He had contributed not a little himself to the difficulties of his brief teaching experience though the confrontations at Klein-Berssen were probably less his fault than that of Father Brand, a stickler of the old school. In its way it was an extension of the conflicts at the *Lehrerseminar*, the forceful self-expression of young men enfranchised by war service and determined on a 'new order' and the intransigence of the old order of Prussian traditionalism. It would engulf Erich far more controversially when he emerged as a best-selling author.

Yet he did not regard his teaching days as a failure. Looking back on them nine years later he would remember them fondly. 'That was a jolly time; the children liked me and I liked them but the life struck me as too cramped for my twenty-one years.'[4]

Or, as he would put it more cogently in *The Black Obelisk*: 'I was sent to a village on the heath where I stayed till I grew sick of dinning into children things I did not believe myself and being buried alive amid memories I wanted to forget.'

Casting himself voluntarily on to the jobless market was a feckless act in the Germany of 1921. They were hard times. The economic catastrophe of the Weimar Republic was already crippling the nation; unemployment figures were soaring, inflation was beginning to bite.

What had probably fuelled Erich's decision to quit teaching and a steady, if meagre income, was the publication of *Die Traumbude* and the modest success of a poem, *Abendlied* (*Evening Song*), he submitted and had published in Osnabrück's daily newspaper, the *Osnabrücker Tageblatt*, in October 1920, a month before his Nahme contract ended. It also appeared in *Die Schönheit* the following month.

A short romantic verse, *Abendlied* expressed the beneficent calming effect of evening light and quiet on a day of turbulent emotions. Readers of both publications responded to it with unexpected warmth and Erich was particularly encouraged by the reaction of Karl Henckell, a German poet of some repute at that time, who wrote: 'It is one of the profoundest love-songs I have ever read', and praised the emotional intensity of the author's language.

The *Tageblatt* claimed Erich as a 'discovery' and declared: 'The extraordinary popularity which the deeply felt poem *Abendlied* has been accorded encourages us to present further contributions by this young and talented poet.' Erich enthusiastically obliged.

Life in the cramped Hakenstrasse apartment with his father, two sisters and a new step-mother was constricting and glum. In February 1919 Peter Remark, after seventeen months as a widower, had married Maria Anna Bahlmann whose names, bizarrely, reversed those of Erich's mother, Anna Maria. There is no record of how Erich adapted to this newcomer in the family. The only reference to her in his surviving correspondence and diaries is to her suicide in 1945.

He would retreat to the room he had made his own on the upper floor with its view over a chestnut tree to the spire of the Saint Katharine Church at the far end of the street. There, on his old Erika typewriter, he wrote poems, essays and short stories for the *Tageblatt* and *Die Schönheit*.

Increasingly he sought refuge from his barren domestic life at the nearby home of Hanns-Gerd Rabe, newly married and embarking on a career as a journalist. Both men found work as theatre critics, Erich for the *Tageblatt*, Rabe for the rival *Osnabrücker Landeszeitung*.

Throughout 1920 he lived a hand-to-mouth existence. The small amounts of money he earned from writing were being daily eroded by soaring inflation. This was the era when workers were paid twice a day and given half an hour's leave to dash to the shops to buy necessities before the next publication of the dollar exchange rate, because by then their money would be only worth half its value. Erich supplemented his income by giving piano lessons and playing the organ for chapel services at the Osnabrück insane asylum. His fee barely covered the cost of the tram fare to the outskirts of the city but on Sundays he received a free meal and a glass or two of wine.

At the asylum he found an unexpected soul-mate in the chaplain, Father Biedendieck, who had been his confessor before the war. He was to be given a key role in *The Black Obelisk* as Father Bodendieck whose philosophical arguments help to salve the young, war-scarred Bodmer's despair and steer him towards a more optimistic future.

It is a true and affectionate portrait of the original: a bluff, bucolic *bon viveur* who was able to offer Erich the intellectual challenges and stimulus he craved. They spent many hours together in Biedendieck's rooms discussing the state of art, literature and the world over endless glasses of wine.

Rabe recalled:

> He was not a spiritual priest but rather a materialist, a lover of food and drink . . . he was tall, a giant of a man, not always popular among his parishioners because he was not slow to speak his mind and let his views be known. He was quite blunt in showing his flock the error of their ways.[5]

By the end of 1920 Erich realized he could no longer afford to drift, however agreeable he found his situation. He would remember that year with nostalgia. As late as 1966 he was to write to Rabe, recalling their days as theatre critics: 'I must say I hold those times in 1920 in tender memory, although naturally I was completely immature as a real critic.'[6] But he now made a conscious effort to confront the realities of the times – the crushing inflation, unemployment and defeatism that were corroding the Germany of the Weimar Republic and opening the gates to National Socialism.

He found work as a book-keeper and salesman with the brothers Hermann and Rudolf Vogt, monumental masons of Osnabrück. His job was to sell gravestones and memorials, a line of business for which he found he had some aptitude. 'I was worth my money,' he wrote years later. 'I sold the oldest, non-selling lines, even relics from the *Jugendstil* [the art nouveau movement, by this time no longer fashionable]. I helped to ruin the landscape with war memorials. We designed and flogged the usual dreadful atrocities – lions with toothache or bronze broken-winged eagles, as far as possible with gold crowns.'[7]

This is the background of *The Black Obelisk*, portrayed with picaresque humour and irony, underpinned by a mood of despair – 'a dark reflection of the Osnabrück of 1923' observed a reviewer in one of the city's newspapers in 1956.[8]

As a sideline he began writing advertising copy for Vogt. It was a providential impulse, which led after a few months to his being offered a job as an advertising copywriter for *Echo Continental*, the house magazine of Continental-Caoutchuk, the international rubber and tyre company based in Hanover.

His move in April 1922 to the sophisticated capital city of Lower Saxony was the overture to his career as a writer, a significance he seems to have consciously implemented by changing his name to Erich Maria Remark.

The decision to substitute Maria for Paul has never been explained. There has been speculation that it was in posthumous tribute to his mother but this seems unlikely. Apart from some natural expressions of grief immediately following her death his subsequent references to her were brief and unemotional, and Maria was, in any case, her second name. Another theory is that he was paying homage to his literary idol Rainer Maria Rilke.

Ironically, after he had been settled in Hanover for six months he received a letter from the Osnabrück schools board offering him a temporary teaching position. He took malicious pleasure in declining with a pompous put-down: 'I am the publicity manager and editor-in-chief of the Continental C and G.P. Co. Hanover'. He signed his letter, 'With great respect, Erich Maria Remark'.[9]

Within a few months, as his correspondence reveals, he had also re-styled his surname. With the move to Hanover and a status he, at least, considered prestigious, his metamorphosis from parochial Osnabrück lad to the urbane sophisticate Erich Maria Remarque had been accomplished.

Remarque's first extant use of the name is in a letter to Karl Vogt, the son of one of his former employers, in August 1923. The young man had written asking for advice about branching out into uncharted career territory. Remarque's considered reply is a gauge of how his own perceptions and unfocused will to succeed had been honed in the months since arriving in Hanover. Gone are the superficial swagger and mannered idealism of earlier days. Economic security and a new sense of self-identity, betokened by the change of name, appear to have given him a measure of acuity, even a veneer of cynicism.

> You are right, the uncertainties in life have a special appeal. Relying on chance gives one's existence a quite peculiar mood, though it takes a certain self-assurance to hit on the right action at the decisive moment . . . And another thing: only put your trust in yourself, never in others. Always see that you have the reins in your own hand. You wouldn't believe how delicate and easy people are to lead. The fellow who says: I can and I want to, always comes through.[10]

His brief at Continental – or Conti, as it was known to its staff – was specifically promotional but allowed him a free hand in disseminating publicity for the firm's multiplicity of rubber-based products. His approach was innovative and imaginative. As well as producing advertising slogans and copy, he wrote articles not only for *Continental Echo* but also for outside magazines on a wide range of subjects – motoring, cycling, boating, travel – always infiltrating subtly concealed plugs for the firm. He created a cartoon strip for *Continental Echo* featuring a pair of lovable pranksters, the Conti Boys, which became highly popular with readers, and another comic character, Captain Hein Priemke, who humorously extolled the firm's range of products from tyres to bathing caps.

It may not have been the area of writing he aspired to but it gave him invaluable technical experience. 'I wrote lots of articles about rubber tyres, cars, collapsible canoes, engines and goodness knows what else, simply because I had to make a living from it,' he said in an interview soon after the publication of *All Quiet on the Western Front*.[11] But in a different interview, he conceded: 'At Conti I learned the editing trade'.[12] It would serve him well. In revising drafts of his novels he was ruthless in eliminating words or passages he considered superfluous.

If he found writing for *Continental Echo* unfulfilling, at least it enabled him to indulge his growing passion for cars – the more powerful the better. Cars and motor racing would become a recurring motif in his novels. In his third best-seller *Three Comrades* (*Drei Kamaraden*), the titular friends are joint owners of a garage, and cars have a symbolic bearing on the narrative. Beautiful women, fine wines and automobiles would form an enduring triumvirate of hedonism in his life.

Conti gave him access to the pick of cars, allowing him to test-drive or motor on business all over Germany, to France, Belgium and Italy, even as far as Turkey. At this time he formed a friendship with the German racing-car ace Rudolf Caracciola which lasted until Caracciola's death in 1959.

Towards the end of 1923, some eighteen months after he had joined Continental, Remarque unwittingly began to follow the advice he had given Karl Vogt – 'it takes a certain self-assurance to hit on the right action at the decisive moment'. A Continental executive passed on to him an enquiry from a Berlin contact about the possibility of his daughter, an aspiring journalist, contributing to *Continental Echo*. Her name was Edith Doerry. More significantly, her father, Kurt Doerry, was a distinguished Berlin sports journalist, who years earlier had founded Germany's first sports magazine, *Sport im Bild* (*Sport in the Picture*). It was now a title, along with *Die Schönheit*, in the Hugenberg empire.

Remarque dutifully contacted Fräulein Doerry and asked her to submit a sample article. She travelled to Hanover in October 1924 to introduce herself and over the following months contributed regularly.

Correspondence between them graduated steadily from the formal to the familiar, with Remarque discreetly hinting that she might return the favour he had shown her by using her influence to persuade *Sport im Bild* to use one of his own articles. She obliged.

As the letters passed between them, Remarque's charm offensive intensified . . . 'By chance it has been brought to my notice that today is your birthday . . . In combining good wishes for your birthday with thanks, I don't need to express them in conventional words.'[13] Edith clearly found herself smitten.

The tactic worked. In January 1925, three months after his first meeting with Edith, Remarque moved to Berlin as an editor with *Sport im Bild*.

5

Berlin and a
Turbulent Marriage

Remarque seemed to be playing a dubious double game, currying Edith Doerry's attraction to him, hinting in his letters at a growing intimacy between them but concealing his new love – for someone else. Edith was useful, not only for her powerful connections but also for practical purposes. In the last weeks of December 1924 she is helping him to find somewhere to live in Berlin: 'Dearest Fräulein', he writes. 'Very many thanks for being so kindly active in the apartment problem . . . I really don't want you to be running around, flat-hunting takes up so much time. Perhaps the singer's (inexpensive!) place is okay for the time being – if she doesn't rehearse too much.'[1]

Edith found rooms for him in the smart Charlottenburg district, at Kaiserdamm 114, but if she had any plans for them as a trysting place she was to be swiftly disappointed. Remarque barely had time to settle in before Edith's mother discreetly intervened by bearing her off to Capri. It was a prolonged holiday, lasting the rest of the year. Whether Frau Doerry was acting on suspicion of her daughter's infatuation with an unacceptable provincial employee of her husband's magazine is not clear, but it looks as if there was an element of calculation involved. Before the year was out Edith had met and married an Englishman, Leslie Roseveare. Remarque, true to his practice of maintaining friendly relations with the discarded women in his life, continued to write to her.

The new woman in his life – and, tormentingly, for the rest of it – now joined him in Berlin and moved into his apartment.

Jutta Ilse Ingeborg Ellen Zambona, née Winkelhoff, a minor actress and dancer, was quintessentially Remarque's ideal of femininity. They had met in Hanover where she worked part-time for *Continental Echo*. Slightly taller than Remarque, she was a Nordic blonde, slim, with the statuesque poise of a mannequin, delicate, almost fragile features, partly due to a recurring though mild tubercular condition, and an innate sense of style in dress and comportment.

Leni Riefenstahl, the actress-turned-photographer who would become Hitler's favourite film-maker, was one of her earliest Berlin acquaintances. 'I saw her for the first time at a premiere in the Gloria Palace on Kurfürstendamm and was greatly impressed by her looks,' she noted in her memoirs. 'She was not only beautiful but also very intelligent. Tall, slender as a fashion model, and strikingly dressed, she had a sphinx-like quality similar to that of the vamp roles later played by Marlene Dietrich.'[2]

At the age of twenty-three Jutta Zambona was already married and obtaining a divorce from her much older industrialist husband when Remarque first met her in Hanover. Mercurial, amoral and demanding, she would cause him unending heart-ache throughout his life, alternately devoted and dismissive, possessive and indifferent. Their relationship was a turbulent one from the start, yet its complexity and unpredictability were probably the forces that bonded them. Jutta was the only woman who would remain a constant in his life, however estranged they would become in the years ahead.

They were married on 14 October 1925 at the register office in the Charlottenburg sub-district of Wilmersdorf where they set up their marital home in an apartment at Wittelsbacherstrasse 5. Edith wired her congratulations from Capri.

Marriage between two such free spirits as Jutta and Remarque was never going to be easy. Within weeks, rumour has it, he had moved out, not returning for nearly a year. The problem was more than likely to have been sexual. While Remarque exuded sex appeal for women and was masterly in the arts of romantic seduction, he appears to have been somewhat less enthusiastic about consummating an affair, preferring the pleasures of the preliminaries and the comforting warmth of intimate physical contact. It was a reluctance that would later characterize his relationships with others. Intimations of his impotence were not uncommon.

Remarque immersed himself in his work and the social world it opened up for him. For a provincial young man eager to live the life of a sophisticate he had timed his arrival in Berlin well. The city was on the cusp of its epochal legend as the permissive capital of Europe. 'Sodom on the eve of its destruction' was how Alfred Döblin described it in his 1929 novel *Berlin-Alexanderplatz*. In stark contrast to the economic ills of the Weimar Republic, now receding, the *haut monde* of Berlin was a maelstrom of live-for-today hedonism and indulgence. 'The city vibrated with life,' Leni Riefenstahl recalled. 'There were parties, premieres and invitations almost every day.'[3]

Sport im Bild, with its masthead tag-line 'The Magazine for Good Society', was one of the conduits for this fevered world, its marketing policy targeted on the burgeoning interest of the moneyed class in sport generally and motoring in particular.

Berliners in the mid 1920s were car-crazy. They flocked to the newly opened Avus racing circuit, famous for its 44° north curve, to cheer on such track heroes as Manfred von Braunitsch in his Mercedes, the Bugatti aces Veers and Charon, and Hans Stuck. When Lilian Harvey, the London-born darling of German cinema, rocketed to fame in 1925 and acquired a white Mercedes, it became as big a star as its owner. Service stations with streamlined petrol pumps and stylish lighting were opening all over the city. A new breed of shops specialized in selling motoring accessories.

The car was a badge of material success and social status and so a criterion of Remarque's fragile self-esteem. Undeterred by Bismarck's canard that 'journalism is the career of shipwrecked lives', he was in his element writing about motoring and consorting with the élite of this sophisticated new vogue. Motor-racing was a passion for him.

While at Continental he had already sold a short story. *Das Rennen Vanderveldes* (*Vandervelde's Race*), to *Sport im Bild*, its eponymous protagonist a racing driver involved with a *femme fatale*, Lilian Dunkerque. Now he began expanding it into his second novel – and indeed would recycle its theme over the years ahead into another short story and a second novel. In his fifth novel and third best-seller, the *Three Comrades* of its title would be co-owners of a Berlin garage, their cars symbolic of their various destinies.

Berlin in the late 1920s, the Berlin of *Cabaret* and *The Blue Angel*, was a journalist's paradise: tough, louche, amoral and a bubbling well-spring of colourful copy. Carl Zuckmayer likened it to a brassy *femme fatale:* 'We called her proud, snobbish, *nouveau riche*, uncultured, crude. But secretly everyone looked upon her as the goal of his desires. Some saw her as hefty, full-breasted, in lace underwear: others as a mere wisp of a thing, with boyish legs in black silk stockings. The daring saw both aspects, and her very reputation for cruelty made them the more aggressive. To conquer Berlin was to conquer the world.' It had 149 newspapers, more than any city in the world, and nearly 400 magazines. Berliners' appetite for news, political comment, entertainment was insatiable.

Remarque was in his element – the country boy making good in the big city. Doors now opened for him. Socially, the interlocking cultural, artistic and media circles of Berlin were compartmentalized into cliques, each with its appointed meeting place in café-bars and private salons. Subtle demarcations defined who should frequent which, roughly according to status, professional inclination or preference for the company on offer. The proclivities or pecking-order of writers, artists, actors could be gauged by the bars they frequented. The most bohemian of them, the Romanisches Café on Auguste-Viktoria Platz, was a favourite of Remarque's, as it was for Heinrich Mann, Bertolt Brecht and Georg Grosz. He also favoured the Eden bar where recognizable faces of the theatre and operetta world gathered.

The theatre producer Rudolf Nelson hosted the most exclusive salon where privileged guests could mingle with such august names as Heinrich Mann, Max Reinhardt and the avant-garde composer Arnold

Schoenberg. Rudolf Nelson's son, the songwriter Herbert Nelson, said: 'If you had already made it, you got invited to my father's. But if you didn't get invited to Betty Stern's, you weren't going to make it in Berlin. It was as simple as that.'[4]

Betty Stern enrolled Remarque in her coterie, not because she detected star quality in him but as a journalist of some influence who could be helpful in promoting the careers of her up-and-coming clientele. She was an unlikely salon hostess, unconnected with show business or literary circles except through her weekly gatherings, but incorrigibly star-struck. She and her compliant husband, a buyer for a textile firm, lived in a modest apartment on Barbarossastrasse off Kurfürstendamm where, Leni Riefenstahl recalled, 'her rooms were so crowded that you couldn't find a place to sit down'.

The German film historian Lotte Eisner thought her 'vulgar' but credited her with knowing 'how to introduce the important people to each other, so that many films and projects began there . . . every famous actor or director strolled through [her] *petit bourgeois* apartment.'

Regulars included the actress Elisabeth Bergner, who was just beginning to make her mark on stage and screen, and her future husband, the director Paul Czinner, the husband-and-wife couple Max Pallenberg and Fritzi Massari, reigning stars respectively of Berlin comedy and operetta, and an unknown revue artiste and film bit-player who Betty judged was 'going to make it'. Her name was Marlene Dietrich.

Remarque and Dietrich must inevitably have encountered each other at this time but ten years or more would pass before they would meet again as world celebrities.

Through the doors of Betty Stern's salon Remarque entered the world of theatre and movie glamour that would be the background to the rest of his life, and at the end of it, nearly fifty years later, he would acknowledge Betty's helping hand by characterizing her as Betty Stein in his posthumous novel *Shadows in Paradise* (*Schatten im Paradies*), a refugee in wartime New York, still resolutely conducting salons that are now sad shadows of their Berlin heyday.

For all the outward trappings of success and his growing sophistication at the heart of one of the world's most cosmopolitan capital cities, Remarque was still beset with social insecurities and inner doubts of his place in the scheme of things. He cultivated an image of man-about-town urbanity. Mindful of his advice to Josef Witt that 'if you want to get on in life, you must set great store by your clothes', he dressed sharply. He still affected a monocle. He had a decorative and desirable wife. His writing was earning a reasonable income. To all intents he had attained much that he had once coveted, but the seam of melancholy in his character acted as a brake on his self-confidence. He craved a firmer reassurance than the superficial acquaintances and attentions of a Betty Stern salon.

On a gauche impulse reminiscent of the Osnabrück affair of the Iron Crosses and officer's uniform he acquired by dubious means an aristocratic title. Berlin rolls of 1926 register him as 'Erich Maria Freiherr (Baron) von Buchwald, called Remarque'. He had allegedly come to a financial arrangement with the real nobleman, an elderly ex-army officer, to have himself adopted for a payment of 500 marks, automatically assuming the title, as sons of aristocrats are entitled to in German law. It also entitled him to display the five-peaked crown of nobility which he duly had engraved, along with the title, on a new set of visiting cards. Though not illegal, such pretensions were socially suspect.

Remarque's ingenuous action again drew reproof from the otherwise loyal Hanns-Gerd Rabe, as his Osnabrück foolishness had: 'I knew this Freiherr von Buchwald. He was an impoverished cavalry captain and, in fact, had wanted to sell me the title earlier. The old man needed the money'.[5]

As he worked at *Sport im Bild* by day and on his new novel at night, Remarque's self-confidence covertly came under increasing strain. Jutta was largely to blame. Theirs was, by agreement, an 'open' marriage, their relationship volatile, careering from reef to reef. But it was Jutta's free-will interpretation of 'open' that fanned Remarque's inner conflicts, driving him to casual liaisons that seemed less an urge for sexual conquest than a quest for consolation. They were never on the flamboyant scale of hers.

Reluctantly he forced himself to come to terms with the reality of her infidelities but not with the frequent bouts of despair they were causing him. After the publication of *All Quiet on the Western Front* he would ascribe them to memories of his front-line experiences, and there can be no doubt that these came back to haunt him in the post-war years. More immediate, however, were his marital problems, and, significantly, he would tell an interviewer a few months after the book appeared: 'I wrote *All Quiet on the Western Front* to escape from something that was depressing me,'[6] omitting his standard qualification that the 'something' was his war memories.

Jutta was quite flagrant in her dalliances. Axel Eggebrecht, a Berlin journalist, claimed in his autobiography that he had an affair with her lasting several months after meeting the Remarques in a bar. 'He was having an affair with another woman, as I soon found out. He remained tolerant towards us; thus when we went away on trips he accompanied us to the train.' He and Jutta, Eggebrecht added, went off together for several weeks in the mountains.

Eggebrecht then casts a light on an unsuspected aspect of Remarque's nature. 'He had her every movement watched by private detectives and soon found out she was meeting – as she had before – with Franz Schulz [a friend of Eggebrecht]. Remarque forced his way into his rival's apartment with a raiding party one night and had him beaten to a pulp'.[7]

It seems an unlikely reaction. Violence was anathema to the mature Remarque. He had seen too much of it in the war. But he had begun drinking heavily at this time and the incident, if true, may be a measure of mounting desperation over the state of his marriage. Another anecdote lends substance to it.

Among his acquaintances was a number of young aspirants in the Berlin film and theatre worlds who would later become prominent Hollywood names: the screenwriter Walter Reisch, the director Robert Siodmak and his screenwriter brother Curt Siodmak and Detlev Sierck who, as Douglas Sirk, would direct such Hollywood classics as *Written on the Wind, Magnificent Obsession* and *Imitation of Life* as well as *A Time to Love and A Time to Die,* based on Remarque's 1954 Second World War novel.

Destined to be the most distinguished of them all was Billy Wilder. Wilder who shared Remarque's birth date, 22 June, arrived in Berlin from his native Vienna as a twenty-year-old in 1926 and began his working life as a journalist on a tabloid newspaper. He was supplementing his income by acting as a taxi-dancer – a paid dancing partner – at the luxurious Eden Hotel, Remarque's favourite drinking retreat.

In his 1987 biography of Wilder, Maurice Zolotow records that he

> was rumoured to have been caught by Remarque in flagrant delectation with the first Mrs Remarque. At least so the scandal went as the gossipmongers passed on this story . . . Anyway, the rumours went that Remarque, like a nineteenth-century Prussian nobleman, had horsewhipped Wilder. Another version was that the confrontation had taken place on a street and that both men had fought with fists until they were bloody and quite bowed.[8]

Billy Wilder would deny the incident in later life, insisting that he had never even met Frau Remarque.

Remarque himself always maintained a strict silence about his private life and especially his early relationship with Jutta, but there is enough anecdotal evidence of her extra-marital activities to indicate the humiliations she caused him.

Leni Riefenstahl was witness to one of them. She had first met Remarque when he interviewed her for *Sport im Bild* and he expressed an interest in meeting one of her friends, the director Walter Ruttmann whose documentary film *Die Symphonie einer Grossstadt* (*Berlin – Symphony of a Great City*) had just opened to critical acclaim. She arranged an informal social evening at her apartment.

> I was surprised when I greeted Frau Remarque, for she was wearing an elegant evening gown, as if she were going to a gala. She looked wonderful with her red (*sic*) curls held in place by jewelled combs, and an almost pure white complexion.
>
> She appealed not only to me and to her husband, but also, and most of all, to Walter Ruttmann – as soon became apparent.

At first it was a lively and cheerful evening. We drank wine and champagne, and perhaps as a result Frau Remarque behaved so seductively that she completely turned Ruttmann's head. At first I thought it was only harmless flirting but as the mood grew more animated Ruttmann and Frau Remarque got up, leaving me alone with her husband. They retreated to a dimly lit corner while I remained with Remarque who tried to drown his jealousy in liquor.

Ruttmann and Frau Remarque behaved as if they were alone and I became more and more distressed, not knowing what to do in this embarrassing situation. Remarque sat on the couch with downcast eyes, his head drooping sadly, and I felt so sorry for him. All at once Frau Remarque and Ruttmann were standing in front of us. 'You've been drinking too much,' she said accusingly, 'Herr Ruttmann is taking me home. I'll see you later.'

I squeezed poor Remarque's hands, then followed by the other two I went to the lift and saw them down to the front door. As we said goodnight, I pleaded, 'Don't make your husband suffer so much,' but she merely smiled and blew me a kiss. I did not shake Ruttmann's hand for I considered his behaviour as awful as hers, if not worse.

When I went back upstairs I found a sobbing man whom I tried in vain to comfort. 'I love my wife, I love her madly. I can't lose her. I can't live without her.' He kept repeating these words, his whole body shaking, and when I offered to call a taxi, he refused; so I stayed up with him till dawn. In the morning light he looked a human wreck, but he didn't resist when I put him in a cab, utterly exhausted. . .

Two days later Remarque called me. His voice sounded hoarse and agitated: 'Leni, is my wife there? Have you seen her, has she called you?' Barely waiting for me to say no, he shouted into the telephone: 'She hasn't come home, I can't find her anywhere.' Then he hung up.

That night he came to my flat and wept without restraint, drinking one cognac after another. He kept answering me that his marriage had been unruffled, indeed very happy, until this meeting with Ruttmann, and he was at a loss to understand his wife's conduct

. . . of course, he would forgive her completely, so long as she came back. However, she didn't come back. Nor did she get in touch with me.

For almost two weeks a desperate Remarque came to my place almost every day. Then, unexpectedly, he told me he couldn't stand being in Berlin any more . . . he simply had to get away.[9]

A few weeks after this incident, Riefenstahl recalled, Ruttmann's wife committed suicide by throwing herself from a window.

'Many men envied Remarque his wife,' Leni Riefenstahl said. Many, too, knew only too well the emotional price he was having to pay for that envy. That he loved her was as self-evident as the brazen-ness of her infidelities, far more uninhibited than his own. Through divorce, re-marriage, exile and his own turbulent affairs she would always retain an empathetic role in his life long after passion had subsided, a complex bond of loyalty and responsibility, sympathy and exasperation.

As he worked on his third novel in the autumn of 1927 his spirit was at its lowest ebb and he pounded all the accumulated poisons of his disillusionment and despair into its pages.

The book that was *All Quiet on the Western Front* (*Im Westen nichts Neues*) and it took him five or six weeks to write – he varied the figure in different interviews – at night in the Wilmersdorf apartment after a full day's work at the magazine. He kept himself awake with large quantities of cigars and coffee.

'I had never thought earlier of writing a book about the war,' he said after its publication in an interview – not without its ironies – with his rival Axel Eggebrecht, 'I suffered from rather violent attacks of despair. In attempting to overcome them I gradually and quite consciously sought the cause of my depression. Through this deliberate analysis I came back to my life in the war. I could see similarities in many of my acquaintances and friends. The shadow of the war hung over us especially when we tried to shut our minds to it. On the same day these thoughts struck me I began to write without much in the way of prior thought.'

The sentences came swiftly and easily, the writing style, governed by the harshness of the subject matter, lean and stark. Remarque had absorbed the rigours of journalistic discipline, and, no less, the rules of expressionist naturalism that was currently fashionable in German literature. The reportage style of his writing could not be further removed from the novelettish *Kitsch* of the two earlier novels.

The second of these, *Station am Horizont*, began weekly serialisation in *Sport im Bild* in late November 1927, continuing until the following February. The Remarque scholar Tiltman Westphalen has dismissed it as 'a jet-set story of the 1920s about motor-races, casinos, Monte Carlo, fascinating women, unrequited love and German melancholy'.[10] The heroine Lilian Dunkerque, resurrected for the first of her two reincarnations in Remarque novels from the short story *Vandervelde's Race* of three years before, was here 'the most difficult, capricious and also unfaithful woman of the season.'[11] An image of Jutta hovers, as it would, intermittently, in various guises over novels to come.

The serial's impact was negligible. *Station am Horizont* was never published in book form until recent times and even now only in a German language edition. If Remarque was discouraged by the reaction to it he left no record of his feelings.

As far as he was concerned there seemed little future or reward in writing novels. He had no idea of the bombshell waiting to detonate in the desk drawer to which he had consigned his new manuscript.

6

All Quiet on the Western Front

G ermany's bookshops were awash with novels and memoirs of the war and by the end of the decade there was a perception in the publishing business that the book-buying public was satiated. In those ten years following the armistice more than 200 war-related titles with respectable sales had appeared, twenty-four of them in the twelve months of 1927/28 alone.

Remarque made no attempt to submit his manuscript. His reluctance remains a mystery he never publicly clarified. Involved as he was in publishing, he may have discerned the prevailing trend, or merely regarded his book as a personal rite of exorcism, for private consumption only. More likely, his chronic lack of confidence prevented him from gauging the true measure of its merits and potential. Billy Wilder allegedly warned him while he was writing it that nobody would want to read 'a grim piece of anti-war realism' and urged him not to jeopardize his job.[1]

At least Jutta had faith in it. Remarque welcomed her comments as he wrote and passed the pages to her for correction and editing. There is evidence that he ultimately made her a gift of the original manuscript. When it mysteriously surfaced for auction at Sotheby's in London in 1995, the anonymous vendor was rumoured to have acquired it from Jutta's estate following her death twenty years earlier.

The manuscript lay undisturbed in Remarque's desk drawer for six months until, pressed by Jutta and others, he decided to seek a publisher.

Tactfully – though with negative consequences later – he discounted his own employers. The Hugenberg organization with its increasingly Fascist stance had no sympathy for anti-war sentiment. Only that year its owner Alfred Hugenberg had been elected leader of the German Nationalist People's Party and would throw in his lot with Hitler five years later.

Instead Remarque sent the manuscript to the Berlin house of S. Fischer Verlag, publisher of Thomas Mann's *Buddenbrooks*. Their reaction to it foreshadowed the impact it was to make. One of the firm's directors Bermann Fischer read the novel at a single sitting, passed it on to his brother and company chairman Samuel Fischer the following morning and urged him to read it at once and draw up a contract with the author without delay 'before any other publisher got sight of it'.[2]

The response of the all-powerful Samuel Fischer was more cautious. He hedged his bets by suggesting they would take the book if no other publisher was prepared to accept it, on the grounds that sales were questionable because nobody wanted to read about the war any more. Privately he felt the novel's style and content did not accord with the Fischer house-image of publishing 'literature' by established authors, a view he maintained even after its spectacular success.

If Remarque was disappointed, Bermann Fischer's enthusiasm compensated and spurred his determination. He promptly sent it to Propyläen Verlag, the book arm of the vast Ullstein publishing company. There have been many versions of the chain of circumstances that turned an unsolicited manuscript into one of the publishing sensations of the twentieth century – and just as many claimants to the honour of 'discovering' it. In a 1963 Berlin television interview – the only one he ever gave – Remarque recollected that a friend, Dr Fritz Meyer, who had contacts with Ullstein, asked his permission to show it to Fritz Ross, one of the firm's editors. 'That did it. I received a letter from Ullstein. Would I like to go along to them?' he said.

But other accounts suggest it was not quite so straightforward as that. Fritz Ross was certainly among the first to read it and recommend buying it. Where the legends diverge is in what happened next. According to some eye-witnesses, Ross's superiors did not share his enthusiasm and it lay, unheeded, on various readers' desks until the production manager Cyrill Soschka, leaving the office one evening, randomly took it home as something to read that night.

The next morning he thrust it to the editorial team, saying: 'I know war, and this is the real war, the truth about war, naked and honest.' And he vowed that if no publisher was prepared to take it, he would found his own company to publish it.

Not without some of Samuel Fischer's trepidation, Ullstein offered Remarque a contract, paying him 24,000 marks in monthly instalments of 1,000 over two years, with a proviso that if the book failed to cover the publishing costs the author would be required to cover the deficit by submitting further writings without payment. Unofficially, however, they signalled a vote of confidence in the book's quality by not demanding any alterations or corrections.

Until the 1995 Sotheby's auction, it was generally believed that *All Quiet on the Western Front* had been originally published exactly as Remarque had written it. In fact the rediscovered autograph manuscript revealed a previously unsuspected opening chapter in which the protagonist Paul Bäumer described his home life and family.

Susan Wharton, Sotheby's specialist in continental manuscripts, said: 'This manuscript shows how it was originally envisaged . . . his second thoughts were really much better than his first.'[3]

While the book was being typeset Cyrill Soschka had galley proofs pulled and sent to the editors of twelve newspapers and periodicals in the Ullstein group, inviting them to bid for serialization rights. Only one responded, Monty Jacobs, the editor of the leading liberal daily *Vossische Zeitung*, the favoured reading of Berlin intellectuals and affectionately known as *Tante Voss* (Auntie Voss). Pre-publication serialization was scheduled to start in November. Ullstein, sensing the expectation that was building up in a book they had been so hesitant about taking, began to plan a promotional campaign unprecedented in German publishing. From press advertising and street hoardings the public quickly became aware that a literary event was in the offing. Booksellers received publicity window displays.

As always, Remarque's reaction was ambivalent: elated by the growing excitement and the justification of his abilities as a writer, enjoying the putative aura of celebrity, yet dismayed by the reality of the media interest it was focusing on him personally. He would later claim to have had no preconception of the book's success.

He had already started work on a so-called sequel *The Road Back* (*Der Weg zurück*) dealing with the immediate post-war problems – loosely his own – that confronted the young veterans of the trenches returning to civilian life in a defeated homeland. But in the run-up to publication of *All Quiet on the Western Front* he found it impossible to write in Berlin and decided to return to Osnabrück. Not, however, to the family home. His advertisement for lodgings in an Osnabrück newspaper brought a reply from a Frau Maria Hoberg, a well-to-do war widow, who would briefly assume the near-status of a surrogate mother to him.

The rooms she offered him in her house on Süsterstrasse were perfect for his writing requirements and state of mind: spacious, quiet, with a terrace fronting a peaceful garden which he could look out on from his desk in the window. Ironically, a neighbour on the opposite side of the street was one of the Vogt brothers who had employed him five years before. Leaving Jutta in Berlin, he moved in on a four-week rental – the period during which his book was appearing in *Vossische Zeitung*. Karla Hoberg, his landlady's daughter, later recalled that he seemed to be in a state of deep depression.

The circulation of *Vossische Zeitung* shot up threefold during the serialization. The instalments carried the title *Nichts Neues im Westen*, a sardonically bitter annexation of the phrase used in official war bulletins meaning 'nothing new on the Western Front'. In the weeks preceding the book's publication Ullstein reversed the words to the sharper, more mellifluous *Im Westen nichts Neues*. The initial print-run was to be 30,000, unusually large for a 'first' novel by an unknown author, but as serialization continued, booksellers' orders increased to avalanche proportions. Another 20,000 copies were added to the run.[4]

Five days after the first instalment appeared Remarque was summarily fired from his job with *Sport im Bild*. Not only had he flouted Hugenberg house rules by failing to give them first refusal on the novel and serialization rights, but the tone of the book was anathema to the company's political ethos. It was a minor indignity in the context of what the future held for him.

By publication day, 31 January 1929, Germany was engulfed in *All Quiet* fever. No book until then in the history of literature had created such excitement. The first print run sold out on the first day. The mighty Ullstein, unable to cope with the printing demand, was forced to sub-contract six outside printers and ten book-binding firms. In the first few weeks sales were estimated at 20,000 a day. By the end of 1929 nearly 1 million copies had been sold in Germany alone.

The pattern, though less frenzied, was repeated abroad. *All Quiet on the Western Front* became an international publishing phenomenon, selling in its first year 300,000 in both Britain and France, 215,000 in the United States and proportionate numbers in smaller markets such as Spain, Italy and the Scandinavian countries.

In Germany, however, the book, unlike elsewhere, quickly became a literary and political *cause célèbre*, polarizing opinion and drawing aggressive critical fire from 'old school' nationalists and military traditionalists for what they perceived as its defeatist, inglorious depiction of German soldiery. Remarque had portrayed life in the trenches as he had observed it, in harsh realism and cryptic neo-documentary sentences. The style of writing, raw, stark and uncompromising, frequently shocking, was unprecedented in fiction. In many respects it prefigured the idiosyncratic style Ernest Hemingway was developing with his First World War novel *A Farewell to Arms* published nine months later in the United States. Even after seventy years Remarque's descriptions of battle and the physical and psychological wounds of its victims still convey a disturbing, piteous immediacy. It speaks for all common soldiers in all warfare and it was this universality that commended it to readers of all ranks and classes.

It was this aspect, too, which determined its impact among politically motivated critics as subversive. They came not only from the right wing. Leftists, too, found cause to attack the book and its author for failing to take an overtly political stance or challenge the social and economic agenda of the ruling classes.

Overwhelmed by the scale of his success, Remarque was totally unprepared for the ensuing controversy, the vehemence of the attrition directed at him personally, not least from fellow authors, impelled no doubt by professional jealousy. Count Harry Kessler noted in his diary the reaction of the left-wing pacifist Arnold Zweig, himself the author eighteen months earlier of a bestselling novel about the war, *Der Streit um den Sergeanten Grischa* (*The Case of Sergeant Grischa*). Zweig 'was venomous about Remarque', Kessler wrote, dismissing the upstart as 'slapdash' and 'a good amateur' who had failed to see the angle from which he should have tackled his subject.

In Remarque's depressive state of mind the onslaughts outweighed the approbations. 'When this success suddenly came upon me last spring, it led to an almost annihilating crisis,' he said later that year, 'I felt that I was finished, vanquished for good. I thought, whatever I write from now on, I would always remain the author of *All Quiet on the Western Front*. And I knew only too well, this book could just as well have been written by anyone else. It was no achievement of mine to have written it.'[5]

More than thirty years later, asked what his reaction had been, he would still remember: 'The feeling of unreality. It never left me . . . I found it to be totally out of proportion. And that it was! Fortunately I always realized this and it prevented me from developing delusions of grandeur. On the contrary, I became insecure.'[6]

The Press clamoured to interview this new literary lion. Veterans organizations and literary groups inundated him with speaking invitations. Remarque went to ground. He had tried to co-operate all he could in Ullstein's pre-publication publicity but the resulting furore cowed him. There was to be no let-up in the months ahead, nor, indeed, were his perceived transgressions to be forgotten in the years to come. The author of the world's most famous anti-war novel was to be hounded by it, sometimes perilously and once shockingly, into middle age. His book became the catharsis of the contradictions in his character: the celebrity and material rewards he revelled in duelling with his lurking sense of inadequacy and instinct for anonymity. He recoiled from the invasion of privacy his sudden fame now triggered.

'I wrote *All Quiet on the Western Front* to escape from something that was depressing me, and when I had finished it I felt free of a dreadful weight of those experiences,' he told an English journalist. 'But now this new terror is hanging over me. I cannot escape from this interest in my own person. People . . . manuscripts . . . the postman . . . everybody I meet, everywhere I go.'[7]

The National Socialists were on the rise and one of the most scurrilous attacks on him was mounted by Hitler's mouthpiece newspaper, the *Völkischer Beobachter*, averring that his real name was Kramer – Remark spelt backwards – and that he was Jewish. It was a myth he tried half-heartedly to correct but which would persist even into some of his obituaries nearly half a century later. Another, with marginally more basis in fact, was that he had never served on the front line and his depiction of conditions and attitudes of the troops there were a falsification.

This touched a nerve. 'The details of my book are real experiences in spite of all the rumours spread to the contrary, which I will not take the trouble to contradict. I was at the front long enough to have experienced personally just nearly all I have described,' he insisted.[8]

He was somewhat placated by the reviews from London when Putnam published A.W. Wheen's superlative English translation in March. Unconcerned with internecine German political polemic, the British Press judged the novel according to Remarque's own ethos, as a commentary on the ordinary soldier in combat, and hailed it as a masterpiece. 'It has marks of genius which transcend nationality. There are moments when the narrative rises to heights which place it in the company of the great,' observed *The Times*. 'So dreadful that it ought to be read by every man and woman who is doubtful about the need for preventing the Next War,' was the prescient advice of the Manchester *Evening News*.

The distinguished critic Herbert Read wrote: 'It is terrible, almost unendurable, in its realism and pathos. But it has swept like a gospel over Germany and must sweep over the whole world because it is the first completely satisfying expression in literature of the greatest event of our time. It is a superb piece of construction.' Demand for the book in Britain necessitated no fewer than eight reprints in the first month and more than twenty by the end of the year.

In the United States some passages in the Wheen translation, mainly referring to bodily functions, were deleted by the publishers Little, Brown to satisfy demands of a lucrative Book-of-the-Month Club contract which they would otherwise have lost. Although the novel has never been out of print in America, the cuts were not restored until 1978 for a new paperback edition.

The world's Press announced in July that the film rights had been sold to Hollywood for $40,000, a record sum for that time. 'A talking film based on the book is to be produced, partly in Germany and partly in Hollywood, in two versions, German and English,' reported *The Times*. In the event it was filmed entirely in California.

Carl Laemmle, the German-born head of Universal Studios, travelled to Berlin to clinch the deal with Ullstein and persuade Remarque to work on the screenplay. Legend has it that he also wanted the author to star in the film as Paul Bäumer. Remarque reluctantly agreed to prepare a treatment but after a half-hearted attempt abandoned the project.

A sequence of coincidences at this point produced a curious align-ment of interests and frustrated cross-purposes between the authors of the two great classic works from opposing sides of the First World War.

On 21 January 1929, ten days before *All Quiet on the Western Front* was published in Germany, *Journey's End*, a play depicting a group of British army officers in the Flanders trenches, opened in London at the Savoy Theatre. Its author R.C. Sherriff, like Remarque, was unknown before overnight success thrust him into the public eye. So was its leading actor, Laurence Olivier. Robert Cedric Sherriff was two years older than his German counterpart but they shared a June birthday.

On its opening night, the play was acclaimed for its realism and anti-war credo, and mirrored the excitement in Germany over Remarque's novel. It was translated into every European language and through countless revivals since has established itself as one of the definitive English-language dramas of war.

Productions of *Journey's End* quickly followed throughout Europe and the United States. Remarque, in the first flush of celebrity, was approached to adapt it for the German stage under the title *Die andere Seit* (*The Other Side*) even though he did not speak or read English. He declined. 'I read it and felt it agreed completely with my own attitude,' he explained, 'But I don't want to be identified with the war and books and plays the war has brought about. I can't escape from my own book.'[9]

Meanwhile Sherriff, in New York for the July premiere of his play, was being approached to write the screenplay for *All Quiet on the Western Front*. Following Remarque's aborted effort, he was the first writer to be considered.

'It was a tempting offer . . . what lured me was the magic spell of Hollywood, a spell I'd been under since my schooldays,' he wrote in his autobiography,

> But there was something pulling harder in a different direction. I was longing to get home. Before I'd sailed we had decided to give the house a face-lift. It was a big old place and we'd never had much to spend on it, but now I'd given my mother a free hand, and all the money she needed . . . I had promised to be home in three weeks and my mother had promised to have everything done and ready for my return. It would be a bitter disappointment for her if I cabled to say I was going to Hollywood instead. So I sent my regrets to Carl Laemmle and booked a passage on the *Mauretania*, sailing the following night.[10]

Two years later he would finally be lured to Hollywood to work on the screenplay of Remarque's *The Road Back*, launching his distinguished career there as a screenwriter.

The two writers were never to meet or communicate with each other, although Sherriff was in Berlin for the German premiere of *Die andere Seit* in the summer of 1929. Years later Remarque hinted that he had regretted turning down the offer to adapt *Journey's End*. 'Had I done it at that time, I would probably have written further theatre pieces, for the theatre fascinates me,' he admitted. So why didn't he? 'Because I thought to rebel. From all sides I was being abused for doing this and that to the poor German soldier. I didn't want to make a business of the war and write about it a second time. Quite stupid!'[11]

Over the years he would attempt and abandon a number of plays before finally making it to the Berlin stage with *Die letzte Station* in 1956.

As income from *All Quiet on the Western Front* soared to unimagined levels, a grateful Ullstein presented Remarque with a bonus – a grey six-cylinder Lancia Cabriolet convertible. Nothing could have pleased him more. It was a dream car. He called it Puma, a pet-name he would recycle in the future.

At Ullstein's insistence he reluctantly submitted himself to a number of Press interviews during the summer months, but avoiding public scrutiny took on a near-paranoid urgency for him. 'I think I should like to disappear, grow a beard and begin a new kind of existence altogether,' he told a journalist that summer.[12] Cars, especially fast cars like the Lancia, became even more central to his life, subconsciously representing, perhaps, a speedy means of escape. 'I spend my free time trying out cars. That's something I do understand. Cars and dogs and fish . . .'[13] He had privileged access to the Avus race-track where he could test-drive various models and where in early 1930 he survived the first of many serious motoring accidents.

In the weeks following publication he and Jutta fled to Davos in Switzerland where she frequently underwent treatment for her tubercular condition. Later he picked up his old friend Georg Middendorf in Osnabrück for an away-from-it-all driving tour through France from Brittany to the Pyrenees, covering 3,750 miles.

But there was no escape from the shockwaves that his book continued to create. It was banned in Italy, already a Fascist dictatorship under Mussolini. In August the Austrian Minister of Defence ordered its removal from all army libraries and 'prohibit[ed] its dissemination anywhere within the precincts of a cantonment'.

Another flurry of controversy followed reports in September that Remarque was to be nominated for the Nobel Prize, with some confusion as to whether it would be in the categories of Literature or Peace. The German Officers' Union promptly announced that it had 'addressed to the Nobel Prize committee an indignant protest against what can only be regarded as an insult to the Army', adding that the book was 'a feeble attempt to misrepresent and discourage the heroic struggle of the united German stock during four years of war.'[14]

Remarque found this rebuke particularly wounding. '[It] makes it difficult for me to imagine how any German officer can really have read into my book an accusation against the heroic spirit Germany showed,' he said. 'The war certainly gave us enough heroes and the only officer I mention is a splendid one who sacrificed his life for his men.'[15]

Like most Germans, he was unaware that the armed forces (*Wehrmacht*), and especially the new younger element of the officer class, was being subtly infiltrated by National Socialist ideology. Such was official concern that General Wilhelm Groener, the Minister of Defence, found it necessary in January 1930 to issue an order of the day. The Nazis, it said, were greedy for power. 'They therefore woo the *Wehrmacht*. In order to use it for the political aims of their party, they attempt to dazzle us [into believing] that the National Socialists alone represent the truly national power.' Soldiers were enjoined to refrain from politics and remain 'aloof from all party strife'.[16]

Far from enjoying his success, Remarque was becoming increasingly soured by it. 'I know nothing of politics and I can only say that the atmosphere of political recrimination which is that of Germany today is hateful to me.'[17]

7

Nazi Sabotage

Women had remained a constant through all Remarque's recent travails, though his relationships with them were more dalliances than affairs. It could well be that he was tacitly acknowledging his own shortcomings as a lover when Robert Lohkamp, the partly autobiographical narrator of his future novel *Three Comrades*, is given the admission: 'I had known women, but they had been fleeting affairs, adventures, a gay hour occasionally, a lonely evening, escape from oneself, from despair, from vacancy.'

With Brigitte Neuner, a married actress, Remarque had maintained a flirtatious contact since the early 1920s. She was jaunty and joky and their letters to each other indicate an almost juvenile interplay of repartee and teasing, verging on the intimate. With the publication of *All Quiet on the Western Front* she voluntarily took on the role of a Girl Friday, dealing with his correspondence, organizing his financial affairs and, whenever he was away from Berlin, acting as an intermediary with his publishers.

Brigitte, was anticipating a divorce. Remarque, too, sensed his marriage was in crisis as Jutta pursued her infidelities, but whether he contemplated a steadier future with her is unclear and probably unlikely. She, on the other hand, seems to have had more serious expectations. They were not to be fulfilled. Within a year their relationship had ebbed away. Another actress, Ruth Albu, replaced her in Remarque's affections and was to play a crucial part in shaping his new life.

Jutta and Remarque were divorced in January 1930. Strangely, little changed in their mutual lifestyle. They both continued to occupy the Berlin apartment, though Remarque also kept rooms in a nearby hotel. They were still seen together in fashionable restaurants and bars, or at the theatre. They frequently travelled together. No sooner had their divorce been granted than they spent two months in Davos and nearby Arosa where Remarque, working on *The Road Back*, was reported to be looking for a house to buy.

The bittersweet bane of the Remarques' lives rested in a tired cliché: neither could live with or without the other. Some acquaintances, like Axel Eggebrecht, accused Remarque of treating Jutta as a token wife, an accessory whose beauty and sophistication lent him the aura of 'class' he had always been conscious of lacking. There was an element of truth in it, but his regard for her was genuine and loving despite the self-evident exasperations she continually caused him and he would continue to bear a sense of responsibility and concern for her. Her feelings for him were less apparent. She revelled in his celebrity and wealth and the privileges they brought her, the *haute couture* clothes, the luxury hotels, the smart resorts, but she gave scant intimation of any deep emotional attachment to him. He was little more than a meal-ticket.

Ruth Albu, ten years younger than Remarque, first met him around the time of his divorce. Petite, vivacious and astute, she was a protégée of the songwriter Friedrich Holländer and had already made her mark in Berlin revues, sometimes alongside Marlene Dietrich, another Holländer favourite. At nineteen she had married Heinrich Schnitzler, son of the Austrian playwright Arthur Schnitzler whose best-known play *Reigen* became an enduring international success as the film *La Ronde* and in recent times on the West End and Broadway stages as *The Blue Room*. She, too, was in the process of divorce.

Puzzled but undeterred by Jutta's continuing presence in Remarque's life, she dedicated herself to him by catering to aspects of it that Jutta couldn't or wouldn't. She set about refining him for the sophisticated new society to which his success now admitted him, ironing out the vestiges of provincialism in his manners and attitudes, cultivating his artistic interests and offering him sound financial advice.

Germany, like the rest of Europe, was feeling the economic shock waves from the Wall Street crash at the end of 1929. Remarque's accumulating wealth was threatened. It was not only deriving from his book and the advances on its sequel. His newly acquired agent Otto Klement had signed a lucrative contract with the American magazine *Collier's* for a group of war-themed short stories, three of which appeared at two-monthly intervals during the summer of 1930, timed to coincide with the US release of the film of *All Quiet on the Western Front*.

Ruth advised him to invest in art at this sensitive time when the art market was depressed. She introduced him to Walter Feilchenfeldt, the Berlin dealer who became instrumental in assembling Remarque's art collection, one of the finest in private hands. With no serious judgement of his own, merely an aesthetic appreciation, he relied on Feilchenfeldt's, buying oriental carpets, Chinese sculpture, Venetian glass and during the early years of his collecting fever, paintings and drawings by Van Gogh, Cezanne, Monet, Renoir, Corot, Degas and Pissarro. He learned to be a connoisseur and an expert on the French Impressionists. Like Edith Doerry before her, Ruth house-hunted for him, finding him a villa in Switzerland that would remain his principal home for the rest of his life.

Ruth Albu fell deeply in love with him. Remarque's feeling for her, as in all the relationships he drifted into at this period of his life, was qualified and reserved: warm, appreciative but stopping short of risking whole-hearted commitment. There was no regularity about their meetings. Their paths frequently diverged, Ruth's in whatever direction her career took her, Remarque's along an escape route from his public persona. He was constantly on the move, to Switzerland, Paris, London, the Riviera and Monte Carlo. And always there was Jutta in the background of his emotions – and often a presence in the foreground.

The final break with Ruth came two and a half years after their affair began, and in his response to a letter from her in which she seems to have been challenging him to declare himself, he hints at the equivocation inherent in his relations with women other than Jutta:

> It's difficult to answer you. What should I say? Words only ruin everything. I can say I have the feeling of riding on an ice-floe which is slowly melting. I can say, perhaps I'm unhappy but I don't want to know it. I can say, yes, I'm a weak character, and tired . . . I can say, yes, perhaps I'm not able to love . . . I can say, yes, go away from me, make yourself scarce. I'm not suited to people who insinuate themselves impetuously and unthinkingly. I'm half, I'm never whole. I am too little. I only take, and give nothing . . . Yes, I can't love as you want and need it . . . Love? Isn't it love if you are in my heart?[1]

Work on *The Road Back* had fallen seriously behind. Not only Ullstein but also the foreign publishers to whom he was contracted were pressing him for a delivery date, anxious to capitalize on the phenomenal sales of *All Quiet on the Western Front*. That summer he retreated again to Osnabrück and the tranquillity of the Hoberg house. It was the last time he would see the city of his youth as he had known it. When he next returned two decades later it had been devastated beyond recognition by Allied bombs.

With his Irish setter Billy for company, he settled in for two months from July to September. In a letter to Frau Hoberg, away on holiday, he wrote: 'The day passes here between work, rain, depression . . . I can't think of anything but work. Besides, I was in a bad state physically for something like ten days. My wife was here one day, but only one day. Work presses me too much.'

Karla Hoberg recalled:

> He worked unflaggingly and with concentration. After breakfast, which he took with my mother and after he'd looked through a

huge pile of mail and occasionally talked about himself and his opinions, he sat at the table which he had moved in front of the garden window and laid out the paper and sharpened pencils, and spoke no more to the world around him.

Overawed by his success and the expectations for his next book, he found writing a struggle. 'He was often depressed,' Karla Hoberg said in a 1969 interview, 'He was not content with his book, he felt he was being rushed.' And she gives a telling insight into his perception of Jutta, still referred to as his 'wife' despite the divorce. 'He felt that she was slowly slipping away from him through all the whirl of his success. He spoke once about it, that he now had so much money and success, but the one thing he was really concerned about – his wife – was slipping away from him more and more.' She added:

> That summer Remarque was always receptive to us and not so depressed as in the previous winter. He was pleased that *All Quiet on the Western Front* was published in so many foreign languages, especially Japanese. He also received letters from all over the world, from war veterans, above all from former enemies who thanked him for showing that men and their problems on all war fronts were the same.[2]

Once or twice, Hanns-Gerd Rabe remembered, he allowed himself a night on the town, inviting old pals from school and the army to join him in a drink in the Golden Hall of the Bavaria Restaurant in the Neumarkt. On those occasions he was 'uncomplaining and cheerful, like a schoolboy'.

The weeks he spent in the Hoberg household remained a happy memory for him throughout his life. In the 1960s Karla, long out of touch, sent him an old photograph of Süsterstrasse as he remembered it. He replied warmly: 'The picture happened to arrive here during a lengthy illness, and I have had it standing by my bed all these weeks. It has aroused so many memories of those days when I wrote my second book in your beautiful house. It was a beautiful time!'

Remarque allowed himself one significant excursion from his writing desk during his Osnabrück sojourn. The film of *All Quiet on the Western Front* had been premiered in Los Angeles in April and on 5 August Universal Pictures arranged a special screening for him in the neighbouring city of Münster.

The film, one of the earliest 'talkies', was as much a landmark in cinema as the novel had been in publishing. Carl Laemmle Jr invested $1.25 million in the production, an unprecedented figure at that time, and considerable risk in entrusting it to a fledgling director, Russian-born Lewis Milestone, and leading actor.

Lew Ayres, a twenty-two-year-old from Minneapolis, had spurned a career in medicine, in which he had graduated from the University of Arizona, for the lure of Hollywood and was talent-spotted in a nightclub where he was playing in a band. A bit part in a minor film led to him being cast opposite Greta Garbo in the 1929 *The Kiss*. With this limited experience he was chosen to play Paul Baumer (the umlaut was discarded for the film's credits).

The film made him a star but was to overshadow the rest of his career and, years later, indirectly ruin it. The influence of Remarque's pacifism in the book was the unwitting cause. The deeply religious Ayres never again achieved a role or performance to equal his Baumer and in playing the character he formed pacifist ideals of his own. With America's entry into the Second World War twelve years later, he declared himself a conscientious objector and refused to join the armed forces. The American public was outraged.

Over the preceding three years Ayres had built a loyal following in the title role of the popular *Dr Kildare* series of movies, starring in ten of them. At a stroke, he forfeited the public good will. Cinemas showing his films were picketed, exhibitors boycotted them and the studios shunned him. Remarque, by now exiled in America, was himself drawn reluctantly into the onslaught of condemnation, and was quoted as saying: 'In this war I think everyone should fight Hitlerism.'[3]

Ayres subsequently volunteered for non-combatant duties as a paramedic and, later, a chaplain's aide, distinguishing himself under fire. 'War', he said, 'is the worst crime. I just couldn't bring myself to kill other men.'[4] Hollywood forgave him and after the war he resumed a low-key career, respected and even nominated for a 1948 Academy Award for his performance in *Johnny Belinda*, but never to regain the status *All Quiet on the Western Front* had conferred on him, the one role for which posterity remembers him.

Remarque's opinion of the film is not recorded but he can have had no qualms about the fidelity and dignity with which Universal had interpreted his book, nor its impact on American critics and audiences. It was generally hailed as the finest anti-war movie of its time – and nowadays of all time. Its overpowering battle scenes and potent imagery of futility and wasted lives set a benchmark for all future war films.

He had no reason to suspect that the increasingly confident Nazis would seize on the film as the hair-trigger for the propaganda thuggery that would come to characterize their rise to power.

The first augury of that phenomenal rise came with the national election in September 1930. In the previous election two years before the Nazis had secured a meagre 800,000 votes, relegating them to a mere ninth position in the strength of parties represented in the Reichstag. In the 1930 election their vote soared eightfold to 6.4 million, winning them second place with 107 seats in parliament. It was the breakthrough Hitler had been dreaming of for ten years.

The citizens of Berlin had bucked the national voting trend. Nazism did not enthuse them (nor ever would). So the National Socialists decided Berliners needed to be 'educated', and the man charged with this mission was the Party's *Gauleiter* for the capital, Dr Paul Joseph Goebbels.

Diminutive and deformed by a club foot, he nursed an almost pathological grievance at not having been considered fit for military service in the war. His hatred for *All Quiet on the Western Front* and, by association, its author was thus as much personal as political.

The Berlin premiere of the German version of the film was scheduled for 4 December at the de luxe Mozartsaal cinema on the Nollendorfplatz. It was to be the most significant film event of the year, a gala opening before an invited audience from the cream of Berlin's society and professional elite.

As publicity and anticipation mounted in the weeks before the premiere, Remarque was surprised to receive a visit from an emissary of the *Gauleiter*. Would Remarque, the aide asked, be prepared to confirm that the film rights had been sold by Ullstein and produced by Universal without Remarque's personal authorization?

Remarque later explained:

> [Goebbels] wanted to use this point as anti-semitic propaganda that I – a non-Jewish author – had been taken advantage of by two Jewish firms for their 'cosmopolitan-pacifist' purposes. As reward, he promised me the protection of the Nazi Party. It didn't bother him that his Party had attacked the book and me with the same reproach. His emissary told me that the public's memory was short and they were getting used to the Party discipline; they would believe what they were told. Needless to say, I declined this nonsense and so missed the possibility of becoming a martyr for the Party.[5]

Goebbels set about planning the Party's revenge, though Remarque was, for him, a relatively minor, if provocative, player in the master plan he cunningly devised to attack his political foes by discrediting *All Quiet on the Western Front*.

For weeks past Goebbels had pursued a vicious high-profile campaign against Albert Grzesinski, the Berlin Police Commissioner and former Minister of the Interior, and his deputy Bernhard Weiss. It had culminated in November with Grzensinski ordering a week's suspension on the official Nazi newspaper *Der Angriff* (*Attack*) which Goebbels edited. In the approaching premiere of the film, the *Gauleiter* and propaganda leader of the Party saw the perfect opportunity to humiliate the police department.

The day before the opening he called a meeting of his cohorts, one of whom recorded the proceedings: 'Within a few minutes he had outlined the project which was to cause a sensation far beyond Berlin.'

The plan was to create mayhem at the screening and trigger a public outcry against the film. Someone asked how they were to obtain so many tickets for the performance. 'Goebbels snapped his fingers. A few telephone calls, and we had the tickets. Half an hour later they had been distributed.'[6]

The actual premiere was allowed to pass without incident. Goebbels shrewdly targeted the following night's performance, the first to which ordinary Berlin filmgoers were admitted, for his demonstration. The audience had to cross a threatening picket line of more than 150 SA 'Brownshirts' in front of the Mozartsaal, watched by a crowd of curious bystanders.

Remarque, warned of potential trouble, mingled anonymously among them. 'I watched the demonstration. Nobody was older than twenty. None of them could have been in the war – and none of them knew that ten years later they would be in another war and that most of them would be dead before they reached thirty,' he wrote later.[7]

Soon after the film started the auditorium erupted. Party members and Brownshirts rampaged up and down the aisles, shouting 'Jews out' and assaulting anyone they thought looked Jewish. They threw stink-bombs from the balcony and as a finale released white mice in the stalls. It was pandemonium. The police moved in but made little attempt to restrain the troublemakers. Instead they ordered the cinema to be cleared. Outside, the audience again had to run the gauntlet of taunting pickets.

The next night Goebbels orchestrated street demonstrations against the film. They continued, with growing crowds, for the following four nights. Fights broke out between demonstrators and police. Whole sections of the city centre were sealed off. A protest march drew 6,000 people (Goebbels claimed 40,000) with Hitler himself taking the salute.

'Over an hour. Six abreast. Fantastic! Berlin West has never seen anything like it,' Goebbels recorded in his diary on 9 December.

The *Vossische Zeitung* described the demonstrations as 'a new variation on Nazi terror tactics' and supported Police Commissioner Grzesinski's declaration that he would safeguard the screening of the film and protect audiences 'from all provocations and violent acts by rowdy elements'.

After consultation with the Interior Minister he took action to ban all outdoor demonstrations, rallies and processions.

It was too late. On 11 December, six days after the first demonstration, the Reichstag debated the situation and voted to ban the film 'because of the danger to Germany's image abroad', its last act before adjourning for the Christmas recess. Grzesinski had been humiliated. So had Erich Maria Remarque.

Carl von Ossietzky, editor of the anti-Nazi newspaper *Weltbühne*, who would later be awarded the Nobel Peace Prize, wrote: 'Fascism has won another battle. Today they have stifled a film, tomorrow it will be something else.'

For the Nazis this first public manifestation of their burgeoning power was, a jubilant Goebbels noted in his diary, 'a victory that could not have been any grander'.

More than eight years later, recording a quiet family Whitsunday in May 1939, he would write without rancour or irony: 'Yesterday: Weather like October. Spend the entire day talking, playing with the children, walking. In the evening, films: *All Quiet on the Western Front*. A very clever propaganda vehicle. At the time we had to sabotage it.'[8]

8

Burning the Books

There was some gratification for Remarque in a coincidence that delivered an unforeseen riposte to the Nazis' campaign. At the height of the uproar, on 7 December, the *Vossische Zeitung* began serialization of *The Road Back*. Even as the first instalment appeared Remarque, not yet happy with his final draft, was still trying to revise it, despite the distractions, in time for book publication, scheduled for April 1931. Again, the circulation figures for *Tante Voss* registered an upsurge, a welcome reassurance for Remarque that his name still had pulling power.

The novel, mirroring the author's own experiences, chronicled the problems that faced the so-called *'verlorene Generation'* – the lost generation of young soldiers readjusting to civilian life in a Germany shamed by defeat and indifferent to their welfare. It was only tangentally a sequel to *All Quiet on the Western Front*, set in a thinly disguised Osnabrück and featuring some of the same characters but with a new protagonist, for Paul Bäumer had been killed at the end of the earlier novel. Remarque was aiming for a hopeful message to contrast with the pessimism of his depiction of war, as he explained in a letter to the distinguished British soldier, General Sir Ian Hamilton, with whom he conducted a thoughtful correspondence about the war and its aftermath in 1929: 'We want to begin once again to believe in life. This will be the aim of my next book.

He who has pointed out the danger must also point out the road forward'.[1]

The Road Back was respectfully reviewed and sold well – 185,000 copies in Germany in the first few weeks of publication – but failed, blessedly perhaps, to generate the controversy or fervour of its predecessor. Its reception abroad was more enthusiastic. In the United States where it was serialized in *Collier's* magazine the *New York Times Book Review* dubbed it 'a worthy successor' and added: 'The world is richer for a great writer, Erich Maria Remarque.' The London *Times*, in a review that verged on damning the novel with faint praise while acknowledging its fluency, observed rather sniffily: 'Herr Remarque's work belongs to that order of realism which a modern French critic has described as "degenerate romanticism".' Remarque himself always considered it the better book.

It was as well for him that *The Road Back* was quietly received, allowing a breathing space for his reputation after the furore that had stormed for the past two years around *All Quiet on the Western Front*, making him an unwilling political pawn. He was not politically committed. 'It is more by good luck than good judgement that I am on the side I now stand on, but I know it happens to be the right one,' he allegedly told Thomas Mann after the Nazis came to power.[2]

He began to realize, nevertheless, that he was a marked man, under surveillance by both the government and the Nazis. His drinking became more intense. In Berlin, when he was not writing he was invariably to be found in his network of favourite bars and clubs – the Romanisches Café, Künstler Club, Neva Grill, the Eden Hotel – with cronies like Carl Zuckmayer.

The dramatist would later reminisce about

> an endless, inexhaustible round of nights together which continued through Austria and Switzerland and all the way to America. The amount of alcoholic beverages of all kinds that we put away would no doubt be equivalent to the stock in the cellars of a large international hotel. Perhaps that had something to do with the war,

which we never alluded to in all our talks, the serious and the humorous ones, but whose oppressive, secret shadow was always present. We felt a sort of taboo about the subject, that it was better to drink the memories away.[3]

Remarque had begun sketching the outline of a new novel but he was edgy. Berlin, once the nirvana of his ambitions, had become oppressive, vaguely threatening. He had a compelling urge to disappear. Most of that summer of 1931 passed in unfocused, anonymous travelling – motoring in his beloved Lancia to the Riviera and Monte Carlo for the Monaco Grand Prix in April, to the fashionable Dutch resort of Noordwijk aan Zee for a prolonged stay in June and July, Switzerland, Paris.

Ruth Albu, still hopeful of a more stable basis for their relationship, joined him for some of the time. They discussed the future – *his* future which, more than ever, seemed to relegate her to its fringes, for all his acknowledgement of her compatibility and sound advice. He was deeply troubled, and he was often drunk.

One July night while at Noordwijk he crashed the Lancia in the nearby city of Leiden, drawing world attention to himself again. The *New York Times* reported:

> Erich Maria Remarque who by ingenious devices had hitherto preserved his incognito while travelling in Holland knocked down a lamp-post in Leiden last night with his automobile which was severely damaged. Herr Remarque escaped unhurt. He immediately paid $48 damages and presented to the Leiden police several copies of his famous book in recognition of their courteous help.[4]

Incognito he may have wanted to be, but he made sure he carried celebrity identification at all times.

That summer he signed contracts for the house Ruth had found him in Switzerland. He paid 80,000 Marks, about £5,000, for the Casa Monte Tabor on the shores of Lake Maggiore at Porto Ronco. The three-storeyed villa, high above the shore-line, its grounds dipping steeply to the lakeside, was a perfect hideaway, screened by lush vegetation, rhododendron, tall cypress and spruce trees, with moorings and a floating bathing deck on the water. Ruth also hired a married couple, Joseph and Rosa Kramer, as gardener and housekeeper. They would remain in his service for the rest of his life, guarding and maintaining the estate, just as he had left it, throughout his Second World War exile.

In later years Remarque attributed to himself a prescience of potential danger and a necessity for flight that seemed fanciful for his motives in buying the house in 1931 when there was, as yet, no inkling of Nazi domination or a coming war. 'I settled in Switzerland as far south as possible near the border where German would still be spoken,' he claimed in a 1962 interview.[5]

He was, in fact, far from 'settled'. For the next twelve months, Casa Remarque, as he now re-named it, seemingly confounding his urge for anonymity, was a transitory bolt-hole from his constant travels and commuting to Berlin. Moreover, it created a new and very unsettling domestic situation for him, with both Ruth and Jutta, never meeting, competing to furnish and decorate it.

With his newly acquired Swiss residence permit, Remarque immediately set about transferring his growing art collection and financial assets to Switzerland where his huge royalty payments were being channelled into Zürich bank accounts. The transactions did not escape the notice of the government in Berlin. Eight months after he bought the property it ordered the confiscation of his assets in the Darmstadt Bank in Berlin on suspicion of illegal currency dealings. The amount was small, no more than 20,000 Marks – just over £1,000 – but the action was yet another ratchet in his perception of official German animus towards him and a sense of insidious persecution. Four months later a Berlin district court issued a writ charging him with illegal currency dealings and threatening a penalty of two months' imprisonment or a 30,000 Mark fine. He paid up.[6]

What wrong had he done? What offence, legal or moral, had he committed? Apart from the records of his so-called Spartacist activities at the *Lehrerseminar* there was no evidence that he had ever engaged in political activity or rhetoric. In the few selective interviews he had given he had scrupulously avoided comment that could be construed as political. He had merely written a novel that spoke as honestly and truthfully as he knew for the condition and attitudes of the common soldier in the war, that had caused offence at certain levels of the military and nationalist establishments but had been admired and endorsed by the mass public. He, a man who hated injustice, was beginning to feel disfranchised by its arbitrary application to him.

At least Porto Ronco was conducive to work. There he could concentrate on his new novel, working title *Pat*, the name he gave to its heroine Patrice Hollmann. Its final title would be *Three Comrades* (*Drei Kamaraden*). The book completes a sequence which, after *All Quiet on the Western Front*, Remarque conceived as a trilogy, each independent of the others but coalescing into an overview of his own generation and paralleling his own experience. Now the backdrop was Berlin in the late 1920s and early 1930s. The three wartime comrades run a garage – a device that enabled Remarque to indulge his passion for cars and motoring.

In a synopsis for publishers in 1931 he wrote: 'The novel is set in the present day . . . a slice of life of young people who have often sacrificed something and begun anew. People who have to fight hard for their existence. People without illusions who nevertheless know that comradeship is everything and fate is nothing'.

Through their interwoven destinies he threads a touchingly bitter-sweet love story between the narrator Robert Lohkamp (Robby) and Pat, played out against a background of the decadent, fun-loving, contemporary Berlin, its bars and cabarets and febrile atmosphere on the cusp of social upheaval. It is a faintly disguised expression of his own times and emotional turmoil, for Pat is unreservedly modelled on Jutta.

> She had taken off her coat and beneath it wore a grey English costume. About her neck was tied a white scarf that looked like a stock. Her hair was brown and silky and in the lamplight had an

77

amber sheen. Her shoulders were very straight but inclined a little forward, her hands were slender, a bit long, and bony rather than soft. Her face was narrow and pale, but the large eyes gave it an almost passionate strength. She looked very good, I decided . . .

Pat, like Jutta, has a consumptive condition. Remarque the author has the means to manipulate her fate in a manner denied him in real life. She dies in a Swiss sanitorium.

The political situation in Germany was taking an alarming turn during the summer and autumn of 1932. The government was crumbling. In Berlin and other cities the National Socialists, scenting the downfall of the republic, fomented unrest. Storm troopers roved the streets of the capital provoking murderous confrontations with Communists and police. Anarchy ruled and martial law was imposed. New elections were called and in November the Reichstag was dissolved, paving the way for Hitler's bid for power.

Despite a political climate that seemed on the verge of civil war Remarque returned to Berlin that month to finish the first draft of *Pat* and consult his publishers. He checked in at the Majestic Hotel, distancing himself from the nearby Wittelsbacherstrasse apartment and Jutta, and safeguarding his seclusion. He remained there for the next two months, apocalyptic days that would determine the nation's dark destiny.

On the last day of January 1933 President von Hindenburg summoned Adolf Hitler and appointed him Chancellor of Germany. Nazi tyranny was about to begin.

That night Remarque was drinking in one of his favourite bars. A friend with links to the Nazis joined him and quietly warned him to leave Germany immediately. He was left in no doubt that he was in danger but debated whether to leave at once or wait until morning. His friend's urgency decided him. In the small hours of Hitler's first day in power he checked out of the Majestic and out of Germany, driving the Lancia through the night, fearful that orders had already gone out to arrest him at the Swiss border.[7]

The following day he was safely in Porto Ronco. He had outwitted the Nazis. But he was now a refugee.

The Nazis wasted no time in serving notice of the fate in store for writers, scientists and scholars they intended to proscribe. On 2 March, barely a month into the new regime, Goebbels's newspaper, the *Volksischer Beobachter*, published an article condemning 'cultural internationalism and intellectual treason' with a long list of names of individuals, living and dead, whose 'pacifist excesses' on the stage and in film, literature and the Press 'are fresh in the memory'.[8]

Remarque found himself in illustrious company. The more notable pariahs also included Professor Albert Einstein, Sigmund Freud, Heinrich and Thomas Mann, Arnold Zweig, Alfred Döblin, Heinrich Heine, Bertholt Brecht, Hugo von Hofmannsthal, Erich Kästner and Carl Zuckmayer. All were to be outlawed on grounds of 'moral decline' or 'cultural Bolshevism'.[9]

Goebbels did not need to order or organize the infamous book burnings that followed. They were orchestrated spontaneously and willingly by the jobsworth leaders of the German Students' Association, one of the university unions. When, three weeks after the article appeared, the first minor portent of the outrage to come occurred on 29 March at Kaiserslautern, a small city in the Rhineland-Palatinate, it was the Remarque name that caught the attention of the foreign Press. The London *Times* reported: 'At a demonstration of "German culture and education" at Kaiserslautern at which several Nazi speakers launched attacks on "internationalism and Judaism and everything alien", seven copies of Herr Remarque's novel *All Quiet on the Western Front* from the municipal library were burned in the public square before a cheering crowd'.[10]

But it was another two months before the barbaric act of burning books – the *Säuberung* ('cleansing') – alerted the world to the true nature of Nazism. Convocations were held in all German universities at which students and academics confirmed their support for Nazi ideology. The ritual was synchronized in the major German cities but it was the scene in Berlin that branded its image on international consciousness. Days earlier students had invaded the city's libraries, stripping their shelves of books by the condemned authors. No attempt was made to restrain them; on the contrary, many among the academic and municipal staffs concerned joined in with enthusiasm. In Remarque's case *The Road Back* was added to the despised *All Quiet on the Western Front*.

On 10 May the thousands of books were loaded on to lorries and ceremonially driven through the Brandenburg Gate and along Unter den Linden, the capital's grandest avenue, to the Opernplatz where the pyre of petrol-soaked logs awaited the torches. In front of the opera house an 'honour guard' of nine representative students each hurled his allotted author into the flames with an incantation of hate.

Goebbels suddenly arrived on the scene to incite them. 'The age of Jewish intellectualism has now ended,' he ranted:

> You are doing the proper thing in committing the evil spirit of the past to the flames at this late hour of the night. This is a strong symbolic act, an act that is to bear witness before all the world that the November Republic has disappeared. From these ashes will rise the phoenix of a new spirit . . . the past is lying in flames. The future shall rise from the flames in our hearts. Brightened by these flames, our vow shall be: The Reich and the Nation and our Führer Adolf Hitler. Heil! Heil! Heil!

The Associated Press journalist Louis P. Lochner reported: 'Every few minutes another howling mob arrived, adding more books to the impressive pyre. Then, as night fell, students from the university, mobilized by the little doctor, performed veritable Indian dances and incantations as the flames began to soar skywards.'[11]

The world shuddered.

9

New Loves

'It was such a shock for me to have to leave Germany that I needed four years to complete *Three Comrades*. I was without a country, like an animal that gets nothing more to eat.'[1]

However artfully Remarque tried to disguise the anguish his banishment from the country he loved and honoured caused him – cushioning himself in luxury, days and nights of drinking with friends, seeking new romances, a compulsive urge to travel – he could not conceal it from himself. In what seemed a calculated decision to repudiate his homeland and all that his past in it meant to him and to initiate a new construct of roots and belonging, he applied almost immediately for Swiss citizenship. His application was rejected. A shadow of melancholy entered his being that would imbue all his work from now on – and inadvertently enhance his attractiveness to women.

'A slightly macabre humour, a breath of sadness surrounded him, and that was his special charm,' recollected an actress, Ruth Niehaus, to whom he introduced himself at a Berlin stage-door in the 1950s and invited to dinner after admiring her in a play.[2] To Marlene Dietrich 'he was in the highest measure melancholy and vulnerable. This quality in his character touched me very much. All too often I had the opportunity of seeing his despair.'[3]

He had all but completed a first draft of *Pat* before his flight from Berlin but much work remained to be done on it. Remarque considered the first draft of any book he wrote merely a sketch to be revised and meticulously refined through three or four further treatments, a legacy of the editing disciplines he had learned at Continental. 'Writing gave him enormous difficulties. He wrote by hand and needed many hours for a single sentence,' Dietrich noted.[4]

One of his last acts before leaving Berlin had been to let his old Osnabrück girlfriend Lotte Preuss – the Lolott whose hands 'I miss often' – read the manuscript. One of his first consolations after arriving in Porto Ronco was her verdict in a letter dated 30 January 1933: 'I howled reading it, I howled writing this. I didn't want to because my eyes are still sore, but I had to. A beautiful poem – the most beautiful romantic novel I know . . .'[5]

Not even Lotte's emotional endorsement was enough to galvanize him into finishing the book. He frittered away the days and months, trying without much success to adjust to his enforced new circumstances, unable to settle to a routine, making desultory attempts to write. Jutta, the inspiration for his heroine, regularly came and went but inspiration failed him. He made some new friends, notably the poet and fellow exile Emil Ludwig who was living nearby in Ascona. His drinking increased.

He was not even technically free to travel outside the area. Under Swiss regulations for his domicile he was required to apply for a permit every time he wished to leave it. Although the rule would eventually be relaxed in his case, he was careful to observe it for the first long months of his exile.

If he felt himself confined in an open prison, Ascona and Porto Ronco were a cell with gilded bars. Ruth Albu had chosen well. The lake shore had been a focus for emigrés, forced or voluntary, since the beginning of the twentieth century, Ascona itself an enclave for writers, artists, philosophers and pacifists, even vegetarians and naturists. The scandalous Isadora Duncan, pioneer of modern dance, had lingered there. It was a favourite retreat of the philosopher Carl Jung. The one-time fishing village, with its quaint streets and Italianate arcades, had acquired a cosmopolitan aura of culture and art. Its beautiful piazza, open to the lake, was studded with chic restaurants and bars, the shore towards Porto Ronco and beyond lined with the luxurious villas of the international wealthy.

From his own terrace Remarque could look out across the lake to the enchanting Isole di Brissago, tiny twin islands with lush sub-tropical vegetation, a botanical paradise and at 193 metres above sea level, the lowest point in Switzerland. A ferry plied between them and Porto Ronco. The shore beyond was Italy. Locarno, stylish and sophisticated, was only three kilometres away. The entire region was a honey-pot for hedonists.

For the next two years he lay low in Porto Ronco, labouring on *Three Comrades*, battling with his despondency. He was surrounded by the trappings of success but, from a creative standpoint, the momentum of that success seemed to have ground to a halt. And his excommunication from the 'new' Germany hurt. Although he was careful not to involve himself publicly in the mounting international concern and condemnations of the Nazi regime, it nevertheless viewed him as a dangerously powerful and persuasive voice, should he choose to speak out. The witch-hunt continued. It became a criminal offence in Germany to own his books and towards the end of 1933 all privately held copies of *All Quiet on the Western Front* and *The Road Back* were required to be surrendered to the Gestapo.

With time the Nazis had a change of heart. A German author of world-wide celebrity and authority was more likely to serve their image as a friend than as a foe, but a conciliatory gesture was advisable. In 1935 the Nazis put out feelers and Remarque agreed to receive an emissary at the Casa Remarque from Hermann Goering who, among his several high posts in the Nazi administration, combined the roles of Minister President for Prussia and Prussian Minister of the Interior. The envoy had a face-saving deal to offer. If Remarque was prepared to let bygones be bygones and return to Germany, Goering would be pleased to appoint him Minister of Culture for Prussia. The idea was laughable. 'What?' Remarque is alleged to have replied, 'Sixty-five million people would like to get away, and I'm to go back of my own free will? Not on your life!'[6]

An even more embarrassing *folie de jugement* soon afterwards was to make the Nazis a national laughing stock – though nobody dared to be seen openly laughing. The party newspaper, the near-bankrupt *Völkischer Beobachter*, printed what purported to be a First World War soldier's front-line reminiscences under the flamboyant introduction: 'After all the lies told by people like Remarque, we now bring you the experience of a soldier who took part in the war, of which you will at once say: that is what it was really like.' Well-versed readers immediately recognized it as a passage from *All Quiet on the Western Front*.[7]

Paris, Davos and St Moritz, Venice, Salzburg . . . Content as he was with his home, the Lancia became his magic carpet for a peripatetic round of travel and extended escapes from the psychological confinement of his new life, between bouts of working on *Pat*. Time and again over the next few years he was drawn to Paris, an assembly point for emigrés lucky enough to have got out of Nazi Germany. For many of them their haven was the Hotel Ansonia, an anonymous establishment in the Rue de Saigon, a nondescript cobbled side-street between the Avenue Foch and the Avenue de la Grande-Armée in the shadow of the Arc de Triomphe, which welcomed refugees without papers, no questions asked. The address, itself a cover for the hotel's clandestine activities and clientele, was in fact the rear entrance to what had probably been the servant quarters of an ostensible grand mansion on the Avenue Foch.

Although Remarque's wealth and celebrity, underpinned by his temporary Swiss identity papers, had accustomed him to the grand hotels of Europe on his travels, he would frequently check in at the Ansonia rather than the Lancaster or Claridge's or the Prince de Galles, his favourite Paris hotels. There he could count on tracking down some old acquaintance or other from Berlin days – cultural exiles he had lost contact with such as Friedrich Holländer, Franz Wachsmann who, as Franz Waxman, would become one of Hollywood's leading composers, the actor Peter Lorre and his wife, even Billy Wilder, all of them dispossessed fugitives who found a transient sanctuary at the Ansonia en route to new lives in America. There, too, he was able to resume his drinking partnership with the Austrian novelist Joseph Roth, author of *The Radetzky March* who lived in Paris until his suicide on the eve of the Second World War.

With so much displaced creative talent concentrated under its roof the Ansonia was a volatile crucible for egos, ideas, aspirations, hopes and despair which coloured and dramatized its spare, shabby ambience. Friedrich Holländer described it in his memoirs as 'this nest for the expelled, refuge of the expropriated, holding tank, transition camp, hotbed for all kinds of premature births – of ideas for the future to suicide plans. The rooms are small but dirty – dirty but cheap.'[8] Billy Wilder remembered: 'No one had much money, but life was cheap. On the street corner there was a restaurant, the Select, with a *prix-fixe* menu of seven francs. We would leave our napkins on the rack to pick them up in the evenings. Very petit bourgeois.'[9]

The emigrés' shadowy world commingled with that of the established colony of Russian exiles from the Revolution in a nocturnal network of bars and clubs where illicit deals were done, forged identity papers bartered, information exchanged about the availability of coveted visas or berths on ships sailing for the New World. And always the fear of arrest and deportation.

Circulating and observing on the fringes of this furtive sub-culture, Remarque was unconsciously accumulating background material for future best-sellers, the three so-called 'emigré novels'. The Ansonia itself was to figure prominently in two of them, *Flotsam* (*Liebe deinen Nächsten*) and *Arch of Triumph* (*Arc de Triomphe*), in which Remarque, with a touch of irony, named it the Hotel International.

> The dining room of the Hotel International was in the basement. The lodgers called it the Catacombs. During the day a dim light came through several large, thick, opalescent-glass panes which faced on the courtyard. In the winter it had to be lighted all day long. The room was at once a writing-room, a smoking-room, an auditorium, an assembly room, and a refuge for those emigrants who had no papers – when there was a police inspection they could

escape through the yard into a garage and from there to the next street. (*Arch of Triumph*).

Following the proclamation of the Nazis' infamous Nuremberg Laws in 1935, defining the status of German Jews and progressively stripping them of their civil rights, the trickle of refugees leaving Germany swelled into a flood, many of them crossing the border illegally into Switzerland.

Even in exclusive Porto Ronco Remarque was made sympathetically aware of them, as he noted in his diary on 19 August 1936 in the cryptic style he used for recording events:

> This afternoon an emigré, 34 years old, Jewish, Ignaz Hain. Had spoken with E. Frank. Gave him money, put him up, rail ticket to Milan. Thought about it all evening. Sad. Decent people for whom there is nothing, probably lost. Was glad to be able to talk. No money – but wore a good suit and snow-white shoes. Bloody shackles over there.

A more sinister incident around this time, officially hushed up, occurred at the Casa Remarque. The body of a refugee was found one morning in the grounds, killed there or dumped during the night. Whether the death was accidental or murder was never clarified. The victim was identified as Felix M. Mendelssohn, a journalist from Berlin and on the evidence of his name probably Jewish.

The incident is mentioned by Thomas Mann in his diaries, presumably because the Swiss police at first confused the man's identity with that of the writer Peter de Mendelssohn, a close friend of Mann's and his future biographer.[10] In the initial confusion immediately after the body was discovered, reports circulated that it was that of Remarque himself.

Whatever the circumstances the refugee appeared to have suffered a sudden and violent death. The fact of his being a Berlin journalist suggested that he may well have been known to Remarque and had been seeking help. And Remarque knew the Gestapo was keeping him under regular surveillance. It was not impossible that he himself had been the intended victim. He never made any public reference to the incident.

Early in 1936 Remarque acquired a new lover, a woman whose identity he resolutely kept a mystery, referring to her in his diaries only as E. Her name was Margot von Opel. As with so many of his affairs it was short lived but conducted with an intensity that precluded all other considerations, even protracted work on *Pat*. And as was his custom with all his romances, he and his lover would remain friends after passion had been spent, meeting up again years later in America as fond old acquaintances.

A new, darker dimension had begun to weave into his sexual tastes. Since his Berlin days he had been stimulated by the thought of casual, often anonymous sex with pick-ups as well as prostitutes. He was only too aware that his sexual prowess and stamina were merely average, if not underpowered. Often he found himself incapable of making love. The word 'impotent' recurs in his diary jottings. The romantic in him idealized his 'official' loves, including his wife; they were not to be degraded by purely physical lusts. For these, he targeted women beneath his own standards of class and intelligence, bar-girls, waitresses, chambermaids. Covert sex brought him reassurance.

Visiting Budapest with Margot in May 1936, he intersperses diary entries noting their lunch with Countess Edelsheim and cocktails with Count Battyani with somewhat less salubrious encounters.

> Sent back [to his hotel] by E. Met Ria. Charming. Wanted to be more than a barmaid. Love. Back to the Moulin Rouge. Then rendezvous in a hotel with a little Danish girl. The weather in the Puszta (the Hungarian steppes) changes quickly. E. superior. Back to the hotel at 5 a.m. Yellow roses in the morning light, God's air, rain-wet and fresh, forgetting everything from before, a little laughter, talk about the day, the great security of being together and the magical shine over it all.

Wrongdoing and deceit are swiftly neutralized by lyrical imagery and the nearness of an idealized love.

On the return journey, without Margot, he stops over in Vienna for a secret reunion with Ruth Albu, their first for three years.

> Tender memories. Tender moments now. Everything is the same, only a rather light shadowing of the years which makes her even sweeter, more imposing and more beautiful. Went to the Grand Hotel in the bar, a couple of Martinis. She was at ease, balanced, happy and, as she assured me, uninhibited for the first time. 'That you are there,' she said, 'That you are alive will always make me happy'. 'It's the end,' I thought.

There were more descriptive diary flourishes the following month when Remarque drove Margot to Venice, garaging the Lancia on the outskirts and drifting romantically on to the Danieli Hotel in a gondola. 'Evening with E. in St Mark's Square. Wonderful, the flying wisps of cloud on the night sky, light and scurrying behind the Doge's Palace which is magical. Lots of wine and scampi.'

They drove on, dreamily contented, down the Istrian coast of Croatia . . . Opatija, Dubrovnik, the idyllic island of Lovran. Back in Switzerland, close to home, Margot left him at Lugano to take a train for Berlin. 'In Lugano to the Lido. Bathed. Then to the railway station. E. leaves. Leaves. On to Porto Ronco alone. Peter [one of Remarque's pet-names for Jutta] there and Bettina [Bettina Hönig, a close friend of Jutta's]. Rather cool welcome . . . A lonely life.'

A month later: 'Phone E. Missing her. Seems very far away.' Further even than he thought. It would be another four years before they would meet again – in American exile as just good friends.

The final draft of *Pat*, its title now settled as *Three Comrades*, was completed by the end of 1937. There was, of course, no question of it being published in Germany and one of the several reasons for its long and troublesome genesis was the need to translate it into English for its first appearance. Serialization started in the mass-marked American magazine *Good Housekeeping* in January 1937 followed by book publication in May. The book touchingly bore a dedication to J.R.Z – Jutta Remarque Zambona.

Reviews were encouraging, if not ecstatic. Comparing the Robby/Pat love story with its equivalent in Ernest Hemingway's *A Farewell to Arms*, the *New York Times Book Review* judged Remarque's 'more than just a little better'. In Britain, *The Times Literary Supplement* thought it 'deeply honest'.

'Good reviews England and America,' he recorded. 'Established that Sweden, Norway, Holland, Denmark have published the wrong, last but one, essentially long-winded, bad version as a result of hanging about and oversight. Stupid!'

English-language sales replenished his bank balance healthily. Film rights had already been sold to Metro-Goldwyn-Mayer in Hollywood and with Universal's delayed production of *The Road Back*, scripted by R.C. Sherriff, scheduled for a Los Angeles premiere in June, a month after the publication of *Three Comrades*, the Remarque name was news again.

Universal's six years' hiatus between snapping up the rights to *The Road Back* and releasing the film had been partially a case of second thoughts. The first flush of enthusiasm following the stunning impact of *All Quiet on the Western Front* had faded all too rapidly. War-related films were suddenly 'box-office poison'. Moreover, the studio was disappointed with Sherriff's screenplay.

'I dramatized it as closely as possible to the story which Remarque had written . . . They liked it up to a point, but this time they had the original novel to compare it with and were disappointed that I hadn't added much from my own resources,' he recalled in his autobiography,

> I told them that Remarque had written such good stuff that it didn't need any artificial flavouring. My job had been to turn narrative into dialogue and to make descriptive passages speak in words, also to distil the essence of a novel of 400 pages into a compact screenplay.
>
> You couldn't explain that to a film producer. All he looked for was stuff I'd invented off my own bat; stuff to make the novel better

than it was when it didn't need to be any better. They accepted it in a lukewarm way, but didn't seem quite sure that they had got their money's worth.[11]

The film, though well enough received, reflected the studio's less-than-wholehearted commitment. 'Big and frequently effective, but a let-down in toto . . . does not compare with *All Quiet* in quality or power,' advised *Variety*, the American screen exhibitors' oracle, in June 1937.

The switch of studios from Universal, who had done well by Remarque so far, to Metro-Goldwyn-Mayer was reputedly instigated by the French actor Charles Boyer, an admirer of Remarque's work. They had met and become friends during one of Remarque's stays in Paris in 1935 when he had visited the set of *Mayerling* in which Boyer was playing the ill-fated Archduke Rudolf of Austria.

Boyer was vehemently anti-Nazi and 'had grasped the reality of the Nazi terror when most people either underrated Hitler or considered him a joke,' his biographer wrote. 'He never doubted that Hitler's Germany was committed to unlimited territorial conquest. In Hollywood Boyer gained early identity with an anti-isolationist element that was regularly accused of war-mongering.'

Boyer was filming *History is Made at Night* in Hollywood when *Three Comrades* appeared. The film's director was Frank Borzage whose credits included A *Farewell to Arms,* and a version of Hans Fallada's *Little Man, What Now?* – arguably Hollywood's earliest, tentative statement of anti-Nazism. Borzage was able to convey characters' inner spirituality, and so was an ideal conductor for Remarque's sensitive portrayal of comradeship and doomed love.

Once *History is Made at Night* was completed, Borzage urged MGM to acquire rights to *Three Comrades* and let him direct the film.[12]

Three Comrades claims a unique place in the Hollywood pantheon: it is the only film which bears the name of F. Scott Fitzgerald as a screenwriter. For the golden-boy of the Jazz Age, the need to seek employment as a studio hack was a low point of his career. Preparing a shooting-script of the Remarque novel was his first important assignment. To his credit he tackled it with zeal enough, but his drinking addiction, prickly reaction to criticism and loss of self-confidence undermined his application to it. To the studio, he represented unreliability and trouble. The writing schedule was constantly plagued by arguments, revisions, re-writes and spats with the production team. Co-writers were drafted in and finally the film's producer Joseph Mankiewicz, an experienced script-writer, overrode Fitzgerald's continual resistance to changes by taking over the re-writes himself. Fitzgerald, battling to the end for the last word, wrote him:

> To say I'm disillusioned is putting it mildly. For nineteen years, with two years out for sickness, I've written best-selling entertainment, and my dialogue is supposedly right up at the top. But I learn from the script that you've suddenly decided that it isn't good dialogue and you can take a few hours off and do much better. I think you now have a flop on your hands . . . Some honest thinking would be much more valuable to the enterprise now than an effort to convince people you've improved it. I am utterly miserable at seeing months of work and thought negated in one hasty week . . .[13]

When the film was released in May, 1938 Fitzgerald was billed sharing the writing credits.

With the Fitzgerald problem disposed of, MGM found itself facing another, potentially more serious problem with *Three Comrades*. The film, like the book, climaxes with the upsurge of Nazi thuggery and street fights between the Nazis and Communists in which one of the comrades is murdered. Remarque, observing the apolitical stance he had adopted at that time, was careful not to identity the opposing parties. The film, while not naming names, was more explicit in showing the accoutrements of dress worn by the Nazi stormtroopers..

Mindful of the German box-office no less than the Reich's political sensibilities, the studio head, Louis B. Mayer, was worried that the Nazis might lodge objections and invited a representative of the German consulate in Los Angeles to a private screening. The diplomat was not impressed by what he saw and pressure was applied to emasculate the offending sequences. Mayer was willing to comply and even Joseph I. Breen who chaired Hollywood's self-regulating Production Code Administration – the notorious Hays Office – threw his weight behind the censorship demand by suggesting the troublemakers should be clearly identified as Communists. Mankiewicz threatened to resign and alert the Press. Mayer capitulated. The film stayed true to Remarque. Soon after its release, however, all MGM productions were banned from German cinemas.[14]

Liberated at last from four years' hard labour on *Three Comrades*, Remarque spent the first two months of 1937 in St Moritz, luxuriating in the company of the famous and the fashionable gathered there for the winter season. The residual Osnabrück provincial in him could still revel in celebrity and the equality of status with famous names it bestowed on him.

'Went walking to begin with; afterwards mostly sat in the bar,' his diary records in a resumé of his stay after his return to Porto Ronco. Then follows a selective list of the people he associated with, among them the American author Louis Blomfield whose most famous best-seller *The Rains Came* was about to be published; the crime-writer Georges Simenon, creator of Maigret, 'who still only writes six novels a year'; Hollywood stars Eleanor Boardman and Kay Francis; Leni Riefenstahl, now Hitler's favourite film-maker following *Triumph of the Will,* her anthem to the Party; the German-born Hollywood director William Wyler, newly divorced from Margaret Sullavan, who would play Pat in *Three Comrades* later that year. Casually infiltrated into the list is the single name Hedy, the only person not fully identified or attributed with an explanatory word or two. Remarque's discretion betrays as much as conceals the degree of intimacy between them.

Hedy Kiesler was already famous – indeed notorious – as an actress in German-language theatre and cinema. She was soon to become world-famous as the Hollywood love goddess Hedy Lamarr. The daughter of a wealthy Viennese banker, she had shocked cinemagoers and Viennese society alike by appearing nude in the Czech film of 1933, *Extase (Ecstasy)*, an exposure that had ensured the film international interest, condemnation and censorship. 'They must have used a telescopic lens,' she conjectured artlessly in her memoirs. She and Remarque no doubt found common ground in their respective experiences of affronting public taste.

At the time of the film's release she had married the much older Austrian armaments magnate Fritz Mandl who spent a fortune trying, with only partial success, to buy up every existing copy and the negative of *Ecstasy*. Marriage to the possessive Mandl was virtual imprisonment and Hedy made several abortive attempts to escape from it. Only a few months before she and Remarque met in St Moritz she had finally succeeded in obtaining a divorce.

Hedy Kiesler embodied all the qualities that Remarque found attractive – a stunning beauty, an actress, sophisticated, louche, German-speaking – and there was no reason why their brief affair might not have developed into another of his idealized relationships. But Hedy had her sights on wider horizons. That summer she embarked on her quest for stardom, soon finding it in Hollywood.

And that summer Remarque met Marlene Dietrich.

10

Marlene Dietrich

V enice. The setting and circumstances could hardly have been more glamorously appropriate for two such inveterate romantics. Dietrich was lunching in the terrace restaurant of the Hotel des Bains on the Lido with Josef von Sternberg, the film director and her sometime lover who had launched her international career in *The Blue Angel* and orchestrated it, Svengali–like, to Hollywood heights. Remarque, alone in Venice, was passing their table. He paused.

'Herr von Sternberg? Madame? May I introduce myself? I am Erich Maria Remarque.'

Dietrich disliked being accosted by strangers in her private moments and would normally rebuff uninvited approaches. But the Remarque name and good looks caught her off guard. 'I almost fell off my chair,' she wrote in her memoirs four decades later, 'That always happens to me if I meet famous, outstandingly good men whom the world talks about. It's always a shock for me if they are suddenly standing there "in the flesh" before me.'[1]

She offered her hand and, charmed by the gallantry with which he raised it to his lips, invited him to join them. Von Sternberg, shortly after, excused himself and left them together.

According to Dietrich's daughter Maria Riva, Marlene claimed they had 'talked until dawn. It was wonderful. Then he looked at me and said "I must tell you, I am impotent", and I looked up at him and said,

"Oh, how wonderful" with such relief . . . I was so happy. It meant we could just talk and sleep, love each other, all nice and cosy.'[2]

The implied directness of Remarque's love-making overture would seem characteristic, but Dietrich's own version is more circumspect, not to say coquettishly romantic.

> I met him for the first time at the Venice Lido. I was there visiting von Sternberg . . . Next morning I met him again on the beach. I had a book of Rainer Maria Rilke under my arm and was looking for a place in the sun to sit and read. He came up to me. He saw my book and said with undisguised sarcasm 'I see you're reading a good book.' I understood what he meant. 'Do you want me to recite some of the poems?' He looked at me sceptically. He didn't believe me. A film star who read?
>
> It was like delivering a blow when I began with *Der Panther und Leda*, followed by *Herbstag*, *Ernste Stunde* etc. All my favourite poems. He said 'Let's go away and talk.' I followed him.

Their affair was to be the apogee of Remarque's emotional life, and if not to the same degree of Dietrich's, certainly a memory she would always cherish. He was, she wrote after his death, 'the last of the romantics. Besides the great writer that he was, he had a capacity few men have. The capacity to understand the emotions of all living creatures. Understand them and soothe aching hearts, including mine, all through the years of his self-chosen exile in America.'[3]

At the time they met Dietrich's *amours* were already the stuff of legend. Apart from Sternberg her lovers had included Maurice Chevalier, the Hollywood actors Ronald Colman, Brian Aherne, Richard Barthelmess, John Gilbert and, most recently, Douglas Fairbanks Jr. Understandably less conspicuous were her lesbian liaisons with Gary Cooper's paramour Countess Dorothy di Frasso and Mercedes de Acosta whose favours Marlene inherited, as she had those of John Gilbert, from Greta Garbo

The anchor of public propriety through all the turbulent *rondes* of these affiliations was her complaisant husband Rudolph (Rudi) Sieber, whom she had married in 1924 and who was the father of her only child Maria. Theirs was an agreed 'open marriage'. Marlene, Rudi and Maria were viewed by the public as an ideal, loving family as the gossip columns recorded their progresses around the resorts of Europe and America, unaware that the 'family' might also incorporate Marlene's current lover (sometimes female) and always Rudi's long-term mistress Tamara (Tami) Matul, a White Russian refugee.

No two anguished souls could have been better programmed to comfort each other than Remarque and Dietrich at this time. Unlikely as it may have seemed to the world at large the star who personified bold, assertive sophistication was going through a period of insecurity. The early heyday of her impact on the cinemagoing public in such films as *The Blue Angel, Morocco* and *Shanghai Express* had passed. Her recent run of titles had been artistic and box-office failures. At the end of 1937 she ranked 126th in the roll-call of Hollywood's bankable stars. It was probably the crisis in her career that had brought her to Venice to consult her mentor, von Sternberg. Rudi, Maria and Tami were, for once, not with her. 'I had nobody, other than myself, who could give me advice, nobody I could ask for advice,' she lamented.[4]

Like the eponymous *Knight Without Armour* of the film Marlene had just completed in London, Remarque rode into her life at a crucial moment. It was almost as though he were a touchstone for reviving her fortunes. Although lavish production costs rendered *Knight Without Armour* unprofitable, it was popular with the critics and public when it was released months later. And it was Remarque who, the following year, urged her to accept an offer to star in *Destry Rides Again*, the film that would transform her screen personality and spirit her back to the top of the popularity polls.

Dietrich, moreover, was waiting for a new man to enter her life. Her four-year affair with Douglas Fairbanks Jr had run its course. As Fairbanks wrote:

> My lovely liaison with Dietrich was not destined to survive much longer. It was too high-powered and sophisticated for me. It was not only the more assured and intellectual German author Erich

Maria Remarque who brought our relationship to an end but my own sudden jealousy was also to blame. Quite by accident, while searching Marlene's desk for writing paper, I came across some intense love letters (from someone I'd never heard of) to Marlene. Although I had no idea of their date or any circumstances of their existence, I blew up in a jealous rage. Marlene's reaction was justifiable anger with me for going through her private papers in the first place. One word led to another and our waning romance fizzled out then and there.[5]

The letters were from Mercedes de Acosta.

Even allowing for Remarque's depressive nature, the problems that had buffeted him in the past had mostly been imposed by outside influences that he was powerless to control. Now they were becoming self-inflicted. During the two months he'd spent in Paris at the end of 1937, ostensibly to gather material for his next book, he had hardly applied himself rigorously to the task. He was by no means sure what the book would be about. He had ideas but no theme beyond a vague impulse to write about the growing refugee situation in Europe. Events in the months ahead would crystallize one for him.

Jutta joined him at the Hotel Prince de Galles. Marlene was also in town with the 'family', but remained discreetly unavailable. Remarque dined separately with Rudi and Tami. The threats of the emotional web he was allowing himself to be drawn into were growing ever more tangled.

'Not happy, not sad. Memory and the present are getting crossed,' he bewails to his diary, 'I could work if I were on my own.'

At least his own emigré status had been regularized. A few months earlier he had finally succeeded in obtaining a precious Nansen passport, so-called after the Norwegian polar explorer and diplomat who after the First World War had campaigned for stateless refugees to be issued with a legal international travel document, a cause for which he was awarded the Nobel Peace Prize. Remarque's papers were authorized by the Republic of Panama.

Jutta's situation was more precarious. Her Swiss visa was due to expire and with the political crisis in Europe growing more alarming by the day she was terrified that the Nazis would prohibit her from leaving Germany.

Remarque agonized over his former wife's predicament and finally offered her a generous solution. 'So that she did not lose her residence permit for Switzerland I married her again,' he later explained in an interview. 'I couldn't allow her to be sent back to Germany just because we weren't in love any more.'[6]

In a perfunctory ceremony at St Moritz on 22 January 1938 Jutta again officially became Frau Remarque.

'This afternoon bath, wash hair, purging – after Hitler's speeches, the pressures of the times and expectations of a gloomy future. This evening a bottle of Wormser Liebfrauen Stiftwein 1934. Necessary.' Remarque's diary entry a month after his remarriage suggests world-weary resignation in his response to the gathering political crisis and his personal circumstances. It was soon to harden into genuine concern and further personal persecution.

On 13 March Europe was stunned by the *Anschluss* – Hitler's enforced political union of Austria with Nazi Germany. 'Speeches, speeches . . . Nobody has done a thing about it – as expected,' Remarque wrote despondently the next day. 'There is already an A. Hitler Square in Vienna. The world consists of lackeys. Except the workers.'

That day Hitler drove triumphally through Vienna, the capital of his native land. Women threw flowers into his open car. Crowds cheered the parading German troops, tanks and field guns. Guests were evicted from the Imperial Hotel, requisitioned for Hitler and his henchmen. Austria had become just another province of Greater Germany.

Austria, one of Remarque's favourite playgrounds, was now closed to him: Vienna with its memories of Ruth Albu, Salzburg where he had enjoyed the festival, the fabulous parties hosted by Max Reinhardt, Germany's great stage director, and all-night drinking sprees with Carl

Zuckmayer. The dramatist, warned by a sympathetic Nazi admirer to flee his home near the city of Mozart, would, within days, arrive in Switzerland as a fellow-exile.

Worse was to follow. Unknown to Remarque, the Gestapo was compiling a damning report on 'the German-blooded writer Erich Paul Remark' for the SS. Among accusations that could barely stand the test of circumstantial evidence, let alone of truth, it charged him with insulting 'the memory of the dead soldiers of the World War' and 'an active social life exclusively limited to emigrants, Jews and Communists . . . associations [which] unequivocally show that he clings just as much as he did earlier to Jewish-Marxist seditious ideas.' The spectre of his brief period as a student activist lingered on his record.

The document was forwarded to the Ministry of the Interior which, four months later in July, announced that Remarque had been stripped of his German citizenship. A similar decree the following November meted out the same sentence on Jutta. Both of them were now officially stateless persons.[7]

Years later Remarque could put a sanguine face on his expulsion. 'My German citizenship was taken away. At the time that was a great honour but professionally a shock, naturally. A writer without a fatherland? What would he write about?' he told an interviewer in 1962.[8] But in that ominous summer of 1938 nothing in the Nazis' campaign of petty harassment left him feeling more wounded and desolate than being deprived of his birthright. Disillusioned and sickened as he was by the political path Germany had taken, he was (and remained) proud of Germany, its language and its cultural heritage.

And he did find something to write about. Galvanized by the *Anschluss*, the mounting tide of people, many of them friends, fleeing the Nazis and his own status as a non-person, he began working on the first of his emigré novels that would bear the ironic German title *Liebe Deinen Nächsten* (*Love Thy Neighbour*) and in English the sarcastically metaphoric *Flotsam*. He would introduce it with the inscription: 'To live without roots takes a stout heart.'

Remarque was finding that he needed no less of a stout heart to cope with his growing obsession with Marlene Dietrich and her mercurial regimen of attachments and fidelities. She in turn was perplexed and resentful of his continuing loyalty to Jutta. She seemed oblivious to the strains her domestic 'establishment' placed on him as an adjunct to the 'family'.

They met up in Paris in July. Remarque was besotted, yearning for a proper privacy in which to conduct their romance but it seemed to him that they could steal only brief moments of intimacy. His diary muses on the complications: 'Marlene reproaches me for remarrying. Rightly and wrongly. Peter [Jutta] reproaches me with furious emotion over Marlene. Rightly and wrongly . . . A bit of a muddle . . . What's more, the Family is always there – friendly, intelligent, good-natured – but always there, even when it's not there.'

Towards the end of their two weeks together – 'tumultuous' is Remarque's diary word for them – Jutta turns up. She is not invited to join the Family. 'Last day in Paris with Peter. Difficult. M. saw us going into Maxim's. Also difficult afterwards. We'll see what will be.'

Remarque intends driving home with Jutta to Porto Ronco but, weakly and against his better judgement, allows Marlene and the Family to pressurize him into continuing with them down to the Riviera, travelling in convoy in Remarque's Lancia and Rudi's Packard. Jutta departs in a huff for Switzerland. After an overnight stop in Lyons, Rudi, driving the Lancia, is involved in a minor collision. The Family drives on, leaving Remarque to deal with the car repairs. There are times when he seems no more than a factotum to them.

At Antibes the party has checked in to the Hôtel du Cap (after finding the Eden Roc 'disappointing') for nearly two months of sybaritic indulgence in this enclave of wealth and privilege where the 'beautiful people' of the 1930s congregated, and still do today. Marlene assuages Remarque's touchy sense of 'coming second' by elevating him to 'head of the table' in the dining-room, displacing Rudi.

The three of them had connecting suites while Tami and Maria were banished to inferior rooms along the corridor. Days were spent sunbathing and swimming from their luxurious cabanas on the rocks below the hotel, evenings passed over cocktails, long dinners and dancing with occasional excursions to restaurants or nightclubs along the coast. They socialized with Joe Kennedy, the American ambassador in London, who was renting a villa nearby for his large family, including the twenty-one-year-old future President of the United States, and were entertained by Elsa Maxwell, the legendary society party hostess.

For Remarque it must have represented the pinnacle of his climb to fame and fortune as he sat, black-tied and monocled, at the head of Dietrich's table. He was in thrall to her. It was too good to last. What began as an idyll soon degenerated for him into an agony of emotional confusion. Ensnared by his infatuation and in bondage to Marlene's mood-swings, he found himself roller-coasting between heights of ecstasy and depths of depression, depending on her whims. Even their most tender interludes together are haunted by his melancholic demons.

'4 August: Rapturous night . . . but as usual over too soon. Lots of small signs: with me, with her: sensitivity, mockery, touchiness. Knowing that this is probably the best and the last. And doing nothing . . .' He soon found he had a rival.

The new and unexpected recruit to the Dietrich entourage was an unlikely contender for her affections. Marion Barbara Carstairs, known as Joe [Jo in Remarque's diaries], was a wealthy, flamboyant lesbian who encountered the Family on the rocks where she was renting an adjacent cabana. The thirty-eight-year-old daughter of a Scottish army officer and his American heiress wife, she had inherited a multi-million dollar fortune from her maternal grandfather, a self-made businessman who had been treasurer of John D. Rockefeller's Southern Improvement Company, later Standard Oil.

The androgynous Joe made no secret of her sexual proclivities. Mannish in appearance and comportment, she wore masculine clothes – a style made shockingly fashionable by Marlene in *Morocco* eight years earlier – and indulged in, for those days, dare-devil masculine sports. Sailing and the sea were her great passion; she had gone so far as having herself tattooed, an inconceivable adornment for a woman outside a fairground booth. She had built boats for competitive racing. She had bought the West Indies island of Whale Cay, where she reigned for the rest of her life as autonomous 'Queen'. There she entertained an inexhaustible succession of female lovers, some of them plain, many beautiful, who included the bi-sexual actress Tallulah Bankhead and Mercedes de Acosta. 'I've never had to go out and race and win,' she once said. 'They just fall in my lap.' At Antibes that summer she added Marlene Dietrich to her sexual trophies.[9]

To Remarque, confused and insecure, the situation was bizarre and vaguely repellent. For all his outward display of worldliness – and only eight years into his own world-wide celebrity – he was still at heart a provincial whose moral instincts and empathy with the mores of his upbringing were closer to the standards of the 'common man' than to those of these pampered, free-wheeling, anything-goes sophisticates. A part of him craved to be included in their world but against a background of political crisis and incalculable human misery in Europe he was guilt-ridden by its self-indulgence – and his own.

Marlene's dalliance with Joe Carstairs became a torment. Almost certainly there was an element of manipulation behind it, her fickle moods testing him, provoking his jealousy, creating situations she could resolve with some generous or affectionate gesture or a brief resumption of intimacy. And Remarque at his lowest emotional ebb was a pitifully easy target for her capriciousness.

His diary entries are a jagged graph of his feelings and his opinion of what he called 'the tattooed woman'. The musical chairs of comings and goings, finding Marlene's door locked against him and knowing Joe is behind it with her, the insouciance of Rudi's response to the situation, the intensities seething below the surface of all their relationships would take on a quality of farce were it not for the anguish Remarque was genuinely suffering.

He tried escaping into work, eschewing the sun-bathing rocks and the pleasure boats to seal himself off in his suite writing *Flotsam*. In spite of the distractions it was progressing well. Some nights he would take himself off on solitary drinking binges.

Maria recalled: 'My mother told everyone how she searched for him in every bar between Monte Carlo and Cannes – afraid he would be arrested and news of his disgraceful conduct hit the headlines,' and, quoting Marlene, 'Everyone already knows [F. Scott] Fitzgerald is a drunkard, and Hemingway drinks only because he is a Real Man, but Boni [Marlene's pet-name for Remarque] – he is a *sensitive* writer. Sensitive writers are poets, so they are delicate, they can't lie in gutters and get sick.' Dietrich's 'searches' were, in fact, more often than not conducted by Rudi on her instructions.

When she slipped away for a two-day jaunt on Joe's cruiser, he was beside himself with jealousy. Yet sometimes there is a suspicion of masochistic self-pity in the detailed introspection he projects:

> 4 September. Strange situation. Sang and began intentionally and unintentionally to cry, very slowly and not much, in front of the mirror, half ironically, half genuinely, half serious and half something else, not play-acting, more curiosity, even wanting to, wanting to get myself in tears, waiting for tears and then there they were: a certain calming down and composure.

At the height of this farrago a note of business-like sanity suddenly intruded. Marlene received a cable from Hollywood sounding her out for the female lead in a film the producer Joe Pasternak was preparing at Universal Studios. Extracts from the script followed. The movie was *Destry Rides Again*, a spoof Western with songs, and the role Pasternak was offering her was Frenchy, a tough, raucous saloon girl who falls in love with a new, mild-mannered sheriff to be played by James Stewart.

Frenchy was unlike any character Marlene had played before, unsympathetic though mellowing under the influence of true love and the high moral values of her lover. Moreover, she dies at the end, stopping a bullet intended for him. Marlene, despite a lack of offers and her own gloomy prognosis for her career, read the script samples without enthusiasm. The role did not appeal to her and the $75,000 offer was a risible one-sixth of the salary she had been commanding before her box-office value plummeted.

Remarque too read the script and glimpsed something of the film's potential. He urged her to consider it. The change of image, he argued, could revitalize her career and, besides, what had she got to lose? So she accepted the offer, not without misgivings, but his advice was proved sound. *Destry Rides Again* would propel her back into the front rank of Hollywood stardom and provide the keystone of her later career as a chanteuse with its classic song *See What the Boys in the Back Room Will Have*. Remarque's reward would be yet another crisis of jealousy, this time in the lanky, laconic person of James Stewart.

Even the hedonistic little world of the Hotel du Cap could not be insulated against the greater crisis threatening to engulf Europe. With Austria firmly integrated into the German Reich new tensions were developing over the Sudetenland, a German-speaking area of the former Austrian empire which had been ceded to Czechoslovakia by the Allies after the the First World War. Following the Austrian *Anschluss* its three million inhabitants had begun agitating for similar incorporation into the Reich. Hitler turned his bullying technique on to the Czech government. Britain and France responded with vague diplomatic warnings. War seemed an imminent possibility.

The Riviera sojourn ended in early September and the Family re-grouped in Paris. Remarque joined them there. So did Joe Carstairs. The emotional fiasco resumed with piquant added refinements. Ruth Albu was passing through. Later Mercedes de Acosta put in an appearance. Remarque and Ruth had several covert meetings, though the old passions were long past.

'14 September: Earlier met Ruth again at the Hôtel Lincoln, said goodbye, was charming. Slept with Puma [Marlene]'. It was some measure of his passion for her that he gave her the nickname he had given his beloved car. The Lancia became Puma I, Marlene was Puma II.

The Czech crisis was dominating his thoughts. The expansionist policies of the Third Reich were beginning to seem unstoppable. Despite Switzerland's time-honoured neutrality, there was good reason to speculate that its German-speaking region could be a future target for Hitler and Remarque, stateless, lacking foolproof papers, a name on the Gestapo's wanted list, was acutely aware of his vulnerability.

Settling in Switzerland 'as far south as possible near the border where German would still be spoken' was no longer the secure option it had seemed four years before.

'Heard that Germans born in the World War are being called up today . . . Sat by the radio till midnight. Ultimatum expired. Eleven deaths. The Czech government called for calm, then negotiations.' He arranged for his bank accounts and various gold items to be transferred from Porto Ronco to a safer deposit in Zürich. The agent for the transaction was Brigitte Neuner, his girlfriend of Berlin days. Discarded old flames always appeared willing and eager to answer his call and do his bidding.

Marlene was no less agitated by the crisis.

> Puma heard that stateless persons in France would be hauled in by the military. Was distraught. I've already been in France for four months and should have had a *carte d'identité* long since . . . Puma was making plans the whole evening. Wanted to go to Porto Ronco for me: to get us all on a ship, to go to the American embassy . . . A call this morning. We are to go to the American embassy at a quarter to three. Situation politically even more intense. A plebiscite which amounts to a breakaway, or war. Relations between Sudeten Germans and Czechs broken off. Already eighteen deaths.

The weeks in Paris were a constant battle of wills and wits between Remarque and Dietrich, she tantalizing and vacillating between possessiveness, tenderness and rebuff, he resignedly, almost slavishly, accepting her inconstancy, even enjoying it.

> 23 September: Fought playfully for two hours. Puma explained how she loved men. Quickly, misty-eyed, unbridled when it comes over her, etc. Then that she doesn't need men. She'd never missed them in bed. Only women – Joe. That's just it . . . Went home. Puma suddenly discovered I've become better trained. Fell in love. After all the talk, suddenly. I wasn't able to do it. Heaven knows why

not. Slept close to one another, Puma clinging tight to me. In the morning Puma in love again.

Later that day, after he had slipped away to say his goodbye to Ruth Albu, they visited the jewellers Van Cleef to choose a wedding ring 'which the Puma wanted to have from me'. When they slept together that night Remarque noticed she was no longer wearing the ring and watch-strap Joe Carstairs had given her.

The Czech crisis was averted temporarily, and shamefully on the part of the British and French governments whose negotiations with Hitler concluded with capitulation to most of his demands and empty guarantees. On 30 September the British Prime Minister Neville Chamberlain returned to London from the Munich conference famously flourishing his slip of paper and declaring 'peace in our time'.

The Family stayed on in Paris. Marlene had accepted the *Destry Rides Again* offer and was due to sail from Cherbourg for New York in November. Joe Carstairs left for London. In the remaining weeks Marlene turned the full mesmeric magic of her attention on Remarque, reassuring him of her love, assuaging his tormented emotions. They were idyllic weeks played out against the mists of a Paris autumn and an intangible mood of foreboding for a future unknown, a sense that civilized Europe was on the brink of an abyss. The atmosphere left a deep impression on Remarque which he would evoke hauntingly in the novel he would write next.

Early in December he returned to Porto Ronco and the home he had not seen for six months. He found everything as he had left it, scrupulously cared for by Rosa, the housekeeper. It was quiet. He was alone and lonely for Marlene. Letters and cables flowed between them. He had the time and the space to put the finishing touches to *Flotsam* and, without a break, start preliminary work on his next idea.

'9 December, Friday: Late this evening wrote the first words of the Ravic novel.'

Ravic was the name he had decided on for the main character of his new novel, a psychological self-portrait, carefully disguised but recognizable. The book would become *Arch of Triumph*, his biggest best-seller after *All Quiet on the Western Front*. It would be suffused with the muse and image of Marlene Dietrich.

11

War and the End of the Affair

With *Flotsam* Remarque broke away from the first-person semi-autobiographical format of his three previous best-sellers and conceived a narrative that was purely fictional. Even so, it was profoundly influenced by the psychological condition of exile and statelessness, his own and that of the emigré friends and acquaintances he had observed in Paris and Switzerland. The 'flotsam' are the dispossessed, the homeless and the hopeless washed up by the tide of politics and events – 'the outlaws and orphans of the twentieth century storm' as the British publisher's blurb described them in 1941. That he would return to the theme in subsequent novels until his last thirty-two years later was an indication of the searing scar the loss of his German citizenship had left on him.

For all the sincerity with which he set about depicting the lot of the 'ordinary' refugee of the 1930s, the theme would bring him further critical onslaughts and abuse in Germany after the Second World War, calling his credibility into question. He had not been a standard refugee. He might understand the psychological stress of being stateless, but his wealth, celebrity and powerful contacts had protected him from the depredations the great majority of enforced emigrés had had to endure. He had not slept in the furtive doss-houses of Prague, Zürich or Paris in constant fear of the police raid he describes so vividly in the opening scene of *Flotsam*, nor had he felt the constant fear of summary deportation, and nor had he experienced the endless, frustrating quest for identity papers and visas. His privileged circumstances did not make his depiction of the refugee's plight any the less authoritative or convincing, but for many of his critics they compromised his eligibility to write so knowingly about it.

Spurred by a deadline for serialization in *Collier's* magazine prior to its American publication, Remarque worked swiftly on the first draft of *Flotsam* through the winter months of 1938/39 at Porto Ronco, distracted only by his longing for Marlene, the death of his beloved dog Billy, accidentally poisoned on his prowls round the neighbourhood, and a letter from his sister Erna informing him that their father was suffering from arterial sclerosis . . . 'Condition almost hopeless. 72 years old. And worked so hard all his life,' his diary records. It was a false alarm. Peter Remark would survive for another fifteen years.

Remarque was never satisfied with a first draft but the lucrative *Collier's* deadline was pressing, and he decided to deliver the manuscript personally. Marlene had been persuading him to pay his first visit to the United States. In March 1939 he sailed from Cherbourg on the *Queen Mary*. Four days earlier Hitler's troops marched into Prague, scorning the Anglo-French agreement of the previous year, and the Czech nation was yoked to the Nazi juggernaut.

On 23 March, he records: 'Very early this morning, around five a.m., the skyline of New York, grey and massive against the light sky, surprising and not surprising, often seen in photos, but splendid naturally . . .'

That day Hitler 'annexed' the former German Baltic port city of Memel, ceded to Lithuania in the Treaty of Versailles, Hungary invaded Slovakia and, in the House of Commons, Prime Minister Neville Chamberlain warned the *Führer* that 'any attempt at world domination would surely bring the same fate that overtook Philip II of Spain, Napoleon and Kaiser Wilhelm II'. The portents of war had never been so grave.

Remarque's agent Otto Klement came aboard to welcome him. So did the posse of reporters who habitually boarded arriving liners seeking interviews with newsworthy passengers. With Klement interpreting, he told them he had come 'to study America, learn the language and write a book dealing with the persecution of the Jews'. Questioned about the situation in Europe, he stated his opinion that 'a world war will break out and there will be a 100,000 killed on the first day,' and added: 'I want to see America because I think this country is the salvation of the world.'[1]

New York fascinated him, from his suite and the bars at the Waldorf-Astoria ('very pretty girls') to the top of the Empire State Building ('wonderful panorama, the multi-towered city cathedral-like'). He lunched with *Collier's* executives and was escorted to Negro nightclubs in Harlem, essential haunts for Manhattan's smart set. In his diary everything about New York was '*wunderbar*'.

Marlene phoned from Beverly Hills, 'offended because I hadn't called her straight away, cool and huffy'. Later, in another call, she was 'sweet'. After two exhausting days he boarded the Twentieth-Century train for Chicago then the Super Chief to Los Angeles and Marlene.

Hollywood, and Dietrich, were an anti-climax. The much anti-cipated reunion was ominously subdued. By agreement she did not meet him at the Pasadena railway station in case reporters were there. Instead she greeted him at the door of her rented house 'in a yellow suit. Beautiful and awkward.' She was unwell. Remarque didn't like the house. Soon they were quarrelling, making up only to resume arguing and sulking. 'Slept alone last night and if this goes on I shall soon be leaving.'

But their respective moods were essentially negotiable, even part of their mutual attraction, and he stayed on, admitted, as much on the strength of his own celebrity status as Marlene's reflected glory, to the high tables of Hollywood where he socialized with such stars as Gary Cooper, Errol Flynn, Constance Bennett, Ronald Colman, Norma Shearer, Douglas Fairbanks Jr (the Dietrich lover he had supplanted), and Dolores del Rio who, in times to come, would briefly be a replacement for Marlene in his affections. Incorrigibly star-struck, he revelled in the glamorous Hollywood ambience, if not in Hollywood itself.

Amid the party-going and emotional storms with Marlene he made time to work on revisions to *Flotsam* for book publication scheduled for 1940, nearly a year after the *Collier's* serialization. The film rights had been sold to Metro-Goldwyn-Mayer. Under the title *So Ends Our Night*, the movie, like the novel, was considered worthy but unremarkable by critics when it was released in February 1941. Overtaken by calamitous events with the outbreak of war, the theme of refugees from Nazi tyranny in the mid 1930s seemed diminished and dated. Unlike in *Three Comrades*, Remarque had specifically identified the Nazis for the thugs they were. Again, as with *Three Comrades*, M-G-M, mindful of America's initial neutrality in the conflict, cautiously avoided any accusatory reference to them in the film's scenario, enfeebling its impact. The novel sold reasonably well, the film was a box-office failure.

Marlene had booked passage for Europe on the *Normandie*, sailing from New York in mid-June. She was not due back in the studios until September to begin rehearsals for *Destry Rides Again*, so there was just time for a break in Antibes. In New York the Family reassembled and in a well-timed flourish of publicity Marlene subjected herself to the ceremony of receiving American citizenship. Less welcome publicity was to follow. As the Family were boarding the liner she was detained by US Treasury agents and charged with American tax arrears. Marlene, if she is to be believed, persuaded the ship's captain to delay departure until the matter was sorted out with a person-to-person call to the Secretary of the Treasury, Henry Morgenthau, in Washington.

The atmosphere in Paris when they arrived reinforced Remarque's instinct that 'a world war will break out': a sense of the lull before the storm. Days earlier Hitler and Mussolini had signed their 'Pact of Steel', committing Germany and Italy to support each other in time of war 'with all military forces'. It was a particularly worrying development for Remarque with his home so near the Italian border. There was no guarantee that Switzerland's avowed neutrality would be respected by dictators who had already proved their disdain for international law.

The swaggering soldier: Erich in 1918 with his 'fashion statement' German shepherd dog Wolf.

A meeting of 'Die Traumbude': Fritz Hörstemeier (left) was mentor and father figure for Erich (right).

Lew Ayres as Paul Baumer in *All Quiet on the Western Front*. The film made him a star and influenced the pacifist views which were to blight his career when America entered the Second World War.

Mexican beauty: wooed by Remarque, Dolores del Rio was acknowledged to be one of Hollywood's most elegant stars.

'A bird of paradise': the fiery Mexican star Lupe Velez whose amorous exploits filled Hollywood gossip columns, coaxed Remarque out of his depression.

Maureen O'Sullivan, 'Jane' of the Tarzan films, was reputed to have become pregnant during her brief affair with Remarque.

Tender interlude: Luise Rainer, a double Oscar-winner, found Remarque 'wonderfully lyrical and romantic', but his drink problem troubled her.

Erich married Jutta Ilse Zambona in 1925. It was a passionate relationship, and far from monogamous on either side.

Paulette Goddard, the star who might have been Scarlett O'Hara, would become Remarque's second wife.

A studio portrait of Marlene Dietrich in 1937, the year she and Remarque began their tempestuous affair.

Greta Garbo: one of the world's most desirable women, her affair with Remarque was a secretive romance of lonely walks and fireside intimacy, defying Dietrich's jealously.

Remarque in 1935, aged thirty-seven: one of the few portraits the camera-shy author permitted after his overnight success.

A scene that shocked the world. Berlin University students burn books proscribed by the new Nazi regime in 1933, including Remarque's two novels.

A louche Remarque in Hollywood, 1940, a few months after his flight from Europe.

Remarque as an actor: he played a small but significant role in the Hollywood film of his novel *A Time to Love and a Time to Die* with John Gavin.

Remarque found serenity and contentment in the early 1960s with his marriage to Paulette and the success of his penultimate novel *A Night in Lisbon*, but the years of hedonism and heavy drinking would soon take their toll.

He hurried to Porto Ronco to supervise the packing and removal of his most valuable *objets d'art*. In a fever of anxiety and activity, pictures, porcelain, bronzes, carpets were all crated for shipment to the United States. The faithful Kramers, Rosa and Karl, gave their word that they would remain as custodians of the Casa Remarque, a promise they were to keep. As he took his leave of them the house he loved seemed empty and echoing. It would be nine years before he would see it again.

When he reached the Hôtel du Cap in the Lancia the normality of routine – at least measured by Marlene's eccentric standards – seemed almost a relief. Joe Carstairs was there. The Kennedy clan was installed in their villa, Jack, Bobby and young Ted among them. There were old Hollywood friends stopping by, Charles Boyer and his wife Pat, Norma Shearer. Yet sheltered as they were from the stark political realities beyond the hotel compound they could not escape the atmosphere of gloom and tension that was engulfing the whole of Europe.

As they were basking in the Riviera sun Hitler now turned his threats on Danzig, another former German Baltic port, this time in Poland and designated a Free City by the League of Nations. Three months before, Chamberlain had warned Hitler that if he used force to seize the city it would mean war. Now Britain, France and Poland were taking steps to mobilize their armed forces.

In mid August Marlene had to return to Hollywood. Remarque saw her off at Nice railway station on the Blue Train to Paris. According to Maria Riva, Marlene took her fourteen-year-old daughter's hand, placed it in Remarque's and, in the finest tradition of grand drama, said: 'My only love, I give you my child. Protect her, keep her safe – for me.'[2] A week later Germany and the Soviet Union signed their infamous Non-Aggression Pact, virtually sealing the fate of Poland and setting Europe on the road to war.

Marlene telephoned from New York 'very agitated'. The following day, 25 August, the French government ordered mobilization of its armed forces. Ambassador Kennedy, in constant touch with his London embassy, shepherded his family back to England and warned those of his friends who could to get out of France. Through his intercession, Marlene organized berths for them aboard the next sailing of the *Queen Mary* scheduled for 1 September.

Jutta telephoned from Monte Carlo, pleading with Remarque to let her join him. He told her he had sent her money and she had best go to Biarritz, close to the border with neutral Spain, and wait there for him to make arrangements. In the weeks ahead he would have a bad conscience about failing to do more to help her at the peak hour of panic. 'Contempt because I'm not taking Peter, the thought and knowledge that it couldn't be, because I don't want to lose the Puma,' he wrote a few days later.

On 26 August the Family fled for Paris, Remarque, true to his pledge to Marlene, taking Maria in the Lancia. It was a nightmare journey. The highways were choked with military traffic, hotel beds for overnight stops were almost impossible to find. They had to lodge in private homes. Most troubling, the Lancia was malfunctioning and running repairs cost precious time.

It finally limped on wrecked cylinders into Paris where Remarque entrusted it to the garage he always used, not knowing when or whether he would see it again. A last dinner at Fouquet in the shadow of the Arc de Triomphe. A final bottle of Champagne at the Sphinx. 'Standing in front of the Triomphe. A beautiful autumn full moon over the Champs Elysées, reddish in the purple mist.' That was his valedictory to the city he loved above all others.

On the day Remarque, with Maria in his care, sailed from Cherbourg, leaving Europe for an unknown future, Germany and Soviet Russia invaded Poland.

The dockside at Cherbourg was a chaos of people frantic to secure passage on the *Queen Mary*'s last peacetime Atlantic crossing. Every available berth was already taken but 250 extra passengers were squeezed aboard. Public areas were turned into dormitories, cot-beds set up in the library and tea-dance salon. The liner sailed with 2,331 passengers, the biggest complement it had carried in the three years since its maiden voyage.

At eight a.m. on Sunday, 3 September, three days into the Atlantic, passengers heard the announcement over the ship's radio that Britain and France were at war with Germany. From London Neville Chamberlain's broadcast was relayed and during a silent lunch they listened to King George VI's sombre speech. The mood aboard the ship was, the *New York Times* reported, 'a sad but calm acceptance of the news'.

The ship was blacked out and set a zigzag course to avoid lurking U-boats. That night somewhere in the North Atlantic the liner SS *Athenia*, bound from Liverpool for Montreal, was torpedoed with the loss of 112 lives, the first British and American civilian casualties of the war. At the same time the *Queen Mary*'s passengers were trying to allay their fears at an impromptu concert organized by the crew. The star attraction was a fellow-passenger Bob Hope who sang his theme song *Thanks for the Memory* with new and topical lyrics he improvised for the occasion.

The scene at the New York pier when the liner berthed was as chaotic as that at Cherbourg had been. Dozens of reporters and photographers boarded the ship seeking first-hand accounts of Europe on the eve of war. Remarque was persuaded to give a press conference. The New York *Times* reported that he was 'obviously deeply distressed'.

'I would like to tell you in a few sentences what I think of the war,' he said with a despairing shake of the head, 'but I can't. I think there is no reason in the whole world for any war, think what you will. This will not be a war on the front. It will be a war on women and children.' Asked if he would fight, Mr Remarque said no. He could not fight against Germany, he said, but he implied that if there were civilian work for him in France he would be willing to take it.[3]

A week later, having cleared his immigrant status with the authorities, he was on his way to Los Angeles again. This time Marlene was at the station to meet and instal him in a bungalow she had rented for him next to her own in the grounds of the Beverly Hills Hotel. Their second

Hollywood reunion was no less fraught than the previous one had been six months before. Marlene was wan and distracted – and with good reason. She had started an affair with James Stewart, her co-star on the set of *Destry Rides Again*, intense on her part, cooler on his. It was no secret in the close-knit movie community, nor, after he had settled in, to Remarque. Again he was racked with jealousy, humiliated by Dietrich's cavalier treatment of him, incapable of confronting her for fear of losing her.

Dietrich had made her pitch for the boyish, unworldly actor, some seven years her junior, from the moment they first met at Universal. 'She took one look at Jimmy Stewart and began to rub her hands. She wanted him at once,' the film's producer Joe Pasternak remembered.

Stewart, more circumspect, admitted in interviews years later that he had been caught off guard by 'her adult concept of life' and 'We dated quite a few times, which was fairly romantic.'[4]

Rumours persisted for years in Hollywood circles that Marlene had been made pregnant by Stewart and at his insistence had had an abortion. Remarque recorded in his diary that she had admitted as much to him but Dietrich's aptitude for fanciful and manipulative exaggeration of her liaisons must always be taken at face value and the evidence has remained inconclusive.

Not that she exaggerated her feelings for Stewart at the time. Remarque was made only too aware of them. The film crew gossiped openly about the long periods both stars spent together behind the closed door of her dressing room. Remarque saw for himself the 'shrine' she created around photographs of Stewart in the bedroom of her bungalow. He haunted the set of *Destry Rides Again*, obsessively watchful and resentful, until the director George Marshall had him prohibited.

'Remarque remained, by day a virtual recluse, forcing himself to write, only to tear up each day's work before my mother returned home from the studio in the evening,' Maria Riva wrote,

> He lived for the sound of her car pulling up in front of her bungalow, the ring of the telephone telling him that she was alone and he was

now permitted to steal across the path, and take her in his arms. Sometimes . . . when she usually didn't appear until the evening of the next day, I sat with him, keeping him company during his sad vigil . . . Remarque not only suffered from utter rejection but . . . from self-hate, because he loved her too much to leave her. He needed to be close to her, just to see her, hear her voice, even listen to her telling him about her new love, which she did, asking his advice on how she could make the moments spent in her new lover's arms even more wonderful than they already were . . . This lovely man had become a pathetic voyeur, a Beverly Hills Cyrano.[5]

A new complication added to his woes. At the end of October Jutta arrived in New York and was detained on Ellis Island while her immigrant qualification was ascertained. Her US visa was found to be invalid and she was ordered to be deported. Her frantic calls to Remarque 3,000 miles away compounded his bad conscience for – as she perceived – abandoning her in Europe. He contacted immigration lawyers who succeeded in diverting her deportation to Mexico where she would have to wait while her US entry papers were processed. At least the Remarque name and influence could expedite the proceedings.

And at least he didn't lack friends in influential positions. In his own right he found a ready welcome and acceptance among Hollywood's elite, as well as from expatriates he had known in Berlin, Switzerland and Paris. He renewed his drinking partnership with Carl Zuckmayer and his friendship with Louis Bromfield. Hedy Kiesler was now well entrenched in her Hollywood career as Hedy Lamarr, though any relationship there had been between them three years earlier had now subsided into a casual acquaintance. The Charles Boyers introduced him into their circle. Studio moguls like Carl Laemmle and David Lewin who had profited from filming his books were kindly disposed towards him, entertaining him in their homes. There was a grim satisfaction in being invited as himself rather than as a Dietrich append-age to a lavish party given by Basil Rathbone and his wife for the pianist Artur Rubinstein and the conductor Leopold Stokowski at which he mingled with Bette Davis, Charlie Chaplin, Olivia de

Havilland, Ilona Massey, Reginald Gardiner, Kay Francis, the director Rouben Mamoulian, all scrupulously named in his diary entry. Indisputably a star himself in his own field, there was still a vestige of the Osnabrück boy in him, impressionable enough to be flattered by the attentions of Hollywood celebrities.

But for all his enjoyment of its social scene the movie capital was an alien milieu which he despised, however much he tried to fit in. The artifice and superficiality of its *modus vivendi* seemed repugnant to Mittel Europeans who regarded themselves as aesthetically superior. As Zuckmayer recorded:

> Experienced fellow exiles told me that the main thing was to be seen – lunching, for example, in the restaurants where the celebrities ate. In order to count for anything you had to live in a top-class hotel or have your own showy home. To prove yourself you had to frequent the expensive restaurants of the movie industry's upper crust. Moreover, if you wanted to 'belong' permanently, you had to begin issuing invitations yourself. You had to act as if you were rich and happy; nowhere have I heard the word 'happy' so often as in that ante-room to hell called Hollywood. And since nobody was, everyone drifted into drinking, even when he was in no mood for it, and ended up in a morass of humourless and dreary night life. Never have I been so wrapped in the mists of depression.

Seeking solace and a compensating sense of reality, he and Remarque 'sat up long nights, drinking rum or vodka, just as if we were still in one of our Berlin nightclubs'.[6]

Many of the exiles were involved in activist, mainly left-wing committees and groupings such as the Hollywood Anti-Nazi League and the Joint Anti-Fascist Refugee Committee but Remarque deliberately kept himself aloof from any political associations. He declined to give interviews on the war situation or contribute to pamphlets. He did, however, make generous, usually anonymous, donations to refugee aid organizations. In the immediate post-war years, as the full horrors of the Nazi era began to emerge, his reticence at taking a more positive and public stand would weigh heavily on his conscience.

David Niven recalled in his memoirs:

> Refugees from Hitler arrived in droves . . . When Erich Maria Remarque was not wrapped around Marlene Dietrich or other local beauties, he acted as a sort of liaison officer between the German-speaking foreigners, the Garden of Allah set and Musso and Frank's Restaurant on Hollywood Boulevard where the brilliant William Saroyan and Budd Schulberg made their headquarters.[7]

The 'literary' German writers exiled in the movie capital, notably the Mann brothers, Thomas and Heinrich, Lion Feuchtwanger and Bertolt Brecht, formed their own clique. Remarque was not admitted to it. His work was considered 'popular', hardly compatible with their own achievements and aspirations, nor did his man–about–town image commend him to them. There was, almost certainly, a touch of envy in their coolness towards him.

Thomas Mann, who arrived in Hollywood from his professorial post at Princeton University in the summer of 1940, confided to his diary a few weeks later: 'Remarque has made it clear he "hates" me. His boorish behaviour had made that clear before, but the feeling of hatred is in itself characteristically inexplicable and it is hard to say when it could have developed.'[8]

Mann's impression was probably an over-reaction. Nothing Remarque ever left in writing or hearsay suggested he 'hated' one of the greatest German authors whom he had read for years with admiration. Rather, he was awed by him and a respectful courtesy may have inhibited any warmth in their encounters. At all events, shortly after Mann's diary comment Remarque was pleased enough to be a fellow-guest with him at a luncheon given by their fellow emigré author Franz Werfel and his wife Alma Mahler, the widow of the composer.

Brecht, too, took a deprecating view of him. They were both guests at a New Year's Eve party given by Elisabeth Bergner in 1941. Brecht writes loftily in his journal: 'Remarque dropped in with a Hollywood Mexican star. Remarque wears a tuxedo . . . his face lacks something, probably a monocle.'

In March 1940 Remarque travelled to Mexico City to meet Jutta, still smarting over his treatment of her, and help her regularize her documentation for entry into the United States. He also negotiated his own visitor papers into a resident's visa, qualifying him to remain indefinitely, and together they entered the US legitimately at the Tijuana border crossing. Jutta carried on to New York where her husband had organized and financed hotel accommodation for her, even though he was preparing to quit the Beverly Hills Hotel and move into a rented bungalow in Westwood.

The Austrian actor Paul Henreid, newly arrived in Hollywood and soon to star in two of its most enduring classics, *Casablanca* and *Now, Voyager*, was also staying at the Beverly Hills Hotel. Before embarking on an acting career the aristocratic Henreid had worked in publishing and had got to know Remarque when he was preparing a special de luxe edition of *All Quiet on the Western Front* ten years before. In his autobiography he recalled:

> When Erich found out that I was going to Hollywood, he advised me, 'The fools all live in Beverly Hills, a congested place I detest. Do you know, Paul, it's a crime to walk in the streets there! Honestly, the police will stop you – and anyway, there's a snobbishness about the place you won't like. You look for a home in Bel Air, Brentwood or Westwood. There are larger lots there and you won't hear your neighbours.'[9]

Henreid took his advice and settled for Westwood too.

Remarque's voluntary removal to 1050 Hilt Avenue, out of the shadow of Marlene, signalled the first crack of their break-up. His remark that 'you won't hear your neighbours' undoubtedly carried deeper significance than Henreid suspected. Dietrich was an addiction and a fetter. He still agonized over her, pandered to her, fought with her in storms of jealousy, but he had begun to realize there was no future for them as lovers. With her ardour for James Stewart cooled by the actor's easy-going, less than wholehearted response, she was now successfully practising her seduction techniques on John Wayne, her co-star in her next film *Seven Sinners*. He, to her fury, turned out to be one of the few men who failed to reciprocate her overtures, explaining to Maria Riva years later: 'Never liked being part of a stable – never did!'[10]

The playwright and screenwriter Clifford Odets, a pillar of left-wing causes, left a revealing study of Remarque's state of mind at this time in his journal. Odets had recently been divorced from the Oscar-winning Viennese actress Luise Rainer whom Remarque would later add to his *Schönheitgalerie* of Hollywood lovers. On an impulse he telephoned Remarque, whom he had never met, and proposed a meeting, possibly in connection with his anti-Fascist activities.

September 6 1940: Called Remarque, the German writer, thinking he might be an interesting man to meet. He answered the telephone but refused to admit that he was Remarque, insistently demanding to know who was calling. As doggedly I refused to tell him unless I knew to whom I was speaking. Finally, with grim disgust, he admitted his identity; a moment later he apologized: 'Excuse me, they are always trying to sell you wine and things on the telephone, or to have long conversations with you'. He said he was finishing the rewriting of a novel and would be happy if I came there for a drink early next week. The other day, seeing her pass by in the Universal commissary, Lewin referred to Marlene Dietrich's 'alumni association'. Remarque seems to be a disconsolate member of it.

September 11 1940: I decided to visit Remarque. It was a very pleasant meeting; for him too, I hope. In one room, where we sat, were four Cézannes, an unusual Utrillo, and a small but first-class Daumier. I admired the paintings very much but said I knew more about the qualities of music; he said he had gone from being a music student to a great lover of paintings.

From the first, excepting a few minutes but not more, we were very easy with each other. He aroused confidence in me, something another person rarely does. He was masculine, strong and yet tender, with a quiet humour which played only around his lips. He has a German solidity but to this is added a slight touch of elegance, something sensitive and sniffing, although he does not point this quality at you. Right now he is finishing a rewrite of a novel which has already appeared in Collier's magazine. In fact it is the story *Flotsam*, which Lewin is now making into a picture.

He said he found this arduous work, a grind, but he was sticking to it so that it might be published before the picture appeared.

I saw or felt that I was trying to pour too much into one hour, ideas of form and technique, ideas of American life contrasted to European, etc., etc. Instead we turned to a discussion of European actresses. This was done by mentioning Luise, whom he had seen once or twice – he knew we had been married. He sighed, groaned humorously, said, 'Do not tell me – I do not ask you – tell me about her only when you like to do it.' He said his father had been a sensible, helpful man in his life, and that he had said, 'Never fall in love with an actress.' His father was right, he had discovered, he said. He said these actresses were so typical that he was sure he would be describing mine if he described his own, meaning Marlene Dietrich. He said such women fell in love with men with minds, loved and admired and built them up for that, but really the only sort of artists they really understood were actors. He laughed as he said, 'Then they hit you hard on the head and you fall, you are stunned. You don't know where you are. But next they are saying, "Why do you have such a long face? That man over there, look how charming he is to me."' Near eight o'clock I left. A kind of sober mask fell on both of us, as if we had been a little ashamed of our garrulity. It seemed to me as if we were two men who had been yearning for weeks to talk to someone. Anyway I was heartily glad to have made the visit. We promised to meet again soon.[11]

Whether he realized it or not, Odets' record caught a sense of the dying fall in Remarque's passion for Marlene. Three months later the affair ended. For just over three years it had been the beacon and the shadow of his existence to the exclusion of any other consideration, even his writing. The only novel he had written during that time, *Flotsam*, was arguably the most superficial and ineffectual of any he wrote. It was not until after they had parted that Dietrich would attain some measure of the influence she liked ever after to lay claim to as his muse. Remarque immortalized her, at least for himself, as the enigmatic, haunting heroine of *Arch of Triumph*.

He needed to put the breadth of the continent between himself and his lost love. In December 1940 he closed up the Westwood house and left for an extended stay in New York. On the eve of departure he received a farewell letter from Marlene delivered by hand. There had, she wrote, been only love, worry and angst between them and now she was full of love and sadness that it hadn't made him happy. She prayed to God to protect him. That night he noted wryly: 'To add to this hair-raising nonsense, she sent a gold St Christopher – and I recognized it with irony as the one which Joe Carstairs had given her last year'.

12

Enemy Alien

Dietrich may have released him – the French actor Jean Gabin now became her new 'great love' – but he could not feel himself completely free of Dietrich. The bond between them would endure, neither of them able to bring themselves to break it irrevocably. 'We were bound by a very special feeling,' Marlene wrote in her memoirs.

At least Remarque had stayed emotionally faithful to her during their affair. The occasional one-night-stand or casual pick-up had been no more than an outlet for his frustrations. Now, almost vengefully, he became a serial lover, embarking on a *perpetuum mobile* of relationships with beautiful and, more often than not, famous women.

The cycle began almost immediately he arrived in New York. At a New Year party he was introduced to Natasha Paley and Greta Garbo. Fascinated as he was by the mysterious actress, who was escorted by her constant companion Gaylord Hauser, the nutrition guru, it was Paley who excited his interest. A few days later he invited her to lunch.

Natasha Paley would become one of the great loves of his life, their affair the longest lasting of all. The thirty-five-year-old, erstwhile actress and photographic model with, in Remarque's diary description, a 'sweet cat-like face' was moderately familiar in magazine fashion pages. She was of imperial Russian origin, a collateral member of the Romanov dynasty. Gossip writers referred to her as Princess Natasha Paley, though in America she was reticent about using her title. She was the daughter of the Grand Duke Paul Alexandrovich, brother of Czar Alexander III, and a first cousin of the tragic Czar Nicholas II, murdered by the Bolsheviks in 1918 when Natasha was thirteen years old. Her commoner mother's marriage to the Grand Duke as his second wife was morganatic and resulted in the couple being banished from the imperial court though Czar Nicholas later rescinded the decree and Natasha's mother was granted the courtesy title of Princess Paley, the name by which she later became prominent in European high society. Their eldest son – Natasha's brother – the twenty-one-year-old Prince Vladimir Paley also perished at the hands of the Bolsheviks in 1918.

Natasha had grown up in Paris and moved to New York in 1935, where she instantly caught the discerning eye of Cecil Beaton, just launching on his period as a fashion photographer for the Condé Nast magazine empire. In his diary, Beaton eulogized 'her quality of beauty so rare and alluring'.[1] Soon she married a member of the Beaton circle, the homosexual Jack Wilson, a marriage which did not subsequently inhibit her from taking Remarque, and others, as lovers.

'Beautiful, clear, quite intense face, long body – an Egyptian cat. For the first time since the Puma, the feeling that one could fall in love,' Remarque noted after their first meeting. The relationship began gently and lyrically with quiet trysts in restaurants, long walks 'hand in hand'. Within days she was writing him a note: 'Tonight I will live with my own so short but so important memories. Thank you for being alive,' and Remarque, transcribing it in his diary, comments: 'I am writing that down so as not to lose it.'

The affair lapsed when he returned to the West Coast a month later, not to resume for nearly another two years, and then with a consuming intensity. But this was a man who 'could never imagine a life without women', and in the intervening months his name was linked with a succession of them, some like Greer Garson no more than Hollywood 'dates', others serious but short-lived, several of a passionate nature.

Garbo was the first. Their brief meeting at the New Year party had aroused a mutual curiosity. It was not just confined to each other. 'Fur will fly if it's true Garbo has taken Marlene Dietrich's best beau, Erich

Remarque, away from her,' the Hollywood gossip columnist Hedda Hopper mischievously hinted in her syndicated column two weeks later.[2] Hopper was prescient. Three months later the affair began in earnest.

'On 1 April called Garbo. Was having her hair cut, etc.,' Remarque reports. On their first recorded date they went to the movies to see *That Hamilton Woman*, the love story of Admiral Lord Nelson and Lady Hamilton, starring Laurence Olivier and Vivien Leigh. 'We munched popcorn [Remarque jocularly uses the verb *fressen* applicable only to the eating habits of animals or uncouth persons]. She cried when Nelson died.'

The star who wanted 'to be alone' was paranoid about intrusion into her privacy, so they went to inordinate lengths not to be seen together in public. The next day they arranged to meet in the Botanical Gardens and wandered among the plantations. 'Went home. Played records. Hungarian music and [Richard] Tauber. Ate together. Hamburgers, then ice-cream with hot chocolate sauce. Sat by the fire . . . At ten o'clock the Puma called. Whether I wanted to go over. Can't. A visitor. Who? Finally told her Garbo. Bomb.'

After he has taken Garbo home, he telephones Marlene. The fur flies, as Hedda Hopper had predicted. In the course of a tempestuous three-hour conversation Dietrich rails against Garbo, informing him that she is arrogant and ugly and has syphilis and breast cancer. Dietrich's professional antipathy towards the Swedish star was legendary. Discussing one of Garbo's lovers once with Maria Riva, she stormed: 'I don't understand how she gets them. He was drunk, the whole evening, but if you have to go to bed with Garbo, you *have* to be drunk . . .'[3] The suspicion now that one of *her* lovers might be doing just that − and obviously wasn't drunk − was a lethal detonator. 'An eruption of jealousy, rage, tears, explanations of what she has done for me and how she loved me,' Remarque reported to his diary. 'I laughed quite a lot.' But he goes to her, finds her in bed 'tired but cheerful', makes chicken sandwiches and Turkish coffee for them both. 'She was tender. I left at five a.m.' The next day he mentions in passing, 'Natasha has written.'

For the moment, though, Garbo commanded his feelings, whether or not he was fully committed to her or using her as bait for Dietrich's jealousy in a spirit of poetic justice. Certainly he was flattered to be the new romantic interest in the life of the world's most mysterious screen star and one of its most desirable, but his private expressions of feeling for her remained muted, almost detached. It was a quiet affair, more a meeting of intellects than of desires, conducted on long walks along the beach at Santa Monica or in intimate evenings of scratch meals and background music in their respective homes, discussing art and literature. Garbo, already interested in pictures, polished her knowledge and appreciation of them at Remarque's knee.

They slept together and Remarque noted his admiration of her tanned body, smooth skin and straight shoulders 'more beautiful than the Puma's whose shoulders are a bit too high', but there seems to have been more aesthetic appreciation than passion in their sexual activity. Years later his second wife Paulette Goddard allegedly told a friend that Remarque claimed Garbo 'was lousy in bed.'[4]

At the time of their romance Garbo had reached a crisis in her career. She was in her mid-thirties. Wearying of Hollywood and bored with films, she had begun to contemplate quitting both, but her contract with Metro-Goldwyn-Mayer called for one more starring role. This, too, presented problems. Various scripts proposed for her were either shelved or failed to materialize until agreement was reached on a lightweight comedy, *Two-Faced Woman,* in which she was to be radically re-packaged as 'sexy'. She had her hair cut into a short bob – possibly the process she was undergoing when Remarque first telephoned her – and began filming in June. It was to be her last appearance on screen. When it was finished she headed for New York and became the world's most famous recluse.

Her affair with Remarque petered out that summer, though they remained friends for years afterwards, always contacting each other and dining out together if they found themselves in New York or Paris at the same time.

Perhaps Luise Rainer whom Remarque would briefly woo the following year put her finger unwittingly on a valid reason for his apparent lack of ardour in the Garbo interlude. 'He liked demanding women and he once told me that Garbo was the only woman he ever met who did not want anything from him,' she recalled, adding with a significant choice of verb, 'He said he liked her very much.'[5]

He was working slowly but steadily on *Ravic*, the novel that would be published as *Arch of Triumph* and his most successful after *All Quiet on the Western Front*. It was personally challenging work, virtually a self-analysis in which he penetrates deep into his own psyche and condition. At its core is the doomed love story of Ravic, a stateless German refugee doctor practising illicitly in Paris, and the rootless, despairing singer/actress Joan Madou whom he takes under his wing.

The book is dedicated to 'M.D.' and Dietrich is the spectral influence for its heroine from the opening paragraph:

> The woman veered towards Ravic. She walked quickly, but with a peculiar stagger. Ravic first noticed her when she was almost beside him. He saw a pale face, high cheekbones and wideset eyes. The face was rigid and mask-like; it looked hollowed out, and her eyes in the light from the street lamps had an expression of such glassy emptiness that they caught his attention.

Remarque was, however, careful to distance his heroine from the real Dietrich. The forlorn, destitute Joan Madou, a chanteuse grubbing a livelihood from the seedier nether-world of Parisian night-life, is a shadow-play of Marlene's characteristics rather than her character, tormenting Ravic with her capricious affections and infidelities, disappearing from his life only to turn up again, re-asserting her need for him.

Marlene had been privy to his early work on the book's first draft – in notes to her at the time Remarque would refer to himself as Ravic – and envisaged herself playing Joan Madou in the inevitable film to follow. Remarque, however, had no intention of advancing her for the role; it would be a casting too close for comfort. He saw Garbo in the part, though this was an ideal he did not communicate to Dietrich. In the event the role would be assigned to Ingrid Bergman.

After the turbulence of the past four years the summer of 1941 was a relatively calm period for him. He dated a succession of attractive women – Frances Cain, a 'sweet, charming' minor actress, Greer Garson, Lady Sylvia Ashley, widow of Douglas Fairbanks Sr and future wife of Clark Gable – all admiringly spoken of in his diary but of no great emotional significance.

One such casual dalliance, however, had unwelcome consequences. In August he enjoyed a brief relationship with the Irish-born, convent-educated actress Maureen O'Sullivan. She became pregnant. O'Sullivan, best known as the scantily dressed Jane, Johnny Weissmuller's jungle mate in the popular *Tarzan* series, had been married for five years to the writer-director John Farrow. They were regarded as one of Hollywood's happiest and most stable couples, a union that eventually produced a total of seven children including the actress Mia Farrow.

The episode was kept secret but the Remarque archive at Osnabrück University attests to his paternity. Remarque notes curtly in his diary entry for 5 October 1941: 'Maureen phoned. Told me it is to happen today.' The archive identifies 'it' as an abortion. If true, it is the only acknowledged instance of Remarque fathering a child.

By this time he was already focusing his charms on yet another star, an unlikely one in the Remarque canon. Lupe Velez, ten years his junior, was known as 'the Mexican Spitfire' and took pains to confirm the soubriquet with her fiery temperament and stormy love life. Her earlier well-publicized affair with Gary Cooper had given the Hollywood set frissons of vicarious entertainment. After they broke up she had married Johnny 'Tarzan' Weissmuller and spiced the gossip columns for the next five years with their volatile public disputations.

She claimed to be the daughter of an army colonel and an opera singer: her closest intimates knew her to be the illegitimate offspring of a prostitute. In the Hollywood pecking-order she was a minor player in B-movies but a star of the gossip columns, an icon of its *outré* glamour image. The décor of her bedroom was reported to be black, silver and gold, offset by a massive polar bear rug. Remarque came to know it well.

In the wake of Dietrich and Garbo's continental sophistication, and Greer Garson or Maureen O'Sullivan's lady likeness, Remarque's attachment to Lupe Velez seemed puzzling in a man of such impeccable tastes, but at the root of it there was genuine affection. She was fun to be with and she had a certain 'tart with a heart' vulnerability that bridged his twin but often conflicting fascinations for refined, unapproachable feminine beauty and the impersonal sex of the brothels he frequented from time to time. Lupe brought out his protective instinct.

Moreover, she had none of the publicity-shy inhibitions Dietrich and Garbo maintained about being seen on the town with him. He enjoyed squiring her in range of photographers' lenses to Ciro's, the Mocambo, the Saturday Club or Saks Skyroom. Provocatively, he took her to Elisabeth Bergner's New Year's Eve party, recorded by Bertolt Brecht who, with Lion Feuchtwanger and their wives, hardly constituted a gathering at which she was likely to feel at ease, but among such cerebral company she was, to Remarque, 'like a bird of paradise'. Another time, at the Mocambo, he was enchanted by her 'shy, slim, cheeky boyishness. Danced around in her rubber belt'.

Lupe was a tonic he needed. She respected him and, though no intellectual, took an interest in his work, once sitting up all night to read *Three Comrades* 'until morning'. Their affair lasted five months until it fizzled out without acrimony. Three years later, after another broken romance, Lupe Velez committed suicide in inimitable style. Having punctiliously kept appointments with her hairdresser and beautician, she took an overdose of sleeping pills in a bedroom filled with flowers for the occasion. Her grand design for a fitting Hollywood dénouement was thwarted by nausea induced by the overdose. She stumbled to the bathroom to be sick. Legend has it that she was found dead crouched over the lavatory bowl, having drowned in its water. 'Lupe took her own life last night, apparently because of an unhappy love affair and because she was expecting a baby by a Frenchman . . . Little to say. She was so full of life. Sad,' was Remarque's diary requiem.

America entered into the war in December 1941 following the Japanese attack on Pearl Harbor. Almost immediately new strains entered

Remarque's life. He found himself classified as a 'enemy alien' along with all other German, Austrian and Japanese residents in California without US passports. He was subjected to a night-time curfew from eight o'clock in the evening to six o'clock the following morning and any movement was restricted to a five-mile radius round his home. Amid fears of a possible Japanese attack on California there was even debate about expelling all aliens from the state.

Two months earlier Remarque had officially registered an application for US citizenship but there was a statutory five-year period before it could be approved and granted. For the time being he was not only stateless but also tacitly interned, virtually a prisoner-of-war. The feeling, he wrote, was eerie. 'How small the world is getting – once from horizon to horizon, then without Germany, without Austria, without Italy – Switzerland, Europe – then without Mexico, only America left, and then still more difficult; travel only with permission and now just five miles in Hollywood.'

To compound this feeling, a few months later he was required to register for the draft and possible conscription into the US army, albeit in the low 3A category as a married man. The dichotomy of being an enemy alien on the one hand and a potential GI on the other afforded him some satirical amusement. He observed that aliens could not be officers, so in the event of being drafted he would be a common soldier again – this time on the opposite side.

Marlene, secure in her American citizenship, tried to be supportive after her fashion, telephoning often if only to unburden herself of her own problems with studio politics and Jean Gabin. He would listen sympathetically but kept his distance.

He frequently flouted the curfew, which 'makes everything unreal, like a glass waiting-room', to attend private parties and date his latest acquisition Vera Zorina. The Berlin-born ballerina had gravitated to acting and Hollywood via the Ballets Russes with which she had danced at Covent Garden Opera House in London and the Metropolitan in New York, and Broadway musicals. At the time Remarque met her she was still married to the choreographer George Balanchine, founder of the New York City Ballet, and was on the threshold of what promised to be a bright Hollywood future. Amid much publicity she had just won the most coveted role of the moment as Maria in the film version of Ernest Hemingway's *For Whom the Bell Tolls*. After the first week of shooting the director Sam Wood realized that her casting had been a mistake and she was summarily replaced by Ingrid Bergman. Her film career never recovered from this humiliation.

The Zorina affair, another passing fancy, was his last fling in Hollywood. The movie capital, the 'glass waiting room', had debilitated him. Its ambience had never seemed to him other than trite and time-wasting. He lacked motivation, the will and capacity to write. Progress on *Ravic* was sluggish. He applied for, and was granted, permission to move to New York.

'New York! That really is a city without the melancholy and oppressive charm of the past. An explosion! The future,' he wrote many years later to his old Osnabrück friend Hanns-Gerd Rabe.[6] For the rest of his life it would be his favourite city, his second home.

He arrived at the end of October 1942 and booked into a suite at the Sherry Netherland Hotel. One of his first acts was to contact Natasha Paley and arrange lunch, another to phone Jutta, permanently installed at her husband's expense in the exclusive Hotel Pierre over-looking Central Park.

Within two weeks of his arrival he had met up again with Dolores del Rio, another Mexican actress whom he had known in Hollywood, and begun a short affair. Del Rio, dignified, elegant and sophisticated, was recently divorced from the art director Cedric Gibbons, and the gossip columnists were busily chronicling her public appearances on the arm of Orson Welles. They were unaware of Remarque's entry into her social life.

'Yesterday flowers, guardedly, to Dolores. In the afternoon, Natasha,' he writes on 11 November. Twelve days later: 'Baby roses from Rainer.'

Luise Rainer has recorded the most detailed and revealing impression of Remarque's personality and attitude to courtship at this time. Her Hollywood career had been short but unique and was virtually over by the end of 1942. Already established in the German and Austrian theatre, the petite German-born actress with her exquisite fragile features and doe-like eyes had caught the eye of an M–G–M talent-scout in Berlin and was persuaded to make a screen test. Louis B. Mayer signed her, reputedly to 'scare Greta Garbo out of some of her arrogance'.[7] His strategy succeeded to an extent even he could not have foreseen. With her second Hollywood film, *The Great Ziegfeld*, she won the 1936 Best Actress Academy Award for a role that occupied barely twenty minutes of the film's three hours' running time. She repeated the achievement the following year with her performance in *The Good Earth*, trouncing Garbo in *Camille* and becoming the first actress to win an Oscar two years running, a record equalled only by Katharine Hepburn in 1967/68.

Luise Rainer was briefly the star of the moment with the public and M–G–M but the studio over-exploited her success by rushing her into a series of mediocre productions. Within two years she was a falling star and had just completed what was to be her final film *Hostages*, a minor anti-Nazi resistance thriller, when Remarque renewed contact with her in New York. Her troubled short marriage to Clifford Odets had ended in divorce two years earlier.

Nearly sixty years after their New York interlude she still remembered Remarque with warm affection.

> I always called Erich God's gift to women. He was a dear, dear man. He was not tall but he was very handsome and he had a combination of qualities that were so lovable, great intelligence and erudition, a great sense of humour. And despite his success he still had humility. I never knew him to be arrogant or vain. He was utterly kind.
>
> I was quite in love with him but it wasn't a great affair. I had no sexual experience with him, though on one of our first dates, when he brought me back to my apartment, he made overtures. But the moment I refused he shied away.
>
> When we first met I knew he hoped I would spend the night with him but I didn't. I was very prudish in those days, I wouldn't go with a man immediately, and that was what he needed in a way, that it should be an immediate thing, but if you drew away he wasn't

aggressive. He was not a brazen fellow. I simply cannot say anything negative about him.

The relationship might have developed into something deeper but for Rainer's reservations about one facet of his character. 'I had a great love for him, but there was one thing that disturbed me. He was very often drunk, and I couldn't handle that. Not that he was anything bad when he had been drinking. He could be very funny, but I was young and didn't know how to deal with it.' Her misgivings were exacerbated by his close friendship with Oscar Homolka, a well-known Hollywood character actor usually type-cast in villainous roles. Rainer had just finished working with him in *Hostages*, which was destined to be her Hollywood swan-song. 'He and Erich were drinking partners at that time. He was not a nice man. I thought he was a bad influence on Erich.'

A year later in 1943 Rainer married Robert Knittel, a publisher – 'He and Erich were strangely alike.' When news of their engagement appeared in the legendary Walter Winchell's column in the *New York Daily Mirror*, Rainer was awakened that morning at five a.m. by the telephone. It was Remarque. 'What are you doing?' he demanded, 'Why are you going to marry that book salesman? Are you mad?'

She and Knittel kept in regular touch with Remarque for the rest of his life, often visiting him and Paulette Goddard at Porto Ronco when they lived for a time in Switzerland and making a foursome for dinner in New York.

In the heady weeks of his courtship, he had showered her with flowers, affectionate, humorous notes and – a particularly cherished memento – a teasing poem dated Christmas 1942, published here for the first time:

Junges Fräulein, ich möcht' fragen	Young maiden, I'd like to ask
Bin ich nicht der rechter Mann?	Am I not the right man?
Hab' ich nicht die Qualitäten,	Have I not the qualities,
Die ein Mädel freuen kann?…	That would please a girl?

(The full version is given in the Appendix on p.213.)

'He was wonderfully lyrical and romantic,' Rainer recalled. 'He had a crush on me. He always said I was "the Spring in life".'[8] It was a tender interlude, the memory of which she would always cherish. They would continue to meet occasionally but her sensitive rejection of him steered him back to Natasha and a repetition of the consuming, tortured state of mind he had endured with Dietrich.

> 6 July 1943: Natasha called. The same old thing – she is slowly going mad, burned out . . . I'm rotten, take her and everything for granted, make no effort etc. She wants Russian drama. I tell her it's better not to speak any more – it would be repetition and agony. If she wants that, okay. But I disagree.

The war increasingly encroached on Remarque's thoughts and diary entries in terse commentaries . . . Fighting around Stalingrad . . . Rommel's attack in Egypt fails . . . Oran taken, fighting in Casablanca . . . Naples burns. But what brought home these faraway conflicts most keenly to him was the destruction of his home town.

> 19 August 1942: Read this morning that Osnabrück lies in ruins and flames, with 50,000 incendiary bombs and two tons of bombs. Erna and Elfriede there. Nothing to be done. Many thoughts. How much more I could have done for them; and for my father. The city, the cathedral, the green St Katharine's Church, the ramparts, the mills, the schools . . . March on, soldier, nevertheless.

For three years, since the outbreak of war, he had heard nothing of his family. It was impossible to get news to or from them. He could not know that Elfriede, the younger of his sisters, was no longer in Osnabrück, that she had married two years earlier and was living in Dresden.

13

Treason and Execution

January 1943. Stalingrad. The German Sixth Army, encircled and demoralized by the heroic Russian resistance, capitulated. It was Germany's first ignominious military defeat, the turning point of the war. Around half a million German soldiers were killed or taken prisoner. Thousands more were to return home mutilated and disillusioned. On the home front British and American air raids were increasingly pulverizing the major cities.

The repercussions on the population after two-and-a-half years of Nazi victories alarmed the regime. Civilian morale plummeted. Anti-Nazi slogans and leaflets appeared on the streets of Berlin and other cities. A putative plot by high-ranking *Wehrmacht* officers was crushed. More openly, a group of dissident students at Munich University calling themselves The White Rose launched a campaign to overthrow Hitler and the movement spread swiftly to the universities of Berlin, Hamburg, Stuttgart and Vienna. Its leaders, brother and sister Hans and Sophie Scholl, were arrested and executed.

To counteract the growing unrest *Reichminister* Goebbels decreed a series of symbolic measures aimed at making the civilian population aware of the sacrifices expected of them. Shops selling luxury goods were ordered to close, fashion magazines were proscribed. Goebbels even tried to outlaw fashion itself on the grounds that women would please 'victorious homecoming soldiers just as much in patched clothing'.

Perhaps it was this decree more than any other, though counter-manded by Hitler himself, that goaded the forty-year-old Elfriede into indiscretion. Since the outbreak of war she had established herself in Dresden as a high-fashion *Damenschneidermeisterin* – master ladies' dress-maker – with an exclusive clientele of officers' wives and local aristocrats.

In 1941 she had married Heinz Scholz, a musician and serving soldier from Hamburg, but the marriage rapidly deteriorated. In 1942 she travelled to the North Sea island of Heligoland where he was stationed to discuss a divorce. According to her husband, she had agreed to one at that time, but later retracted and in the spring of 1943 he took the initiative and instituted proceedings in the Dresden courts. In the meantime Elfriede Scholz concentrated on building up her business from her Dresden apartment.

In September 1943 the Gestapo arrested and charged her with 'defeatist talk' and 'subversion of military strength'. She had been denounced by two women whom she regarded as friends: her landlady Frau Toni Wentzel and a young customer Frau Ingeborg Rietzel with whom she socialized outside business hours and whose husband was a serving officer at the front.

The Gestapo clamp-down on even the most trivial actions or remarks they could construe as 'defeatism' exposed the divisions between moderate criticisms by ordinary citizens and the fanaticism of com-mitted National Socialists among the civilian population. In this atmosphere of suppressed terror nobody could be trusted. A casual remark could bring frightening retribution.

In the wake of the Stalingrad defeat there was a spate of such arrests and accusations. Victor Klemperer, a Jewish professor at Dresden University whose diaries give an unparalleled picture of life in the city throughout the Third Reich, makes a number of references to the arrest of civilians on similar charges in 1943:

> 11 May – . . . the arrests are attributed to 'politically suspect conversations' which have somehow been overheard, denounced, perhaps inadvertently betrayed . . . What is a politically suspect conversation? Everything and anything.

20 August – Only one thing is surprising about the talk: people's courage and lack of caution, because the papers are full of prison and death sentences for every kind of 'defeatism'.

13 September – The same newspaper . . . reports the carrying out of two death sentences for defeatism and betrayal of the people. How many have been carried out? How long can they act as a deterrent?

15 September – Two people, another two!, executed for 'undermining the fighting strength of the armed forces'.[1]

The indictment against Elfriede is chilling evidence of the prevailing climate of suspicion and treachery. It reads:

Frau Scholz has struck her landlady Frau Toni Wentzel in many conversations as a woman who does not believe in our victory, who admits to such and who asks scornfully, after some setbacks, whether she (Frau Wentzel) still believes in victory.

Moreover, Frau Scholz has for months had an undermining, defeatist influence on Frau Ingeborg Rietzel. She knew Frau Rietzel as her customer – she is a dressmaker – and had already made friends with her. So they sometimes met in Frau Rietzel's apartment and sometimes came to Frau Scholz's apartment together.

According to Frau Rietzel, she (Frau Scholz) revealed to her her scornful and ironic state of mind, particularly in remarks about the progress of the war. She said she did not believe in victory and asked whether Frau Rietzel still believed in it.

Once she said to Frau Rietzel, 'What luck has he (Hitler) brought us? Everyone who goes to the front is mere "cattle for slaughter", which he has on his conscience. If I had the chance, I'd put a bullet through his head myself. I would gladly take the consequences. At least then the German people would be rid of this man. I would gladly sacrifice myself.'

Or 'Is this idiot going to destroy all our cities before he makes peace?' Or 'I have travelled the world and met many people. When the enemies get here it won't be so bad. They are much better than we are given to believe and Germany is so hated by the whole world through its own fault.'

Or 'I wish that the women who are still for this war will lose their husbands (in battle) and that the wives and children of the men who fight so fanatically will be killed by bombs.'

Frau Elfriede Scholz admits that she has made negative remarks about the outcome of the war out of a general feeling of pessimism. But she says she only did it to give herself strength. She knew that Frau Rietzel is a believer in National Socialism and that Frau Rietzel's husband is an active officer, a soldier in body and soul and a believer in National Socialism. She thought she could take new heart from the pair of them. She said she did not say the things Frau Rietzel said.

She has never had the intention of allowing Frau Rietzel to convert her to National Socialism; on the contrary she has tried to destroy Frau Rietzel's beliefs.

Frau Rietzel has informed the court of the above remarks and Frau Scholz's scornful and ironic demeanour without any hatred and with such convincing certainty, and given the impression of a thoroughly credible person, aware of her responsibilities as a witness, that there can be no doubt that it was as she has said. Moreover, Frau Scholz's attitude, as conveyed by Frau Rietzel, tallies exactly with Frau Wentzel's account. Neither lady knew each other when they first became involved in this case.

If Frau Scholz wants to blame her pessimism partly on the influence of her brother, the author of the notorious shoddy effort (*Machwerks*) *All Quiet on the Western Front*, that cannot excuse her because, by her own admission, she has not seen her brother for thirteen years.

Rather, she is a shameless traitor to her own and our German blood, to our life as a people, a propaganda agent who stirs up defeatist attitudes in favour of our enemies. There can be only one punishment for a woman who has so forgotten her honour and who will therefore be forever without honour: the death penalty.

Elfriede was taken to the Nazi prison for 'enemies of the state' at Plötzensee in Berlin. On 29 October she was put on trial before the *Volksgericht*, the much feared People's Court established to deliver quick verdicts on traitors to the Third Reich. Its hearings in a chamber of the Berlin Law Courts were dominated by three huge swastika banners and busts of Frederick the Great and Hitler. Its presiding judge was the dreaded Dr Roland Freisler, known as the 'hanging judge' who would habitually hurl abuse at defendants, denouncing them and threatening dire punishments. The hearings were held *in camera*. There was no appeal against its verdicts.

Observers afterwards reported that Elfriede remained calm and composed throughout the hearing, even when Freisler pronounced his verdict. He sentenced her to death 'as a dishonourable subversive propagandist for our enemies'. The prescribed form of execution in the *Volksgericht* was beheading by guillotine.

Barred from appealing against the sentence, her woman lawyer entered the next best thing, a plea for clemency, submitting that 'the condemned woman has always contested the remarks attributed to her by Frau Rietzel and points out that Frau Rietzel is the only one to claim that she made such remarks.' Frau Rietzel, the lawyer stressed, was 'an extremely young witness' who had been a friend as well as a customer of Frau Scholz for years and remained a friend despite her knowledge of Frau Scholz's anti-war remarks 'which is inexplicable given Frau Rietzel's claims to be one hundred per cent behind National Socialism . . . None of the other hundred or so customers of Frau Scholz, the majority of whom came from officer circles, reported hearing treacherous remarks.'

A plea was made on the grounds of Elfriede's failing health. She was, it claimed, 'a pessimist by nature as a result of her illness – a weakening of the bones – which means she can only work if she takes constant doses of medicine. She also has acute anaemia and only survives thanks to liver sprays.' She had made remarks about not believing in the war after her sister Erna had been bombed out of her Osnabrück home and her husband's family had suffered similarly in the fire-raid on Hamburg just before her arrest.

And for full measure, the lawyer added: 'The fact that she is the sister of the notorious Remark (*sic*) and frequently heard him air his views in her youth naturally plays a role as well. Being wise, she did not adopt them herself but it has meant that she has not explicitly come round to a positive viewpoint either. Since she has not been in contact with her brother for thirteen years, he can no longer be said to have a powerful influence on her.' The lawyer tactfully evaded the fact that Elfriede's last contact with Remarque thirteen years earlier was some three years before the Nazis came to power and therefore any 'views' he might have had on National Socialism would have been immaterial.

It was all to no avail. The plea for clemency was rejected. But the curtain, when it fell, ended only the first act of Elfriede's ordeal. The date of execution was fixed for 25 November. That morning her head was shaved and she was granted a final interview with a priest. Then she waited for the warders to come for her. She waited all afternoon until at four p.m. she was informed that her execution had been postponed. Vital legal papers had been destroyed in an air-raid and the formalities had to be re-processed.

She waited twenty-one days, not knowing each dawn whether that was to be the day she was destined to die. She received a touching letter from Erna who, in poignant innocence, wrote, 'I am mad with worry about how you have withstood the terror attacks. Can you imagine how I felt when I heard the bombers had been over Berlin?' The letter went on: 'Sometimes I think that my broodings and thoughts will drive me crazy. I can no longer laugh . . . I go to Mass every day for your sake.'

A second plea for clemency was entered in which the lawyer submitted: 'The condemned woman asks whether this fearful state of constantly expecting execution might count as punishment and atonement enough and whether she might be pardoned on account of it.' It enclosed a statement from one of Elfriede's aristocratic clients, the Gräfin (Countess) Monika Finckenstein, who, at considerable risk to herself, stated that in all the years of their acquaintance she had never heard Elfriede say anything subversive and that her two accusers were 'extremely unreliable'. This plea, too, was rejected.

Her agony ended on 16 December 1943.

At 1304 hours the condemned woman, her hands tied behind her back, was led out by two prison officers. The executioner Roettger from Berlin stood ready with his three assistants. After her identity was confirmed, the condemned woman, who was calm and collected, lay down without resistance on the guillotine block whereupon the executioner carried out the beheading with the guillotine and then announced that the judgement had been carried out. The execution from the prisoner's arrival to this announcement lasted eight seconds.

A month later Erna, to whom Elfriede had granted power of attorney, wrote a sycophantic letter through a lawyer to the court requesting the bill for the costs of the trial, imprisonment and execution. She signed it with the salutation Heil Hitler.

The Remarks had plumbed the depths of despair and degradation: Peter and Erna bombed out of their Osnabrück homes, Erna's husband a prisoner-of-war, Elfriede branded and beheaded as a traitor. Peter Remark's wife Maria Anna, unhinged by the catastrophes that had befallen the family, committed suicide in September 1945, four months after the end of the war. 'My daughter was unjustly executed,' Peter wrote to a friend. 'My wife fell into a depressed state and came to an unhappy end.'[2]

Records of Judge Freisler's summing up at the end of the trial were among the documents destroyed in the air-raid during Elfriede's incarceration but in pronouncing sentence he allegedly stated: 'We have sentenced you to death because we cannot apprehend your brother. You must suffer for your brother.'[3]

Freisler was killed just over a year later when American bombs destroyed the Plötzensee court house while he was presiding over another treason trial.

Belated as it was, the shock Remarque felt over the fate of his favourite sister was profound. How quickly he learned of it is unclear. Elfriede's 'crime' was only one of many brought to trial in Nazi Germany that year and received scant coverage in the press. There was no way the family could contact him; they did not even know where he was. No mention of it appears in his diaries until June 1946, two and a half years after Elfriede's execution:

> 11 June: The first news out of Germany. A few days ago, letter from my sister Erna. Living near Leipzig, alone. Husband in captivity. My father still seems to be alive. She saw him in 1944. His wife had just become mentally deranged, committed suicide. My sister Elfriede imprisoned in 1943 because of anti-state remarks, sentenced by a People's Court, executed in December 1943.

Such a spare, unemotional recital of the facts suggests he may have merely been confirming what he already knew. Certainly it was not in his nature to react so matter-of-factly to such devastating news, even allowing for the long years of estrangement from his family. At all events, the studied refusal he had maintained throughout his exile to be publicly drawn on the subject of the Third Reich or the prosecution of the war, conditioned no doubt by a sense of self-preservation, underwent a drastic revision in the final stages of the war, suggesting he had had earlier intimation of Elfriede's fate.

'He believed that he had shirked his responsibility,' Marlene Dietrich wrote after his death, 'that he had not sufficiently struggled against Nazism, and often he would say, "Talk is easy, action is much more difficult".'[4]

From this time he began to take – arguably too late – a pro-active stance. In *Arch of Triumph*, on which he was still working in 1944, the brutality of the Nazis is uncompromisingly represented in the person of the Gestapo agent Haake whom the refugee protagonist Ravic murders in revenge for the torture and death of the wife he has been forced to leave behind in Germany.

In June of that year, days after the D-Day landings in Normandy, Remarque was approached by the American Office of Strategic Services (OSS) with a request to lend his name and time to a programme of 'denazifying' propaganda being prepared for the conquest of Germany. He agreed and three months later began working on *Practical Educational Work in Germany after the War*, a blueprint for the post-war political rehabilitation of the German people. Soon he would be breaking his avowed silence by giving a number of interviews to newspapers and magazines on the same subject.

A few weeks later he is discussing an idea for his next novel with an executive from *Collier's*. 'Soldier returns' is the only intimation he gives in his diary of the theme that would evolve into *A Time to Love and A Time to Die* (*Zeit zu leben und Zeit zu sterben*) which he would develop into a Second World War resonance of *All Quiet on the Western Front* as a study of soldierly disillusionment with Nazism and corrupted militarism. He began writing in January 1945 while still revising the final draft of *Arch of Triumph* but it would be another nine years before he completed it. Confirmation eighteen months later of Elfriede's fate shocked him into shelving work on it. Instead, a month after receiving the news, he wrote the opening sentences of the novel that would be his tribute to her. *Spark of Life* (*Der Funke Leben*) carries the dedication 'To the memory of my sister Elfriede'.

When the German edition was published in 1952 the dedication was omitted, a snub for which no reason or explanation has ever been advanced, but it was indicative of a covert, sullen resentment towards Remarque in post-war Germany which manifested itself obliquely in reviews of his books and, frequently, the expressed views of its readers. To many among the intelligentsia and the general public the author of *All Quiet on the Western Front* was still the traitor to the Fatherland he had been in 1930.

The Remarque scholar Tilman Westphalen has speculated: 'Did it seem inopportune in 1952 to remember the sacrifice of the Nazi terror via the close family of this famous author? We don't know.'[5]

Arch of Triumph, seven years in the writing and the longest of his novels, finally appeared at the end of 1945, following serialization in *Collier's* – 'our book' as he described it in a covering note to Marlene Dietrich a few months later when he sent her a copy of the first German language edition, published in Zürich, adding, 'Can you possibly make time for a meal and a laugh with me?'[6] It was an instant best-seller and a critical success. 'The best he has written since *All Quiet on the Western Front* which means that it is very good indeed,' wrote the *New York Times*. American sales alone topped 2 million copies.

The film rights were snapped up for $235,000, a record for the time, in a deal with the newly formed Enterprise Pictures which also included a number of short stories and scenarios Remarque had written several years earlier with a view to film production. Lucrative it may have been, but it was not to prove a happy arrangement.

However the money was welcome. For the six years of the war, since the publication of *Flotsam* in 1939, he had been living on his diminishing American royalties, and living at a high level of expenditure. His capital in Switzerland was frozen. His tax affairs in both Switzerland and America were in disarray and early in 1946 he was summoned to appear before a New York Internal Revenue inquiry into them. He was introduced to a lawyer, Harriet Pilpel, whose consummate expertise would be the bedrock of his American business affairs for the rest of his life.

More immediate and unsettling was the impoverishment of spirit he felt as the war ended. Apart from his writing there was an aimlessness to his life, a sense of wasting the years that should have been the peak period of his achievement. Much as he loved America, and New York in particular, he was, and felt, alien and rootless, still stateless, a non-person.

He was living at the Ambassador Hotel on Park Avenue, a few blocks from Jutta at the Pierre. They dined out frequently, their relationship generally convivial now that her jealousies had subsided – or, at any rate, been philosophically accepted – and her income ensured. Remarque assigned her a percentage of his *Arch of Triumph* royalties as maintenance. It would amount to a sizeable sum over the years.

Natasha remained the keystone of his emotional life and, as with Jutta and Dietrich before her, it was a volatile, on-off affair, almost as though, for Remarque, deep and committed love had to be tortured to be true. Her capricious moods, by turns loving or indifferent, tantalized and tormented him; in periods of depression – and they were becoming increasingly intense – he would seek solace in brothels or with women he picked up in bars.

Enterprise Pictures, founded on high ideals, was a bold, but risky, bid to break the established Hollywood mould for the new post-war era, producing quality films with everyone involved, from management and stars to the lowliest technician, working on a profit-sharing basis. 'Equality and Fraternity At This Studio' proclaimed the headline on a profile of the project in *Picturegoer* magazine describing how two of Hollywood's 'thinking' producers, David Loew and Charles Einfeld, were aiming 'to individualize their organizations' with an independent studio 'where people would feel happy, free and, regardless of their status, responsible'.[7] On paper at least, it was a scheme that accorded perfectly with Remarque's social conscience.

Loew and Einfeld were both known to him. Six years earlier Loew had co-produced *So Ends Our Night*, based on *Flotsam*. By acquiring the film rights to *Arch of Triumph*, the bestseller of the moment, and launching their plans for Enterprise with the announcement that it was to be the studio's first production, the producers sent a charge of excitement and anticipation through the entire movie industry.

The production, though, was beset by troubles from the start. Budgeted at $750,000, its costs eventually topped $5 million, the most expensive production since *Ben Hur* twenty-one years before. Ingrid Bergman, embarking on a freelance career now that her contract with David O. Selznick had expired, reluctantly agreed to play Joan Madou, a character totally alien to the heroines on which she had built her career and popularity.

'*Arch of Triumph* was one of the few films in my life that I felt "wrong" about,' she wrote nearly four decades later. 'I really didn't want to do it and I told them so, but they persevered, and there was Charles Boyer in it and Charles Laughton, so I decided it was ridiculous not to do it. But I was always unsure of myself, concerned that I would not be "believable".'[8]

Charles Boyer, Remarque's old friend, was even less enthusiastic at being cast as Ravic/Remarque. He told David Lewis, the producer assigned to the film: 'I am a Frenchman. For me to play a German would be ridiculous. And for me to play a *good* German, that would be impossible. I would not know how to begin to act such a part'.[9] The impasse was resolved by Remarque himself. He agreed that any specific reference to the character's German nationality in the script should be removed, so that Ravic became, literally, a stateless person. Boyer waited until after Remarque's death to reveal that he had hated *Arch of Triumph* at his first reading of it. He had admired the three early novels and, ingenuously perhaps, considered *Flotsam* his masterpiece.

The director was Lewis Milestone who had directed *All Quiet on the Western Front*. At the outset Remarque, unaware of the dormant doubts, had good reason to believe his novel was in capable hands. He trusted Lewis and Milestone; Boyer was an old and valued friend whose intellect chimed with his own; and, inevitably, he was enchanted by Ingrid Bergman.

Whether he practised his well-tried seduction techniques on her is questionable. At the time *Arch of Triumph* went into production Bergman's marriage to Dr Petter Lindstrom was in serious trouble and she was deeply involved in an affair with Robert Capa, one of the most celebrated war photographers of the era, whom she had met in Paris the previous June, a month after the war ended. Capa followed her to Hollywood when she began working on *Arch of Triumph* and became almost a fixture on the set, photographing her unofficially.

What isn't in question is the warm, affectionate relationship that blossomed between Bergman and Remarque, expressed in many letters to each other, with more than a hint on Remarque's part that he might be hoping for a more intimate friendship.

In one he wrote floridly but with a whisper of lovesickness:

> These days of September. They go like arrows through one's heart. Floating, full of nameless goodbyes, sustained hopes and promises, golden and quiet without regrets. To keep the intensity of youth clearer by experience comes the mystic ninth month of the year;

the beginning of the second life – conscious, but without resignation. There exists a wine like it. A 1937 Oppenheimer of which I snatched, in a lucky hour, a few bottles. I have them here. Please do call me when you are here, and tell me you will stay – and let us have one of these September wines. But don't do it too late – life and wines don't wait . . .[10]

After seeing a rough-cut of the movie, he wrote to her:

Strange, I know that having seen Joan on the screen, I will not be able to recall her face back from my imagination. It will be from now on always your face . . . I believe she looked like you . . . From now on nobody will ever think of her in other forms than in the storms, lightnings and landscapes of your face, and I, wanting it or not, will be included in the magical exchange. So hail and farewell. She died a beautiful death in your arms.[11]

Marlene, his muse for Joan Madou, had, it seemed, finally been exorcised.

Yet the film was ill-omened for Bergman, the prelude to a downward spiral in her career and popular image which plunged to its nadir with the international scandal surrounding her adulterous, highly public affair and subsequent marriage to the Italian director Roberto Rossellini. David O. Selznick would write in one of his famous memos: 'Her downfall started with her very first picture after leaving us, *Arch of Triumph* . . .'[12] It would be another ten years before Hollywood – and her public – welcomed her back to the fold.

Production, starting in June 1946, was scheduled to last twelve weeks. It lumbered on for twenty weeks, with Lewis Milestone drafting in new writers and eventually taking over the script himself. Bergman was committed to start rehearsals for a Broadway play, Maxwell Anderson's *Joan of Lorraine*, and her scenes had to be rushed and compressed so that she could be released, leaving Boyer to film additional scenes alone. At its first screening the film ran for 224 minutes, three minutes longer than *Gone With the Wind*, and had to be cut to a more manageable 120 minutes, still an excessive length for those days. Boyer, asked if cutting the film had improved it, is alleged to have retorted: 'It has improved it considerably. It was terrible for four hours but now it is only terrible for two hours.'

Arch of Triumph, trumpeted as the emblem of a new, democratic ethos in studio management and production, augured instead the death-knell of Enterprise Pictures. Post-production problems and revisions delayed its theatrical release for nearly two years. When it finally opened in New York in February 1948 the critics were largely scathing – 'overdrawn', 'dismal' were just two of the dismissive epithets.

Enterprise, in the intervening months, had pressed on with another Remarque property. *The Other Love* was based on an unpublished short story *Beyond* he had written in the early 1940s. It was merely a re-working of *Das Rennen Vanderveldes*, the first story he had sold to *Sport im Bild* twenty years before while working for Continental in Hanover and later developed into his second novel *Station am Horizont*. The movie starred Barbara Stanwyck as a consumptive, demanding concert pianist undergoing treatment in a Swiss sanatorium, David Niven as the doctor who falls in love with her and Richard Conte as a racing driver with whom she has a fatal, defiant affair before reconciling herself to death and the doctor's comforting arms.

A prototype 'woman's picture', modestly produced, it was released before *Arch of Triumph* and proved reasonably successful at the box-office. But too late for Enterprise. *Arch of Triumph* was a financial disaster, one of the most costly flops in cinema history. After producing one more film, *No Minor Vices*, a negligible comedy, the studio was declared bankrupt.

For Remarque the Enterprise experience, initiated with such amicable, not to say lucrative, intentions and hopes, ended in sour recriminations. A year later he sued the company in a Los Angeles court for $10,000 he claimed was due to him on his contract. It was the only time in his life that he indulged himself in litigation. He never got the money.

14

Switzerland Again

Remarque was granted American citizenship in August 1947 following hearings at which he was interrogated about Nazism, Communism, political memberships, whether he had broken the curfew during the war, why he lived apart from his wife . . . 'And about Marlene. Whether etc. I am now forty-nine years old and have to answer to this.' Jutta, legally still his wife, also swore allegiance to the United States of America.

He was no longer stateless, a refugee, an emigré, yet there was a curious dichotomy in his reaction to this all-important confirmation of a status he had been trying to attain for the past five years. The idea of being American pleased him. 'I am not German any more, for I do not think in German nor feel German nor talk German. Even when I dream it is about America and when I swear, it is in American,' he told a *New York Times* interviewer. Yet, with a passport now secure in his baggage, his thoughts turned increasingly and yearningly towards his natural and spiritual home, Europe.

He had just completed first drafts of both *Spark of Life* and *A Time to Love and a Time to Die* but more research was necessary, especially for the concentration camp background of *Spark*. 'Better, perhaps, to work in Europe,' he noted. But even three years after the end of the war, the bureaucracy that harassed private individuals requesting visas to enter the military occupied zones of Germany was formidable. Remarque's application was refused.

However there were no restrictions on visiting Switzerland, and he longed to return to Porto Ronco. On 12 May 1948 he sailed for Europe. His emotions as the liner approached the shores of the Old World are reflected in the stark, compelling catalogue of impressions in his diary – 'the English coast and then the French coast. The pilot boat. A clear sky. Le Havre. The cliffs. Ruined houses.'

And more so later in Paris as a taxi takes him from the Gare St Lazare to his hotel, the George V, nostalgically feasting his memories on changeless landmarks, street scenes, remembered bistros. A drink that evening in the Plaza Athenée Hotel, dining at Fouquet in the shadow of the Arc de Triomphe. Lingeringly, he details every sight and small experience of the Paris he loved in the three days he spends there, as though they are signposts gently directing him back into his former life and ways.

Natasha Paley was in town and their reunion did nothing to dispel the differences between them, the least of which was that she had a new Italian lover in tow. She and Remarque spent time together but the familiar routine of bickering and rows was quickly re-established, invariably at Natasha's instigation. She tried to dissuade Remarque from travelling on to Porto Ronco and instead accompany her to Biarritz, a particularly insensitive suggestion: she must have been conscious of the anticipation and excitement he was feeling at the prospect of returning to his beloved house for the first time in nine years. The old fire between them was dwindling. Natasha had not been part of his Paris. She seemed almost an intruder on the memories. 'Nothing stirred. After all I had lived here in earlier days with Marlene.'

They went their own ways, Remarque stopping off in Zürich to spend two nights with the Feilchenfeldts, Walter the art dealer, and his wife Marianne, who introduced him to his godson, their nine-year-old Walter.

And then on by train to Ascona, registering every detail, relishing it . . . 'Bellinzona in the rain. Roses in bloom. Lake Maggiore in the rain. Rain, rain, well-remembered. Out of the rain the house . . .'

The faithful Kramers, Josef the gardener and Rosa the housekeeper, were at the door to greet him. So was *Der Alte* (the old man) – his father, now an infirm but jovial eighty-one-year-old, for whom he had arranged permission to travel to Switzerland three months earlier. It was the first time they had seen each other for sixteen years. Remarque was overwhelmed by emotion.

He toured the house and grounds with Rosa and Joseph. Nothing had been changed or even moved. 'Everything as I had left it. Toothpaste, letters, pencils, paper in the same place. A Rip van Winkle; A Sleeping Beauty dream. One wakes up – it is ten years later. Emotion and ghostliness . . .'

But none of these shadows from the past gave him more joy than finding Puma I, his talisman motor car, his beloved Lancia, in the garage. Astonishingly, it had survived the Occupation, languishing in the Paris garage where he had left it nine years before and probably saved from Nazi requisitioning by its neutral Swiss registration plates. It had been reclaimed after the war and refurbished for him by the Swiss Automobile Club.

That evening, after dinner, he sat in the kitchen with Josef and his father, reminiscing, catching up. They drank a bottle of Cognac. He was home.

For a week or two he yielded to the contentment of renewing half-forgotten domestic ways and being cossetted by Rosa's housekeeping. It rained incessantly, encouraging him to work on *Spark of Life*, but the presence of his father pottering aimlessly around the house looking for something to do was becoming an irritant. Worse, he began to miss the social stimulus of New York.

Wanderlust quickly repossessed him. Barely a month after his return he took the train to Rome where Natasha was visiting. It was a city he didn't know – it would become a winter retreat for him in later years – and they followed the route of all first-time tourists, taking in St Peter's, the Sistine Chapel, the Villa Borghese, the Diocletian Baths. They also followed the rocky, well-worn path of their relationship. Natasha was unwell and diffident. She wanted to go to Palermo; he didn't. Another prickly parting. He solaced himself with heavy drinking and casual pick-ups. But if his charm over women needed more positive reassurance, it was soon provided by Ellen Janssen, the daughter of his Porto Ronco neighbour. Nearly thirty years his junior, she began working for him as an unofficial secretary, typing up the hand-written pages of *Spark of life*. Soon they were lovers.

The ravages of alcohol, cigarettes and anonymous sex were beginning to take their toll. He had quietly celebrated his fiftieth birthday three weeks after his return to Porto Ronco; he looked older, handsome still, but well-worn, his features increasingly puffy and lined, his eyes pouched. In late October he met Jutta in Paris and together they headed back to New York and, unsuspectingly, towards his first serious health crisis.

Waking in his suite at the Ambassador Hotel one morning three weeks after his arrival 'the room suddenly began to go round and round . . . then [I] threw up.' At first he blamed food-poisoning but the sickness persisted and two doctors summoned to him diagnosed Ménière's disease, a condition that usually occurs in middle age, caused by excessive fluid in the labyrinth of the ears. The symptoms, difficult to treat and for which there is no certain cure, include tinnitus, deafness and dizziness and unless responsive to treatment can result in permanent deafness.

He was checked for tumours and thrombosis and found negative but the recurring dizziness confined him to his bed for four weeks. Marlene and Natasha were both in town. Dietrich, in residence at the Plaza, bombarded him with concerned telephone calls and notes – 'Dearest, have been trying to reach you but in vain . . .10,000 kisses, Your Puma.'[1] The ties that bound them still held. Jutta came to sit with him. Natasha visited 'not too often'.

Indeed, Natasha, he later noted in his diary, visited him only twice throughout the month of his confinement and the widening cracks in their relationship were uppermost in his thoughts as he slowly convalesced. The relationship, by now the longest he had ever sustained with a woman, was crumbling. His diary entries during the following weeks reveal the depths of his depression, intensified by his illness, over her detachment, her rejection of his sexual advances and often calculated humiliation of him – her 'pettishness, blind egotism, lack of understanding and prejudice'. When he telephones her she isn't available. If he leaves messages she doesn't call back.

The weeks dragged on. Bouts of dizziness kept recurring. He couldn't work although the deadline for delivering the manuscript of *Spark of Life* was approaching and he had fallen seriously behind with it. The Natasha affair sidelined every other consideration as it lurched acrimoniously to its end-game.

It came in April, six months after he had returned to New York. Remarque presented her with an ultimatum before he was due to leave for Europe. Her reply, in English, is quoted in his diary:

> Darling, I know that the appearances are against me, and I don't ask for forgiveness – between us it could never exist. But what you must know . . . is that you have and will always have my entire devotion and affection, in spite of what you think. There are crises in life, as we know, that only oneself can surmount and only by oneself. I am in the middle of that and I need loneliness and reflection and to get in my own shell for a while. If you don't want to see me before you sail, I will submit to your decision but I will not understand it . . . Keep well and God bless you always,
> N.

Remarque, approaching his fifty-second birthday, was well aware that his health, mental as well as physical, had become a prime concern. His drinking was out of control, his nerves were in shreds. He was lonely and bored and apprehensive, and to compound his depression he had to acknowledge that his state of mind and body was largely self-induced. As if ordained, help was at hand. Among his neighbours was the German film actress Brigitte Horney, a popular star during the Nazi years who had fled to Switzerland in 1945, as the Red Army approached Berlin, and re-invented her career in the Zürich theatre, eventually settling in Porto Ronco. Her mother was the world-famous psycho-analyst Karen Horney whose practice was in New York. Karen Horney happened to be visiting her daughter when Remarque returned from New York in June 1950 and Brigitte arranged for them to meet.

In a series of therapy sessions over the next two months Karen Horney talked him through layers of suppressed neuroses and emotions as far back as his childhood. His diary notes matter-of-factly that he had subconsciously felt neglected by his parents in the shadow of his elder brother's protracted illness and early death, a sense of personal ugliness, his craving for love, a lack of self-confidence compensated for by exhibitionism and self-aggrandizement – the illegitimate officer's uniform and Iron Crosses of the First World War, the fast cars and racy life-style of Hanover and Berlin days, the compulsive need for the company of glamorous women. 'Day-dreaming; building castles in the air – my great burden – typical for alienation of self.' At the end of a lengthy summary he enthuses: 'Important, important day'.

Karen Horney soon calculated that Natasha was at the source of his melancholia and from her questioning constructed an identikit of her character. The type, she deduced, was the woman who, once she had a lover in thrall, lost interest in the affair, but wouldn't let go of it; only her feelings were important. She counselled Remarque to write about the Natasha episode, which he did, but not for some years, in *Shadows in Paradise*, his last incomplete novel published after his death. By then he was secure enough in himself to name the character, a mercurial, manipulative New York model, Natasha, and to recognize the self-inflicted failings in his own nature that had helped to fuel the breakdowns in his most significant relationships with women:

> She took my arm. I felt an almost anonymous tenderness, a tenderness that still had no name and was attached to no one. Yet it was not pure, but a mixture of different feelings; there was fear in it, fear that the past might rise up again, and fear that something might yet go wrong in this mysterious interval of helplessness between peril and salvation; there was a groping for anything that would give promise of security. I was ashamed to be dissecting my emotions and ashamed of what the dissection revealed, but I consoled myself rather lamely with the thought that Natasha's feelings could not be far different, that she, too, was a tendril clinging to the nearest support, without even asking herself to what extent

her heart was in it. She didn't want to be alone in a troubled period of her existence, and neither did I.

That he benefited rapidly from the analysis is reflected in his diary entries. Almost immediately his spirits have lifted; there is a new vigour in his jottings – and, evidently, in his application to his writing. 'Yesterday evening at home,' he notes five days after beginning the therapy, 'Worked on the terrace. A new moon for an hour before it vanished into the west behind the mountains . . . Good, free mood. Relaxed. The swing of the pendulum. Jupiter above the house. A feeling of how it could be if the Natasha pressure fades.'

There is a harsh irony in this glimpse of Remarque working on *Spark of Life* in such an idyllic setting. It is the bleakest, most harrowing of all his novels, the first for which he had no personal experience to draw on other than the emotional impact on him of Elfriede's fate. In a handwritten note appended to the original manuscript he recorded: 'It was very difficult to write the book. But the author felt a compelling obligation to write it. Many of his friends and also of his family became sacrificed to the Nazis.'[2]

Set in a Nazi concentration camp on the outskirts of a city that is recognizably Osnabrück in the final months of the Second World War, it charts in graphic and disturbing detail the day-to-day existence and struggle for survival of a group of male political prisoners. In tandem and counterpoint, the approaching end of the war and of the Third Reich is interwoven in the growing panic of the camp commandant and his family as Allied air-raids systematically devastate the city and the investment properties he has plundered from Jewish owners. The sight of the spire of St Katharine's Church – the church Remarque could see from his boyhood home – ablaze after an air-raid represents to the inmates of the camp on the hill a beacon of hope – a spark of life.

In amassing his documentary research for the book, Remarque had to read copiously and interview scores of concentration camp survivors, an exercise new to him in preparing a novel, and one that partly explains the length of time he took to write it. But the one example most personal to him and uppermost in his mind – Elfriede – he scrupulously avoided reinterpreting for the story. The only oblique reference to her ordeal is put, ironically, into the mouth of the Nazi commandant when he warns his wife against 'defeatist talk'. 'Take care, for God's sake! Where's the maid? If anyone hears you, we're lost. The People's Court knows no mercy. One denunciation is enough.'

Spark of Life marked a conscious shift of emphasis in Remarque's writing, a more overt political stance crystallized in a belief in the dignity of the individual and an implacable resistance to the totalitarian tyrannies of the twentieth century. He had hinted at it – or as Marlene Dietrich would later indicate, guiltily skirted round it – in earlier novels but, liberated from the threat of potential Nazi reprisal against either him or his relatives, from now it was to be a thematic imperative. As Hans Wagener observes, 'The principal theme in the novel is not merely an impersonal love of life or the survival of life against all odds, but a personal humanism, a proclamation of man as the ultimate value, of human beings free from any ideologies, whether National Socialist or Communist.'[3]

The American edition, published in January 1952, was judged respectfully, if not fulsomely, by the critics and entered the *New York Times* best-seller chart at No. 4. 'No actual survivor of a concentration camp has been able to draw up such a savage or eloquent indictment as has Erich Maria Remarque in *Spark of Life*,' wrote Quentin Reynolds in the *New York Times*.

The actor/director José Ferrer floated the idea of dramatizing the novel for the theatre. Remarque was interested, and doubtless flattered. Ferrer was very much the theatrical man of the moment. During the previous twelve months he had won the best actor Academy Award for the film *Cyrano de Bergerac*, directed two Broadway hits, *Stalag 17* and *The Fourposter*, and was currently starring on Broadway in *The Shrike*. Remarque, moreover, had long nurtured an ambition to write for the stage. Meetings took place between the two men and a contract was drawn up, but the project came to nothing.

Remarque's satisfaction over the novel's American launch was soon clouded by a contractual dispute with the Swiss publisher who had won the German language rights. He was aware that the book was likely to cause controversy, even hostility, in Germany but he was hardly prepared for the reaction of his Swiss publisher.

In a memorandum he deposited with the manuscript copy in the Library of Congress, he recorded:

> The biggest Swiss publishing house which had made a contract for *Spark of Life* refused to print the book after it was delivered, and gave as a reason that the book and all other books of the publisher would be boycotted in Germany if it appeared. Other publishers wanted changes. When the book finally came out in Germany the reaction was, to a large part, hostile, guarded and resentful – to a smaller part, the book was received without objection.[4]

To its credit, the Cologne publishing house of Kiepenheuer & Witsch took the novel and published it in July 1952. From that date Remarque stayed loyal to the firm known as KiWi which remains his publisher to this day.

Perhaps the ultimate verdict on *Spark of Life* was recorded privately by Winston Churchill. On holiday in the South of France in 1953 and suffering a bout of depression during his second term as prime minister, he wrote to his wife, Clementine: 'Today I went into Monte Carlo and bought a grisly book by the author of *All Quiet on the Western Front*. It is all about concentration camps, but in good readable print which matters to me. It is like taking refuge from melancholy in horror . . .'[5]

Remarque had planned to be in New York for the novel's publication but on the point of leaving Porto Ronco that month he suffered another attack of Ménière's disease. However much his spirits and self-esteem had benefited from the consultations with Karen Horney – they had continued in New York during his visits the previous year – he was still drinking excessively; his diary entries are littered with 'drank too much' and 'hangover', particularly during his times in New York. Also, he was still finding it difficult to rid himself psychologically of Natasha. There were the usual one-night-stands and short-term liaisons, though he was keenly aware that his libido was showing signs of waning.

But benefits there definitely were. He was writing more enthusiastically – starting work on *A Time to Love and a Time to Die* even as he was polishing the final draft of *Spark of Life* – and in New York, with Natasha no longer in the picture, he made a momentous decision to buy a lease on a permanent pied-à-terre. After eight years of suitcase life at the Ambassador Hotel he moved into an apartment on the fifteenth floor of the Ritz Towers, a block at 320 East 57th Street in one of the city's wealthiest districts. From his windows he had a magical view of the Manhattan skyline.

Jutta supervised the décor and furnishing. She was still a willing dinner partner and a conduit for his moods and confidences, the one woman he felt he could turn to now that all past passions and emotional claims on each other had subsided into comfortable, well-worn companionship.

But her days, and the status she so enjoyed, as Mrs Erich Maria Remarque were numbered. A casual meeting had brought a new woman into his life, one who would remain constant and unchallenged for the rest of it.

15

Paulette Goddard

Remarque had met Paulette Goddard casually in Hollywood during the 1940s when she was a top star at Paramount Studios and a leading lady in the film colony's social set. By April 1951 when he encountered her in New York, walking on Fifth Avenue, her screen career was in decline but her celebrity status and public image were still potent, if focused more on her private life and tastes than on her canon of personable but largely unexceptionable movie roles.

Paulette was nothing if not personable. The product of a broken home, she was born Marion Levy, or Levee, in New York in either 1905 or 1910, depending on reference sources and her whim. She naturally preferred the later date, just as she arbitrarily chose to call herself Pauline when she gained a foothold in show business, later adjusting it to Paulette. The family circumstances she was born into were moderately comfortable but at some stage in her early childhood her father walked out, leaving mother and daughter to face increasing poverty.

Driven by her mother's as much as her own ambition, she was modelling clothes at fourteen and two years later had gravitated to showgirl in a Ziegfeld revue on Broadway. Her dazzling looks and effervescent personality swiftly drew attention. Almost instantaneously they also brought her a rich husband. At sixteen she eloped with Edgar James, a North Carolina lumber magnate twice her age. It was the first step in a lifelong odyssey of accumulating wealth which would culminate in her owning one of the world's most valuable jewellery collections.

As the wife of a Southern gentleman and nominal mistress of a gracious mansion at Asheville, North Carolina, Paulette took full advantage of the opportunity to hone her personality and social accomplishments. She learned to ride and rode with the hunt. Inquisitive as well as acquisitive, she began tutoring herself in literature, art and general good taste. She was not yet twenty when she divorced James after three years of marriage. She accepted a $375,000 settlement and headed west for Hollywood, taking as her professional name Goddard, her mother's maiden name.

After two struggling years of bit parts, cushioned by a bank balance larger than those of many an established star, fate suddenly dealt her another winning hand. In July 1932 the producer Joseph Schenck threw a weekend party aboard his yacht and chose Paulette to be one of the decorative entourage of starlets he invariably recruited to enliven proceedings. Among the guests on board was Charlie Chaplin.

According to Chaplin's biographer David Robinson it was, perhaps not surprisingly, a matter of money that ignited the initial spark between them. 'Chaplin was delighted at this first meeting to give Paulette some financial counsel. She was still naïve enough in Hollywood ways to be contemplating investing $50,000 of her alimony in a dubious film project. Chaplin was just in time to prevent her signing the documents.'[1]

He was entranced by her and immediately set about grooming her. He bought out her studio contract. He persuaded her to abandon her Hollywood platinum blonde and revert to her natural brunette. When he saw her off at Los Angeles airport on a flight to New York two months after the Schenck party, a press photograph of their farewell kiss made front pages across America. Paulette casually told reporters that she was to be his next leading lady.

The film was *Modern Times*, released in 1936. Chaplin created the role of the Gamine specially for her. It made Paulette Goddard a star, and established her immutably in Hollywood circles as Chaplin's property in more ways than one.

The date, the circumstances, indeed the authenticity of Chaplin's marriage to Paulette remain one of Hollywood's abiding mysteries. No documentation of it has ever been traced. One school of thought claims they wed in China, another that the ceremony took place at sea. Certainly, two weeks after the premiere of *Modern Times*, the couple embarked on a four-month cruise through the Far East, accompanied by Paulette's mother, Alta Goddard. At all events, Hollywood and the rest of the world came to accept them, if dubiously, as man and wife, though, paradoxically, neither of them publicly acknowledged they were married for years and in the higher echelons of the film capital they were deemed to be 'living in sin'. To add to the confusion, at their divorce hearing in Juarez, Mexico in 1942 corroborative evidence was filed claiming that they had married at Canton, China in 1932. The mystery remained as to why they persisted in concealing the fact of the matter and declined to spare themselves a continuing aura of gossip and innuendo.

As Chaplin's presumed third wife, Paulette found herself step-mother to his two young sons who adored her. Three decades later, in his memoir *My Father, Charlie Chaplin*, Charles Chaplin Jr wrote of her:

> We lost our hearts at once, never to regain them through all the golden years of our childhood. Have you ever realized, Paulette, how much you meant to us? You were like a mother, a sister, a friend all in one. You lightened our father's spells of sombre moodiness and you turned the big house on the hill into a real home. We thought you were the loveliest creature in the whole world. And somehow I feel, looking back today, that we meant as much to you, that we satisfied some need in your life too.[2]

Public perception of Paulette the star as beautiful, slightly dizzy, hoydenish, fun-loving was only superficially accurate. Her vivid personality and charm were deployed at full power on the Hollywood social circuit but they concealed a quest for knowledge and intellectual self-improvement every bit as thirsting as her pursuit of jewels. Her friend Anita Loos, author of *Gentlemen Prefer Blondes*, described her as 'extraordinarily intelligent'.

When she first met Chaplin she was paying a University of California professor to coach her in English literature and other tutors to teach her French, Spanish, history and economics. Her circle of friends, some of them lovers, included the authors William Saroyan, John Steinbeck, Michael Arlen, H.G. Wells and, closest of all, Aldous Huxley who, it has been suggested, drew on Paulette for the character of the Vamp in his 1939 novel *After Many a Summer*. Christopher Isherwood noted in his journal: 'I do like Paulette; she is tough and good-humoured.' Michael Arlen thought her 'the most civilized girl in Hollywood' and William Saroyan commented: 'What she has is an inner twinkle, and it goes around in a strictly non-sorrowing frame; all of it attractively tough, challenging, mischievous, coquettish, wicked and absolutely innocent.'[3] George Gershwin fell passionately in love with her and introduced her to the great Mexican artist Diego Rivera who adored – and painted – her. He became her lover, too.

Anita Loos, a close companion throughout her life, probably knew her better than anyone. 'Paulette is one of the most complicated, intelligent, fascinating people I've ever met in my life, and she and I became great, great friends from the time she first came to Hollywood,' she once said, 'She is an absolutely astounding woman, She is the most cultured and best-read woman I know in show-business. Which nobody is aware of, because her looks have always stopped it. She used to say to me: "If you tell anybody I'm taking lessons in political economy, I'll never speak to you again," and I would say: "Why not?", and she would say: "It makes me seem so dull!".'[4]

Paulette's status in the Hollywood hierarchy was consolidated when she emerged as front-runner for the role of Scarlett O'Hara in *Gone With the Wind*. As David O. Selznick's search for the actress who would play the most coveted role in film history neared its climax in a blaze of publicity, the betting was on Paulette. 'I saw the [Paulette Goddard] test and thought there was an enormous improvement in her work – so much so that I think she is still very strongly in the running for

Scarlett,' Selznick wrote in one of his memos a month before shooting was to begin in December 1938. Three days later he was writing: 'I think we should make clear to Katharine Hepburn, Jean Arthur, Joan Bennett and Loretta Young that they are in the small company of final candidates . . . I think the final choice must be out of this list plus Goddard and our new girl [an unknown actress called Doris Jordan], plus any last-minute new-girl possibility that may come along.'[5]

Alas for Paulette, a new-girl possibility *did* come along at the last minute. Her name was Vivien Leigh. Nothing if not resilient, Paulette put the disappointment behind her and concentrated on maintaining a star career over the next ten years in such box-office hits as three Cecil B. de Mille spectacles, *Reap the Wild Wind*, *North West Mounted Police* and *Unconquered* as well as Chaplin's *The Great Dictator* and a clutch of other productions. In one of them, the 1942 *Hold Back the Dawn* which co-starred Paulette with Charles Boyer and Olivia de Havilland, the screenplay involving European emigrés illegally entering the United States across the Mexican border was uncannily reminiscent of Remarque's experiences in both his own arrival and Jutta's.

Divorce from Chaplin in 1942 brought her a settlement estimated at $1 million and his 32 ft luxury cruiser *Panacea*. They remained on amicable, though distant, terms. Years later both had homes in Switzerland, Chaplin at Vevey, Paulette at Gstaad. Once asked by an interviewer if they ever met up, Paulette cryptically replied: 'We live on different mountains.'

Paulette's next marriage in 1944 to the actor Burgess Meredith broke up after three years.

'I was fascinated by the impact she had on people,' he wrote in his autobiography. 'Her presence was strong; she was more attractive in life than on film. She sometimes became tense facing the camera – not all of the spontaneity and fire of the lady came across. But in life she was bright, funny, sensual – you felt the vibrations when she walked into a room. She had an intuitiveness, a kind of ESP, that told her where people's thoughts were. She understood the id of the male animal. She was flattering in conversation and attractive physically'.[6]

Never short of admirers, she had a series of affairs after her divorce, one, highly publicized, with John Steinbeck who once teasingly presented her with a trunk full of cheap paste jewellery he had bought at a five-and-dime store,[7] another with the director John Huston. Her gem collection fared no better with Clark Gable for whom she discarded Huston. Gable was noted for his parsimony.

A widower since the death of Carole Lombard in an aeroplane crash in 1942, he and Paulette had known each other casually over the years before suddenly in 1949 they embarked on an intense relationship. Heedless of the publicity, they were seen dining or dancing together nearly every night. The gossip columnists predicted a marriage. Then, just as suddenly, it was over. The reason became, embarrassingly for both of them, public knowledge.

Paulette was due to fly to Mexico and Gable presented her with a gold Saint Christopher medallion, the first and only piece of jewellery he gave her. When she wore it she noticed her skin turned black, revealing, to her irritation, that its gold standard was less than genuine. She told friends, and the story got into the papers. A furious Gable abruptly terminated the affair.

Her appetite for jewels was a byword in Hollywood social circles, and one of the characteristics her detractors scoffingly held against her. She made no secret of it, fuelling envy and resentment in many of her female rivals. Once, when told that only Sonja Henie, the Norwegian ice-skating movie star, flaunted jewellery as conspicuously as she did, Paulette retorted: 'But Sonja *buys* hers.'

Although her screen career was declining rapidly by the end of the 1940s her business interests absorbed her. She owned a lucrative antiques dealership and dabbled in various film production projects and property speculations, most of which brought good returns. 'Paulette has a flair for business. She has the easy manner of the born salesman, all the externals of persuasiveness and the hard-bitten instinct for closing a bargain just at the right moment,' observed the Hollywood columnist W.H. Mooring. In 1949 she was rated among the ten wealthiest stars in Hollywood.

Dining at El Morocco, Copacabana, Pavillon or the other goldfish bowls of fashionable New York, Remarque and Paulette soon became an item in the gossip columns. Remarque revelled in her company, much as he had in the company of Lupe Velez. Paulette had a similar tonic effect on him – the same qualities of vivacity and *joie de vivre* but without Lupe's coating of vulgarity. On the surface at least, she could be very much the lady.

One person who didn't think so was Marlene Dietrich. She was appalled when she learned that Remarque was dating her. Barely a month after their encounter on Fifth Avenue he was noting in his diary: 'Marlene called. Tore Paulette to pieces. I pointed out that, all the time, everything she mentioned was something I particularly liked. She dropped it.'

That 'her' Remarque had become involved with 'that terrible woman' must have been specially hurtful to Dietrich whose contempt for Paulette dated back to earlier days in Hollywood. Maria Riva has recalled a story her mother enjoyed relating to friends. Dietrich and Paulette happened to be travelling on the same train, and Paulette came to Marlene's drawing-room. 'Now, you know me,' Marlene would say. 'I must have been *very* lonely to want to talk to Paulette Goddard.'

The conversation got round to a man who had treated Dietrich badly.

> She stood up, left, then came back schlepping a large jewellery case – a trunk! Like those that jewellers use when they come to your hotel to show you their whole store – they are made of ugly Moroccan leather and have drawers. Well, Goddard had one of those in *alligator*, and it was full! Nothing but diamonds! Like rocks! And she says to me, very serious, like a professor: 'Marlene, you have to get diamonds. Coloured stones are worth nothing. Only pure white stones have lasting value. A man wants you? It's easy! You say no, right away. The next day he sends you long-stemmed roses, you

send them back. The next day, when his orchids arrive, you send them back. His little gifts, expensive perfume, handbags from Hermes, mink coats, things like that, you send everything back. Rubies and diamond clips – back, even emerald and diamond pins. When the first diamond bracelet arrives, it's usually small, so you send it back, but you call him and say thank you, sweetly. The next day, when the larger diamond bracelet arrives, you send that back, but now you let him take you out to lunch – nothing else! The first diamond *ring* never is big – give it back but say yes to dinner . . . go dancing. The only thing you have to always remember: *Never, ever* sleep with a man until he gives you a pure white stone of at least ten carats.'

Dietrich would then add: 'It's true! She really said all that to me. It must work. She has all those enormous diamonds. Terrible woman! But isn't it amazing how those women do it? Get away with it like that?'

Marlene no doubt kept her own counsel when Remarque dined with her the following month in Paris en route for Porto Ronco. Here he dallied for several weeks – for once a free spirit inasmuch as there was no one demanding woman to be answerable to. Though not feeling at his best – neuralgia was a new complaint – he pursued a hectic social round, meeting Jutta, dining with old friends including Karen and Brigitte Horney, attending race meetings at Chantilly with Coco Chanel. And drinking heavily again.

Then to Porto Ronco where he found, after months of laboured writing, that he was able to work conscientiously on the final revisions to *Spark of Life* while he waited for Paulette to join him. Thanks to her invigorating influence, his writer's block had been breached.

Her introduction to the Casa Remarque, a house she never grew to like, was not auspicious. She arrived at the height of a violent storm after wading waist-high through flooded streets in Locarno and, with her customary initiative, finding a post-bus that would take her through the tempest to him.

Blissful days followed, swimming, lazing in the sun, Paulette pottering around the house 'happy, purposeful and seemingly without complexes'. When, after 'two drinking nights', he suffered an attack of Ménière's she dealt capably with the situation. 'Good, slightly guilty [regarding work etc.] days with Paulette.'

With revisions of *Spark of Life* completed, he began work in earnest on *A Time to Love and A Time to Die*.

In July 1952, after twenty turbulent years of exile, he returned to Osnabrück. It was to be the main background, re-named Weiden, of the new novel and he needed to see for himself how it had weathered the war years. This, rather than sentimental considerations, seems to have been his motivation and was probably the deciding factor in finally persuading the allied occupation authorities to approve a visa for him to visit Germany.

He and Paulette sailed from New York to Rotterdam and spent a few days together sight-seeing in Amsterdam and being entertained by his Dutch publisher Rinny Van der Velde and his wife.

Whatever the state of his emotions as he crossed the frontier, a free man, into his native land, he conceals them in customarily cryptic, almost detached impressions and observations. 'The border near Bentheim. German officials in green uniforms. One who checked my passport: I had never expected to see you. Asked for it back again; wanted to show it to a colleague who doesn't believe it's me. Drive on. Ems [the river] country. Grey sky. People on bicycles. In fields. Not very cheerful'. The Dutch student he has hired as a driver asks him how it feels after twenty years. 'That it's raining.'

Finally Osnabrück. He made a quick survey of the city centre with-out, apparently, getting out of the car, suppressing afterwards any emotion he might have felt at seeing the legacy of destruction – making sure, nonetheless, that he viewed the landmarks of his good memories.

Katharinenkirche [St Katharine's Church] tower without its cladding. Ruins. Hakenstrasse 3 (the last family home he had known) no longer there. Bierstrasse. Grossestrasse. Almost everything new, low-income housing. Johanniskirche [St John's Church] practically intact. Süsterstrasse destroyed. The Vogt house too [the home of

his employer when he worked for the funeral monument firm].
The Hoberg house and garden a little [where he had taken refuge
from the uproar over *All Quiet on the Western Front* and worked on
The Road Back; he would later use the house and garden as
background for a key romantic interlude in *A Time to Love and A
Time to Die*]. All these seen only driving past.

A short 20-kilometre drive south of the city brought him to Bad
Rothenfelde where his father now lived, with his sister Erna, her
husband Walter Rudolf and their fourteen-year-old son Klaus, the
nephew Remarque had never met. 'Driving up, saw my father on the
balcony of a pretty house . . . Father seems to be in good shape. Sister
pretty, sometimes a bit "wilted" [he uses the English word] – have to
remember that she is fifty-two-years-old.' As the barriers broke down
in the short time he stayed with them, he found himself growing fond
of his young nephew.

He travelled on to Berlin where he spent two weeks, looking up
those old friends he could trace – including an embarrassing reunion
with Lotte Preuss, the 'too fat' one-time girlfriend who still carried a
torch for him – and gathering 'material' for future use. He was appalled
by the scale of destruction and by the many harrowing reminiscences
of life and survival in the last weeks of the war that he coaxed from
Berliners he knew: stories of arrests and torture, hunger and deprivation.
On a pilgrimage to old haunts he found Wittelsbacherstrasse 5, the
apartment block where he and Jutta had set up home, still standing.

> The house next door in ruins. Roof destroyed. Looked inside. On
> to the Hotel Majestic. Destroyed. Only the part left where my room
> was. The piece of garden. The garden entrance to my apartment
> now the entrance to the Red Mill Art Café – tired, 1920s drawings
> on the walls, black, gold, lesbians, gentlemen in capes and evening
> dress, sadists in boots with whips . . . This was where my apartment
> had been.

Paulette was at his side throughout this journey back in time but judging from his diary record of it she melted into the background, a silent witness. She is mentioned only glancingly, a mere letter P. in references to restaurant visits. What she thought of his family, how they responded to her is left unsaid. It's as though Paulette, the star attraction, had for once accepted a supporting role, a sympathetic bystander in what must have been for Remarque a sobering emotional odyssey.

From that summer of 1952 their lives wove into a regular though flexible routine of togetherness and separation, an unwritten accord to go their own ways whether by whim or necessity. Paulette spent several weeks away filming in Barcelona. The movie was *Babes in Bagdad*, a title which, along with those that followed it in 1953 – *Vice Squad, Paris Model, The Sins of Jezebel* – reflected the penny-dreadful depths to which her screen career was plummeting. Paulette was unconcerned. She cheerfully accepted that her best movie years were behind her and signed the contracts for one reason only: the money to finance her shopping sprees and extravagant tastes.

Remarque was happier, more confident and focused than he had been for a long time. The turning point had been his consultations with Karen Horney. They had clarified and resolved many of his self-doubts and inhibitions, replenished his self-esteem. Horney's death from cancer at the end of 1952 upset him but at least he was no longer dependent on her ministrations.

A few days later, in New York, he spent an evening with Dietrich at her Park Avenue apartment. 'Gave me a meal. Ate potatoes with butter herself. Glued to the television set . . . everything false, exaggerated. No affinity any more. The half-furnished apartment – too little light in the living-room; the sickening blond and beige of the floor, walls, furniture; the many mirrors; no affinity, Hollywood elegance . . . insincere personality . . .'

His disenchantment was, perhaps, premature, a knee-jerk reaction of self-denial to the pleasure he now found in Paulette's spontaneous, uncomplicated attitude to life and to himself, and coloured by the all-too-aggravating knowledge that Marlene was conducting a highly public affair with Yul Brynner, currently the sensation of Broadway in *The King and I*, and twenty years her junior.

Karen Horney's death was the first of several losses that affected him deeply in the following twelve months. Josef Kramer, for thirty years his gardener and man-about-the-house in Porto Ronco, died in the summer of 1953; Walter Feilchenfeldt, the art dealer, close friend and father of Remarque's godson, at the end of that year. As though to emphasize awareness of his own mortality, he was found to be suffering from diabetes in addition to the recurring attacks of Ménière's.

Contrarily, his will-power and energy seemed recharged. He began for the first time to think about writing for the theatre, sketching ideas simultaneously for three plays, *Die letzte Station* (The Last Station), *Die Heimkehr des Enoch J. Jones* (The Homecoming of Enoch J. Jones) and *La Barcarole*. Once, when asked what he regarded as the key to his success as a writer, he replied: 'Perhaps because I am a playwright manqué. All my books are written like plays. One scene follows on another.'[8] To another interviewer he confided: 'I write by ear. I hear everything that I write. I choose words for their sound . . . my novels all sound good when they are read aloud. I find easy what other authors find most difficult – writing dialogue.'[9]

Of the three projects only two were completed and only *Die letzte Station* would achieve a modicum of success in Berlin. *Die Heimkehr des Enoch J. Jones* was given a one-off production in Osnabrück after his death.

But the work that monopolized his attention at this stage was *A Time to Love and a Time to Die*. By the end of 1953 it was completed.

16

A Time to Love

A Remarque novel which attempted to confront and question the attitudes of the German man-in-the-street to Nazi tyranny was bound, even calculated, to be contentious in the light of the emotions aroused by *All Quiet on the Western Front*. Tilman Westphalen, in his Afterword to the modern German edition of *A Time to Love and A Time to Die*, observes: 'Remarque faced the German people with the unavoidable question about guilt and collective guilt after the end of the war in September 1954 when the book appeared for the first time in the Federal Republic, and he hoped for an honest answer from his readers.' Many of the 'answers' would, for Remarque, be woundingly honest.

He was prepared for controversy, but hardly for the objections and problems raised by his publishers when they took delivery of the German-language manuscript. The book, dedicated to 'P.G.' (Paulette), had appeared in America and Britain five months earlier to encouraging reviews and immediately went into the best-seller lists. Germany was not to be so readily accommodating.

The novel's hero Ernst Graeber, schooled from youth in Nazi doctrine, is a young *Wehrmacht* soldier on the Russian front in the final stages of the war, increasingly disillusioned by the atrocities he witnesses but torn between duty and conscience. He returns on leave to his home town – geographically but anonymously Osnabrück – to find it devastated, his home destroyed and his parents missing. In his attempts to trace them he is helped by an old school friend, now a senior SS officer and fanatical Nazi, further compromising his ethical instinct. He finds romance briefly with another friend from earlier days whose father has been denounced and sent to a concentration camp. He meets his old teacher Professor Pohlmann, a humanitarian intellectual who has been hounded out of his job and is secretly sheltering a Jew. In the course of Ernst's leave, Pohlmann is arrested by the Gestapo and disappears.

'I would like to know how far I am involved in the crimes of the last ten years,' Ernst says to his teacher, 'and I would like to know what I ought to do.'

In a tacit remembrance of Elfriede, Remarque has Pohlmann reply: 'Do you know what you are asking? People are beheaded for less than that nowadays.'

Ernst says: 'I have seen certain things, and I have heard a great deal. I know too that the war is lost. And I know that we are only continuing to fight so that the Government, the Party, and the people who caused it all can stay in power for a while longer and create more misery . . . I know it now. I've not always known it.'

He finally has to return to the front and survives a battle which, for him, signifies the beginning of the end of the Third Reich. Put in charge of a group of captured Russian partisans, he is ordered to shoot them by Steinbrenner, a brutish Gestapo officer. Instead he shoots the officer and allows the prisoners to escape – a small gesture of redemption. As they scurry away, disbelievingly, one of the Russians produces a concealed rifle and shoots him dead.

Remarque, through his mouthpiece Ernst, was effectively imputing complicity in the Nazi terror to the German people as a whole, and he would not be allowed to get away with it.

A Time to Love and A Time to Die is no *All Quiet on the Western Front*. More reflective and considered, it lacks the anger, the edge of despair, the tangible fear and immediacy with which Remarque conveyed bombardment and battle in the earlier novel. There are, nevertheless, sequences of disturbing imagery, most potently in the opening paragraphs describing the ghoulish emergence of long dead corpses, Russian and German, as spring sunshine begins to melt the snows of winter . . . 'when they lay in the sun, the eyes thawed first. They lost their glassy brilliance and the pupils turned to jelly. The ice in them melted and ran slowly out of the eyes – as if they were weeping.' Similarly, Remarque graphically depicts the annihilation of a German city – his Osnabrück – and the degradation of its bombed-out inhabitants.

Judged too strong meat for sensitive domestic digestion, many such impressions were toned down or expunged for the German edition. Tellingly, the most significant omission from the original German edition occurred during Ernst's showdown with Steinbrenner: '"Murderer," he said once again and meant Steinbrenner and himself and countless others.'

Through the spring and summer of 1954 Remarque was distracted by negotiations with the publishers over deletions and revisions. In March, at the height of them, he crashed his car in Locarno. The circumstances have remained a mystery, as has the extent of Remarque's injuries, but they must have been fairly serious. He was incommunicado for three months during which time his secretary Olga Ammann conducted and signed all correspondence relating to the forthcoming publication.

German reviewers were generally tolerant, if judiciously subdued, about the novel. The criticism and a controversy, which faintly echoed the furore over *All Quiet on the Western Front*, came from the readership, reflected in letters and articles in the press. At the heart of it was resentment that Remarque had spent the years of the Third Reich in safe, comfortable exile. He was not 'one of us'. He had no right as an absentee German to judge fellow-countrymen who had endured Nazism whether or not they had subscribed to it.

'Remarque is an emigrant,' wrote a correspondent to the Dortmund *Ruhr-Nachrichten*. 'He did not live in Germany for a single day of the war. Antipathy towards the SS, venom against the Nazis, fierce arrows against loudmouths cannot conceal that Remarque warmed his feet at American and Swiss fireplaces when these were dragging their horrors through German cities. One cannot subsequently spoon up this 1944 life out of a preserving jar.'

Remarque, another wrote in the *Münchener* (Munich) *Illustrierte*, saw events of those times 'from the perspective of a disgusting corpse-maggot which feels good in the garbage and lives off it.'

The Hollywood director Douglas Sirk who was to direct the film version two years later, and himself an emigré from Nazi Germany, would later write:

> They couldn't allow a refugee to give any kind of an interpretation of what life was like in Germany during the war. In Germany then, in the late Fifties, everyone was full of self-pity. And today people are still, at least the generation of the war. I meet someone I knew from way back and he keeps telling me how bad things were for them, how they suffered, how they endured, how many examples he could give me of courage, and so on, and how splendid, comfortable and serene the life of an emigré must have been.

To some degree, however, Remarque had already forestalled such accusations and set his agenda eight years earlier in an interview – conducted in New York – for the Vienna magazine *Europäische Rundshau*. 'I myself have lost a sister and many friends who were murdered by the Gestapo,' he said. It must follow, he went on, that 'the majority of the German people takes on board the responsibility for the slaughter, for the occupation of foreign countries, for the murder of six million Jews.'

Such were the German readership's sensibilities that three decades would pass before the original 'uncensored' text was published in German in 1989, nineteen years after its author's death.

Peter Remark died in June 1954, three days short of his eighty-eighth birthday. Two days earlier he had walked to church in the rain without a coat – in order, according to family reports, to impress a lady-friend – and caught a chill which developed into a fever and caused an embolism. Remarque travelled by train to Osnabrück for the funeral and a reunion with family members, aunts and cousins, he had not seen since his youth.

Grief for his father, tinged with guilt, is palpable in his account of the occasion.

> Later in his room. Looked at his things, clean, orderly, he had never wanted to give anybody the least trouble. The room empty . . . nothing left of him. Looked at photographs, his meagre possessions. He didn't have a single book of mine – I never thought to give him any. Wanted to bring him the last one for his birthday. Too late. Many things too late. Why didn't I come to see him before? Could have done. Why haven't I done so many things?

The day after the funeral, before leaving for home, he made a solitary pilgrimage to his father's grave.

The distant past, memories, regrets, nostalgia had already begun to cast their long shadows over his consciousness in his fifty-sixth year. The new book he had started working on immediately after completing *A Time to Love and A Time to Die* would develop as a lightly fictionalized case history of his last months in Osnabrück (Werdenbrück in the novel), part wistful, part bitter. The underlying theme of *The Black Obelisk* (*Der schwarze Obelisk*) is the rise of Fascism during the Weimar Republic and the conditions that seeded it. Its first-person protagonist Ludwig Bromer – Remarque himself – is a young former school teacher and soldier reduced to working as a salesman and advertising manager for a graveyard monument business run by two brothers (in real life the Vogt brothers). For the German edition Remarque provided a wry sub-title: *Story of a Belated Youth*. The narrative, less a plot than a representation of linked events, has a picaresque quality, veering from black humour to stark social com-mentary. Cumulatively, it captures a vivid impression of the city and the times as he knew them and the ominous stirrings of Nazism as he faced an uncertain future.

Shortly after returning to Porto Ronco from his father's funeral, he was approached by the veteran German film director G.W. Pabst to adapt a film script titled *Der letzte Akt* (*The Last Act;* alternative UK/US titles *Ten Days to Die* and *The Last Ten Days*) from *Ten Days to Die*, a book about Hitler's final days in his Berlin bunker. The American author Michael A. Musmanno had been a judge at the Nuremberg Trials of Nazi war criminals.

It was a subject that chimed with Remarque's self-appointed obligation to help alert international opinion to any potential threat of a resurgence of Nazism and, putting *The Black Obelisk* aside, he tackled what was for him a new and untried medium with enthusiasm. Working with Pabst, one of the great German directors, was an honour. His First World War film *Westfront*, released a few months after the publication of *All Quiet in the Western Front* but without causing the same degree of controversy, and *Pandora's Box*, which elevated its star Louise Brooks to lasting cult status, had become screen classics. In the following months Remarque immersed himself in the work, driving with Paulette to meetings with Pabst in Austria where the film was being shot, indulging himself for three days at the Salzburg Festival, enjoying a reunion with Ingrid Bergman in Munich with her husband Roberto Rosselini ('not getting on together; but three children and so much publicity, divorce almost impossible').

Remarque was quick to realize the film was going to be a disaster. After his first sight of it at a studio preview, he noted his 'annoyance' at a weak screenplay, unnecessary dramatic insertions, a flabby ending and phony psychology. In spite of its lack of impact in Germany it was chosen to open the 1955 Edinburgh Film Festival. When, months later, the English-language version was released in London, the *Daily Mail* critic dismissed it as 'one of the most diabolically pathetic films of the war ever seen'.

But at least it offered Remarque a platform for driving home his ominous fears of a Nazi revival. To coincide with the London premiere in 1956 he contributed an article on the subject to the *Daily Express*, the only time he allowed himself to express a fixed and cogently argued political viewpoint in a newspaper.

It appeared on 30 April, the anniversary of Hitler's death. Under the headline BE VIGILANT! the *Express* introduction read:

Adolf Hitler died this day eleven years ago; his mystique did not. It still lives deep in the militant soul of Germany. The man, dead, is still dangerous. To publicize the danger and to demolish The Myth, Erich Maria Remarque has co-operated in the writing of a film which will shortly be seen in London. It is called *Ten Days to Die* and it is a relentlessly truthful documentary-dissection of Hitler's last wretched days in his Berlin bunker.

What followed was Remarque's thesis that former Nazis were still covertly active, even occupying positions of responsibility in German society and in exile.

He concluded:

The great part of the German people want peace and democracy and have had enough of Hitler and his associates; nonetheless the forces of reaction are not dead. They are agitating and working and waiting their chance, and they do not consist solely of former Nazis; they also include those circles that helped the Nazis to power, which did nothing to check them when they could still have been stopped, which put false patriotism above the concept of personality and responsibility, and which worked hand-in-hand with the Nazis for their own ends.

Let us hope God will never allow them to come back to power. But simply hoping is not enough. Education in active democracy is more important. Twelve years of education in intolerance and a couple of hundred years of training in blind obedience cannot be so easily eradicated.

That is why this film was made. That is why its last words are:
BE VIGILANT!

It was hardly surprising that, coming hard on the heels of the controversy over *A Time to Love and A Time to Die*, the article was not picked up by the German press.

Remarque had high hopes for his first venture into writing for the theatre, collaborating excitedly on the final rehearsals of *Die letzte Station*, now retitled *Berlin 1945*, before its premiere opened the Berlin Festival in September 1956. Its story of a young escapee from a concentration camp in the last weeks of the war in Berlin amplified themes he had been exploring in his last two books and the Pabst film script – youthful disillusionment with the Third Reich, repudiation of Nazi tyranny, suspicion that the Nazi virus had merely gone underground to resurface later. 'The combination of a life-threatening situation and a love story is obviously vintage Remarque,' Hans Wagener has observed.

His euphoria was short-lived. Although *Berlin 1945* was well received by its audiences, the critics were lukewarm. Plans for a Broadway production came to nothing. With another title change to *Full Circle* it was eventually given an off-Broadway production in 1976, four years after Remarque's death, directed by the film director Otto Preminger with Leonard Nimoy – Mr Spock in the television series *Star Trek* – in the leading role. After three decades audience interest in the Second World War as a dramatic basis had waned. Remarque, too, had begun to pass out of fashion. The production made a negligible impact.

Encouraged by Paulette, he had invested a great deal of faith and energy into what he had envisaged as a new career in theatre and screen writing – the 'playwright manqué' as he had once described himself to an interviewer – so the relative failure of his attempts was a considerable disappointment to him.

Universal Pictures had bought the rights to *A Time to Love and A Time to Die* and assigned Douglas Sirk to direct it. As Detlef Sierck, Sirk had been part of the young artistic crowd Remarque had mingled with during his Berlin years. In the Hollywood of the 1950s his reputation was riding high on a wave of box-office hits with such lush romantic melodramas as *Magnificent Obsession*, *All That Heaven Allows* and *Written on the Wind*. He invited Remarque to collaborate on the screenplay.

For the first time in fourteen years Remarque found himself back in Hollywood, his aversion to it tempered by his enthusiasm for the way the production was shaping and for his contribution to it. He set himself a rigid working routine, writing every day from nine a.m. to six p.m. in a bungalow on the Universal Studios lot but Sirk was not satisfied with the finished screenplay and brought in a seasoned Hollywood dialogue writer to refine the final version. Yet again Remarque, proud and confident of his fluency with dialogue in his novels, found his ambitions for script writing thwarted. 'Nobly, as Remarque was, he waived his royalty because of that,' Sirk said.[1] He also declined a screen credit and when the film was released the screenplay was attributed to Orin Jannings.

It was a measure of consolation when Sirk had the imaginative idea of casting him as Professor Pohlmann, a small but crucial role embodying the conscience of anti-Nazism at the heart of the story. Remarque was in Los Angeles for two months working on the script before rejoining the film unit in Berlin where his scenes were to be shot. Finding himself transported back into a replica world of the Third Reich was eerie and disturbing.

> When I opened the door to the studio it was like a bad dream. So unbelievable that it seemed almost credible. There they were again: the swastika flags, the black SS uniforms, the atmosphere of corruption and confusion . . . a couple of days later we drove to a street in the city and on the way had to fill up with petrol. In the car were three actors dressed as SS officers. The woman petrol pump attendant turned round and yelled 'Run, Otto! They're here again.' Memory can be a strong seducer.[2]

For someone who had never acted before he acquitted himself honourably, receiving generally favourable reviews, although one dissenter, the *New York Times* film critic Bosley Crowther, dismissed him as 'stumbling around in a small role'. Though brief, his performance and characterization give the film a thought-provoking dimension at its core. More interesting perhaps, it preserves a unique, 'live' portrait of the man himself. In his sixtieth year, his face reveals the depredations of his drinking and smoking, worn but still handsome; his voice is deep and sonorous, with a quiet Germanic accent. There is a sense of gravity and world-weariness demanded by the role but which was endemic in the personal Remarque. Recalling his performance years later, Sirk told an interviewer: 'The melancholy came through wonderfully in his expression.'

The interplay of Ernst Graeber, played by the American actor John Gavin in his first major screen role, and Professor Pohlmann can be viewed as a composite image of Remarque's own rite of passage: Graeber the disillusioned, questioning young soldier he had been himself and Pohlmann the humane realist he had matured into.

When production had wrapped, Remarque told Sirk resignedly: 'Your film won't be successful in Germany because it's a Remarque'.

The gossip columnists had been speculating for some time about a likely marriage between Remarque and Paulette. So, to himself, had Remarque, but he was not yet sure. Nevertheless he was, subconsciously perhaps, preparing the ground. In May 1957 he and Jutta were divorced by mutual agreement, if marginally less mutual on Jutta's part. It was she, however, who brought the suit before a judge in Juarez, Mexico. Remarque was not present. Jutta, still living, largely at Remarque's expense, at the Hotel Pierre in New York, had become increasingly neurotic and hypochondriacal as the years passed. Despite his generosity and genuine, if sometimes exasperated, concern, she continued to feel ill-used and neglected, but after nineteen estranged and sterile years of their second marriage-of-convenience she had sense enough to realize she had no role to play in his life and a diminishing claim on his sense of integrity.

The divorce may have regularized his marital status but he was still uncertain where his future lay. According to Douglas Sirk, Remarque mused on it weeks after the divorce while they were working together in Hollywood. Dietrich still exercised a hold on his emotions.

'I remember having lunch with him one day,' Sirk would recall,

> and he suddenly looked up at me and said, 'Douglas, I have a terrible problem.' So I said, 'Oh, really, Erich, what is that?' and he said, 'Well, there are these two women who are in love with me, and

they are both after me.' So I said, 'Oh, really, Erich, that sounds terrible, who are they?' 'Well,' he said, 'one of them is Paulette Goddard and the other is Marlene Dietrich.' So I said, 'Well, Erich, my God, you're in real trouble here.' But he was deadly serious. 'Which one do you think I should go for, Douglas?' 'That is a terrible dilemma, Erich, I mean, my God, this is something we have to think about very carefully.' 'You know,' he said, 'Marlene is very attractive, but Paulette is really good at the stock market. I think I should go for Paulette.' So I said to him, 'Well, Erich, the stock market is very important, no doubt about that.' And that's who he married – Paulette Goddard.[3]

There is a flippancy about the conversation that suggests Sirk suspected Remarque, despite being 'deadly serious', may have been teasing him, but Dietrich's daughter Maria corroborates the general drift of his 'dilemma'.

'Remarque announced he was thinking of getting married to – of all people – Paulette Goddard,' she wrote, 'My mother was appalled; I have to admit, so was I. "What insanity! He is not really going to marry that Goddard woman, is he? Doesn't he know she only wants him for his paintings? I am going to talk to him." And she did.'

What Marlene told Remarque is not recorded but Maria Riva confirms that he asked her to marry him, with the last-ditch ultimatum that 'if she refused, he was marrying Paulette, which he finally did.'[4] Technically, Dietrich was still married to Rudi Steiber, and would remain so. She declined. Paulette, unsuspecting, won the toss of the coin.

The marriage took place on 25 February 1957 before a judge at Branford, Connecticut, a small town near New Haven. If, by choosing such a secluded venue, they had hoped to avoid publicity, they were mistaken. The ceremony was besieged by 150 reporters and photographers.

Dietrich, who had loathed Paulette from their earliest encounter twenty years before, pronounced her valediction: 'Now, just watch. Now she'll try to kill him. He was a great writer, but about women – always so stupid.'[5]

17

A Settled Life

Dietrich was not alone in her reaction to the marriage. Other, less prejudiced friends of Remarque privately questioned his decision and Paulette's motives, but his obvious happiness and devotion to her effectively quelled most of their misgivings. 'We saw each other often in Switzerland and New York as friends, my husband and I and Erich and Paulette,' Luise Rainer said, 'I think it was a happy marriage. He could give her a lot of jewellery and that's what she loved. George Gershwin had once told me years before that Paulette was a little gold-digger, and I'm sure she was perfectly aware of Erich's money, his art collection, his beautiful house when she married him.'

What Paulette was not aware of, as she once confessed to Rainer, was the modest limits of his sexual appetite and prowess. 'She told me after he had died, "You know, when I met Erich I thought I was getting a flamboyant, fantastically sexual man. But none of it. None of it". She was not very enthusiastic about his virility, but she certainly loved him.'

Remarque's reputation as a great lover among the social set he moved in derived less from anecdotal evidence than from the received image of the alluring women his name had been linked with, archetypal love-goddesses like Dietrich and Garbo, Lupe Velez, Dolores del Rio and now Paulette herself.

He was a romantic. He idealized beautiful women and love for beautiful women, and while the act of love was relatively important to him it was not of paramount interest. Rather, he found emotional fulfilment in the old-fashioned sense of 'making love' – the challenges and intricacies of wooing, courting and winning the affections of his objective, even the agonies and jealousies of sharing her with another man. More often than not his overtures could be easily deflected, as Luise Rainer had found. There was, too, an element of submissiveness, if not masochism, in his perception of such women, as Rainer identified: 'He liked the type of woman who was absolutely in command.' For full gratification when he needed it, he was more likely to resort to the anonymity of one-night-stands with bar-girls, chamber-maids and, *in extremis*, prostitutes, for which his sensibilities were not engaged.

Of Marlene Dietrich's claim that he had told her he was impotent, Luise Rainer contended:

> I don't believe for one moment that he was impotent. It would be just like Erich to say that. A joke. One reason I think he didn't totally go for me in those days was that he liked demanding women and I didn't come into that category. I distinctly remember him once telling me, with the greatest glee, how Lupe Velez had on one occasion taken off one of her shoes in a tantrum and hit him hard with it, and he thought that was wonderful. But he would never talk about his affair with Dietrich. In that respect he was a perfect gentleman.[1]

For twenty years and more Remarque's love life had been, in the words of Tilman Westphalen, 'mentally straining and very wearing', a long roller-coaster ride of angst-ridden, emotion-draining relationships with Jutta, Marlene and Natasha. But in a perverse and significant sense the principal women in his life had made their contribution to his creative acumen, modelling and defining the female protagonists in his novels: Jutta in *Three Comrades* and the book he was now working on, *Heaven Has No Favourites*: Marlene, with a wisp of Garbo's enigmatic mystery, in *Arch of Triumph*; the fickle Natasha in his last, posthumous work, *Shadows in Paradise*.

There had to be a certain irony in the fact that, after a long succession of relationships with such introverted, capricious, unpredictable women, it was Paulette, out-going, down-to-earth and fun-loving, who brought him emotional stability and contentment in his final years. Any demands she might have made of him were largely materialistic – and he could cope with those cheerfully. 'He loved giving Paulette jewels,' said Rainer.

Nobody who saw them together doubted that he was entranced by her. 'They often smile and laugh at each other,' Cole Porter reported after visiting them.[2] Even a teenage boy, a namesake, was astute enough to note his devotion. Erik Lee Preminger, the son of Gypsy Rose Lee, the famous striptease artist, and the Hollywood director Otto Preminger, was on a holiday tour through Europe with his mother when they called on Remarque. Gypsy, her fading stardom and finances recently boosted by royalties from the hit Broadway musical *Gypsy*, based on her life, had starred some years earlier with Paulette in the film *Babes of Bagdad*, and was minded to renew their acquaintance.

Erik Lee Preminger would recall years later in his memoirs,

> From Paris Mother had telephoned her good friend Paulette Goddard who lived in Ascona, Switzerland. Her husband Erich Maria Remarque answered the phone. Paulette was in the States. He and Mother had never met but he knew of her from Paulette and when he heard we were passing nearby, he insisted we join him at his villa for dinner.
>
> Remarque was warm, generous and not the least condescending toward me. He went out of his way to make us feel welcome. He was a man of few but intense passions: his wife whom he missed terribly and talked of at great length; writing; his wine cellar which he both showed off and shared; and his collection of oriental carpets which covered the floor of his living room in layers.

It was one of Remarque's quirks to lay several carpets on top of each other and delight in visitors' admiration as he turned them back, layer by layer, for their inspection. Gypsy disgraced herself at the end of the evening by over-indulging Remarque's wine cellar and vomiting over the topmost, priceless carpet.[3]

Mr and Mrs Remarque settled into a mutually agreed, free-and-easy pattern of living, frequently apart for long weeks at a stretch when she was working on television shows in New York and Los Angeles. For Paulette the Casa Remarque was little more than a *pied-à-terre*. Much as she valued the house, and its contents, she would never come to regard it as her home and would quickly become bored with its enclosed ambience and the relaxed, (to her) 'small town' character of Locarno and the social set Remarque moved in. 'I'm a Gypsy who likes to go first-class,' she was once quoted as saying. 'I've never had a permanent home. I have property, but no home . . . I love being wherever I happen to be.'[4]

In New York she leased an apartment on the floor above her husband's at the Ritz Towers on East 57th Street, an arrangement which raised some eyebrows, but a practical one, enabling them both to work without getting in each other's way.

Heaven Has No Favourites (*Der Himmel kennt keine Günstlinge*), the novel Remarque was now working on, was a deliberate departure from the themes he had consistently pursued; a story, in Tilman Westphalen's words, 'of bitter-sweet love, reason and madness, the nature of life and feelings, melancholy and death', shorn of the political and societal conditions and questions that had delineated the fates of characters in his previous books. For this reason it was widely judged, when it appeared, to be his weakest novel.

For some German critics there lurked, too, a suspicion that he was running out of ideas. He had been toying with this one for more than thirty years, originally as *Vandervelde's Race*, the short story he had written in 1925 while working at Echo-Continental in Hanover and sold to *Sport im Bild*, expanded two years later as *Station am Horizont*, the novel serialized in the same magazine, then in the early 1940s in Hollywood as *Beyond*, the unpublished short story adapted for the Barbara Stanwyck/David Niven film *The Other Love*. Each plot-line differed substantially while preserving the two main characters – a racing driver and a dying woman – in some form or other. More manuscripts exploring the same theme are in the Remarque Archive, including one, *The Last Life of Lillian Dunkerque*, dating from 1948, the year after *The Other Love* had utilized it. It was as though the situation, or the character, were a recurring obsession for him.

The novel's plot is signposted with resonances of Remarque's past. The principal setting is a sanatorium for tubercular patients in the Swiss Alps, well remembered from Jutta's sojourns in such a one in the 1930s. The hero, Clerfayt, is a racing driver in his forties and nearing the end of his career and his run of good luck on the tracks – a nostalgic token of his own passion for the sport. Clerfayt's sports car becomes virtually a character in its own right, and the name of the German racing ace Rudolf Carraciola, Remarque's lifelong friend since their Berlin days together, is admiringly cited several times in the narrative.

Clerfayt is visiting a one-time co-driver who is a patient at the clinic and there meets a fellow TB victim Lillian Dunkerque – the name Remarque had given in various forms and spellings to each of the female protagonists of the earlier stories. Enigmatic, capricious, with a shadowed past, she is an archetypal Remarque woman, resigned to the imminent possibility of death but defying it as she seeks some purpose and fulfilment to what is left of her life. She finds it in a love affair with Clerfayt which culminates in an irony no less cruel for being inevitable. 'We're alike, she thought, both of us have no future. His reaches only to the next race, and mine to the next haemorrhage.'

Uncompromisingly romantic, Remarque nevertheless weaves into the story seriously thoughtful reflections on life and death and the tenuous psychological skeins of fate that both link and hold the couple apart. When Lillian discharges herself from the sanatorium to accompany Clerfayt to Paris for what she believes will be a 'last fling' of life and freedom, he breaks the journey at Porto Ronco where, he tells her, 'I lived for a year after the war.' It is Remarque's device to express what his home meant to him. 'I wanted to stay a few days, but I stayed much longer,' Clerfayt recalls, 'I needed it. It was a cure of loafing, sunshine, lizards on the walls, staring at the sky and the lake, and so much forgetting that after a while my eyes were no longer fixed upon a single point; they began to see that nature had taken no notice at all of twenty years of human insanity.'

In a pre-publication advertisement in the German Press in 1961 Remarque, perhaps inadvisedly, allowed himself to be quoted as saying: 'I believe this novel is one of my most important works'. In a personal sense it probably was, representing as it did a clean breakaway from what had become expected of his books. He had wanted 'many times' to break with the political shadings his novels had been identified with, he told a German television interviewer in 1963, two years after its publication. 'That's what I tried to do with *Himmel* . . . to get away from political and emigration fates. It's very difficult because the overall background of the world today is decided by politics and earlier wars. You can't avoid it. But I very much wanted to write something different.'[5]

German reviewers were not convinced. The *Frankfurter Allgemeine Zeitung* magazine dismissed it as 'the weakest of all the weak books the world-famous author has published'. The critic of *Die Zeit* wrote: 'The style is shameful, the sentimentality dreadful, the experience repulsive'. Habitual German hostility towards the world-famous author had failed to be purged by a book with none of the expected political overtones, accusatory wartime references or censure of collective guilt.

Perhaps most woundingly, several reviewers conjectured that the book had primarily been written as a prospective film subject (as indeed the story had been in a previous incarnation) and no doubt felt vindicated by the news that Columbia Pictures in Hollywood had paid $350,000 for the rights before publication. The stars first considered for the projected movie were Audrey Hepburn and Laurence Harvey but immediate production was shelved and the rights were eventually sold on. Drastically reworked in time, names, character and mood, it was not filmed until sixteen years later in 1977, seven years after Remarque's death, as *Bobby Deerfield* starring Al Pacino and Marthe Keller.

As his health deteriorated and the physical reminders of advancing years began to beset him, accentuated by the vivacity of a wife some twelve years his junior and still mercurially active and high-spirited, his thoughts and memories increasingly returned to Osnabrück and youth. Paulette's zest and encouragement had given his writing process renewed incentive; her extended absences even facilitated it, however greatly he missed her. With only the widowed Rosa in the house, still taking good care of him, he wrote regularly and speedily, only too keenly aware that age was overtaking him.

'I have always had the worst conscience in the world [about writing],' he said in an interview towards the end of his life. 'If only I had written as regularly as other writers [he had always admired and envied Thomas Mann's rigorous application], I should have had a much happier life. Only now am I beginning to get some pleasure from my work. Ever since the doctor has tried to prevent me from writing, the whole business has acquired something dangerous and attractive.'[6]

In the new book he was working on, *The Night in Lisbon* (*Die Nacht von Lissabon*), he was returning to the wartime emigré theme that had served him so successfully in *Flotsam* and *Arch of Triumph*. Again Osnabrück, no longer disguised, is one of the backgrounds to the story. Now, for the first time and clearly as a gesture of his nostalgia for his native city, he accords it its true name.

In the 1950s he had resumed a regular and affectionate correspondence with his youthful Osnabrück friend Hanns-Gerd Rabe who still lived in the city. Rabe frequently entreated him to pay a visit to Osnabrück, chiding him for not doing so and charging him with harbouring 'a strange love-hate' attitude towards his home town. Remarque had clearly been stung by the accusation, protesting his fondness for the place in his reply from New York in 1957:

> Odd that you believe I have a love-hate for Osnabrück. Nothing could be further from the truth. For the past four years I have wanted to come back there but if I travel to Europe l go to my house in Switzerland and time always passes so quickly that I suddenly have to return without seeing Osnabrück. The city lies precisely on my heart as on yours; after all, we were born and grew up there. To you over there I am regarded as a 'worldly fellow', here my friends

call me 'the Osnabrück kid'. One should never disown something, and, as you know, all my books have a bit of Osnabrück background'.

In 1965 he was still promising Rabe that he would pay a visit to the city that autumn and was looking forward to 'a journey of contemplation into the past, bowing to the fount of memory – and also to Osnabrück beer . . .' Two years later, his health failing after two heart attacks and under doctor's orders, he writes: 'Nothing will come of my trip to Osnabrück this year; it is too far, too exhausting, and emotional, strange as that may sound . . . Please send my greetings to all my school friends again and tell them that I often think of the very happy old days of our youth . . . that is probably always the case when one gets older. Youth then often seems strangely close, as if it were only a few years past instead of half a lifetime away.' And the following year from Rome: 'It is strange how vividly the picture of our home-town stays with me. . .'[7]

It was probably Rabe, a writer and journalist himself, specializing in the city's history and memories, who badgered the Osnabrück authorities to recognize the international standing of its most famous son with an official honour. At the end of 1963 the City Council announced it was awarding him its most prestigious accolade, the Justus Möser Medal. The citation formally recorded the city's appreciation of his 'loving remembrance of his birthplace'.

Rabe no doubt calculated that the honour would induce Remarque back to the city for a ceremonial visit. It didn't. Instead, nearly a year after the announcement of the award, it was the civic dignitaries led by the Bürgermeister, eleven representatives in all including Rabe, who made the long journey to Porto Ronco in October 1964 for a presentation in the garden of the Casa Remarque. 'Touching and boring,' Remarque noted. 'What should one do with eleven people with whom one has nothing to discuss?'

It was a long and tedious day. Remarque, ever the perfect host, had arranged to entertain the delegation to dinner at a local restaurant, felicitously chosen; he knew the manager also hailed from Osnabrück.

A special cake bore the city's coat of arms and the titles of all Remarque's novels in marzipan. The menus had ribbons of black and white, the colours of the city. The grandees were duly flattered and impressed. The Bürgermeister asked if he might take the marzipan crest home with him. 'I was glad when it was over – tired and bored, but touched that the eleven had come so far and had not even had good weather here,' Remarque wrote that night.

In the same mood of nostalgia, especially during the lengthy separations from Paulette, his memories would stray to Marlene. The bond between them still held, and they corresponded periodically, a secret he concealed from his wife. 'Dearest,' Dietrich writes in February 1962, soliciting his advice on a film script she is considering, and concluding, 'I yearn for you every second for all eternity, Your Puma.' He replies: 'Magical One, Your letter touched me so much,' and after furnishing his advice, continues:

> I am alone here for several weeks past in order to write, a book (*The Night in Lisbon*) which I think you would like, with a big, touching woman's role. Outside, a cold spring lies over the camellias, mimosa, tulips and the unquiet lake. Cats are wandering round; it is midnight, and it was from here, just before the great European destruction, that I telephoned you in Hollywood – conversation always came so readily. Orion hung over the mountains, and how young we still were. Almost as young as now. Photographs of you are always coming with the newspapers. How nice that we are still in the land of the living.'

He signed himself 'Ravic'.[8]

He and Paulette were apart for most of the summer of 1963 while she was in Rome shooting her first film for ten years. It would also be her last, an ignominious finale to a sparkling movie career. *Time of Indifference*, based on a novel by Alberto Moravia, was a mediocre Italian production targeted at the English-speaking market, in which Paulette co-starred with Rod Steiger, Claudia Cardinale and Shelley Winters and, now in her mid fifties, realistically swallowed any vestigious pride to play Cardinale's mother, an aging countess.

There was an amiable rivalry between Paulette and Shelley Winters who recalled in her memoirs:

> I think my scenes with Paulette Goddard were very funny. I remember one in which I was giving her a facial. I had worked with her in *The Women* and she had worn different sets of jewellery every day, and she did the same in this film. It was rather difficult to get around her diamond necklaces while I was giving her neck and face a facial . . . She was indeed fun to work with in this film, rather zany, and she would tell me long, rambling stories about how stingy Charlie Chaplin was, ignoring the fact that she was the only woman in his history who got a lot of money and jewels from him.[9]

Remarque, lonely and pining for her, joined her in Rome as the production neared completion and when it had wrapped they travelled on to Naples. It was there that he had his first stroke.

18

A Time to Die

For a time he was partially paralyzed and his speech was temporarily impaired. The attack hit him hard. For most of 1964 he was sunk in deep depression, conscious of his mortality and brooding over the past. Paulette was away for long periods. She was not cut out to be a nurse, and convinced herself that in the devoted care of 'Röschen' – Rosa, the housekeeper – and his doctors he was in good hands.

'I have the feeling that the solitude here isn't of any use to me,' Remarque wrote in his diary. 'At the same time, the feeling of a wasted, missed life, with so many opportunities and so few taken – have lived without living.'

Not even the success of his latest novel was much of a solace. *The Night in Lisbon* was published in America and Britain in March 1964 and immediately went into all the leading bestseller lists, his biggest seller since *Arch of Triumph* nineteen years earlier. It stayed in the *New York Times* Top Ten for the next five months.

'Remarque's best novel in years,' John Barkham wrote in the *Saturday Review* while Maxwell Geismar, with a prescience, perhaps, that this could well be the ailing author's last novel, used his *New York Times* review to offer a considered assessment of his career and reputation.

Remarque's most brooding and thoughtful novel; it is the novel most involved with the destiny of twentieth-century man. It is the novel in which the artist most fully comes to grip with the meaning of his own life and his own historical period, and which he leaves to us as the testimony that art is always the final witness to history . . . it may not quite be a great novel, but it is surely one of the most absorbing and eloquent narratives of our period.

In some respects Erich Maria Remarque has had a curious career, but it is a great tribute to this aging literary veteran of World War I that now, at the age of 66, he has produced what may be his best novel. A famous European counterpart to Hemingway, Remarque has, through the years, almost converted a handsome minor talent into a major one; whereas Hemingway almost reduced his own large talent into a more limited one.

In London *The Times Literary Supplement* called the book 'inspiring', and the *Daily Telegraph* 'a profoundly moving and absorbing experience'.

The Night in Lisbon completed what has come to be known as Remarque's 'emigré trilogy' along with *Flotsam* and *Arch of Triumph*. The idea for it had been germinating since 'the Hitler period' in the 1930s, as he explained to a Swiss journalist: ·

At that time I knew an emigrant in Paris who had decided to go back, at least for one day, in order to see someone he would otherwise never see again. A woman, naturally. He was so desperate, his situation was so desperate, that it didn't matter anymore.

Did he go back? I don't even know that, but what that man told me at that time struck me to the core. For I too could not suppress the thought: What would actually happen if I were to go back? It was a nightmare that never quite left me. I did not really think seriously of going back although, as you know, all sorts of proposals and promises were made to me.

The nightmare . . . to go back, to see how it is . . . didn't we all have it?[1]

In Remarque's novel Josef Schwarz, the refugee who 'went back', tells his story in the course of one Lisbon night to a fellow fugitive desperate to obtain tickets and visas for himself and his wife for a ship sailing the next day to America. Schwarz offers him his own as long as he keeps him company through the night. Part adventure, part morality tale, Schwarz's suicidal oddysey on the eve of the war takes him back to Osnabrück to see for possibly the last time the wife he has had to abandon. She opts to flee Nazi Germany with him and after a tense flight through Switzerland, France and Spain, hunted by the wife's ruthless SS brother, they reach the relative safety of Lisbon and a poignant climax which reveals the reason for his generosity in surrendering his tickets to his companion of the night.

Remarque had loosely based the couple's flight to Lisbon on the experiences of fellow author Hans Habe, a near-neighbour in Ascona who had become his closest friend. The two writers had much in common. Both had begun their careers as journalists – though Habe's career in this field was the more distinguished – and had made their names with controversial war novels. Both bore the honourable distinction of having had their books ceremoniously burned by the Nazis. And both, in their times, had been voracious womanizers, though Remarque's track record paled into insignificance beside that of his friend whose current wife, Licci, was his sixth.

As a young reporter on a Vienna newspaper in the early 1930s, the Jewish and Left-leaning Habe, born Jean Bekessy in Budapest, had researched and secured a scoop that caught the imagination of the world. He was the journalist who revealed that Adolf Hitler's family name had originally been Schicklgruber. His father had changed it thirteen years before Adolf's birth to Hitler, a variation on Hiedler/ Hüttler, the surnames of previous generations of the family. Schicklgruber, a coarsely rustic name in German, became a derogatory epithet for the Führer throughout the duration of the Third Reich, invoked by satirists and opponents the world over to taunt him in song, speeches and articles.

Habe's revelation had inevitably made him a marked man even before the publication of his first novel *Three Over the Frontier* in 1937. This was the first German-language novel to deal with the flight of refugees from the Nazis and was duly burned in public when they marched into Vienna a year later. Habe had fled to France where he joined the French Army and in 1940 was taken prisoner in the first days of the German invasion. He escaped and made his perilous journey to Lisbon much as Remarque's Josef Schwarz does in *The Night in Lisbon*. Habe's own account of the fall of France and the ineptitude of the French military command in his semi-autobiographical novel *A Thousand Shall Fall* became one of the earliest Second World War best-sellers when it was published in America and Britain in 1942, and was filmed by Metro-Goldwyn-Mayer as *The Cross of Lorraine*.

Fate was kinder to Hans Habe than to Josef Schwarz. He spent the rest of the war in the United States, took American citizenship and in the immediate post-war period was responsible under the American occupation powers for reorganizing the German Press while continuing to produce such best-selling novels as *Aftermath* and *Off Limits*. These, too, gave him a link with Remarque, dealing as they did with the immediate post-war German experience in the same way Remarque had portrayed the post-First World War experience in *The Road Back*, *Three Comrades* and *The Black Obelisk*.

The Remarques and the Habes were a regular foursome for convivial evenings in each others' homes and local restaurants, Paulette as ever the life and soul of the party. Out of consideration for her, conversation would generally be in English. She spoke French and a smattering of Italian, the principal language of the Locarno region, but no German. She professed to detest her husband's native tongue, possibly a sub-conscious expression of her revulsion for Fascism in general and Nazism in particular, possibly a guilty justification for not having mastered it since marrying him. 'We speak English the whole time,' Remarque revealed in a 1963 interview. If he and Habe occasionally lapsed into German during their evenings together, Paulette would become tetchy, feeling herself excluded.

Although Remarque's friendship with the Habes was instinctively warm and genuine, it was reinforced by their ready acceptance of Paulette who was not universally popular among the social set they moved in. Her Hollywood mannerisms, her ostentatious display of wealth, her occasional hauteur and hint of vulgarity grated in the conservative milieu of Locarno society.

Patricia Roc, a leading British film actress of the 1940s who had settled in Locarno with her Swiss husband soon after Remarque's death, remembers:

> I knew Paulette well when she lived here. We lunched and dined together fairly frequently. Her house on the lake was very beautiful. She always looked great but she tried her best to still be the film star, in her manner and dress. It was a pity she found it so difficult to grow old gracefully – but who doesn't?[2]

One particular dinner party at which she and Paulette were guests stands out in Roc's memory. Only twenty minutes after they had arrived for drinks, Paulette suddenly announced: 'I'm going into the kitchen because it's time we ate,' and, to the consternation of the hostess, disappeared to chivvy the cook. Ten minutes later she re-appeared and said: 'Well, we can eat now.' The party had just finished the main course and were enjoying an interlude before the dessert when Paulette abruptly stood up and said: 'Well, I can't wait any longer. I've got to go home. You know I have to go to bed early.' The hostess protested that the dessert had been prepared specially for her, but Paulette was adamant. 'She didn't say good-bye to anybody,' Roc recalled, 'Just stood up and walked out. I found it so ill-mannered.'

Remarque himself was always a model of courtesy and gracious manners. That such behaviour should have been tolerated at all by the Remarques' circle of friends was a reflection of their regard for Remarque himself and recognition that, plainly and simply, he adored her.

In January 1965 they were spending a few days in Milan when he was struck down by a second stroke and admitted to hospital. Safely home in Porto Ronco the following month he sensed death closing in and his thoughts winged back across the years to unquiet memories of Ypres and the trenches of Houthulst Forest for an analogy of his fears. He muses in his diary:

> The condition now similar to the war, where one lay in a position that was more dangerous than when it was quiet, but not so

dangerous as the front. It could strike – more often than in peace – but not like in a continuous bombardment. You live there and are almost contented. So it is with heart disease.

Paulette, too, was fearful, if not so much for his chances of survival, certainly for the constraints his illness placed on her freedom to travel as she pleased. Conscience troubled her. A few days after their return home he records:

> Slight problems with P. It's hard for her. What is there for her to do here? On our own, I don't talk much. She has hardly any acquaintances; it's quiet. Who is there here who even speaks English, and she can't spend all her time reading. On the 25th she wants to go to Paris. What should I do? I still can't travel. The medicine makes me moronic.
>
> Poor P. She has so much merriment and so little natural ease! But everything here is like lead for her. And I can't give up everything and take her away. Where to? The winter has been too long for her. We wanted to go to Cairo, but didn't go. And it was just as well. The attack got me in Milan.

One reason Remarque didn't 'talk much' was that he was devoting as much time and energy as his condition allowed to a new novel. 'I'm a one-track-man when I'm writing,' he told Franz Baumer in 1969, using the English idiom.[3] All too conscious that it was likely to be his last, he worked doggedly through a number of drafts during the remaining years of his life, and fearful perhaps that he would not live to complete it, he steadfastly refused to divulge information about it to anybody – not to his agent or his publisher, least of all to his friends. Paulette knew but, as was his practice with any work-in-progress, he avoided discussing it with her. 'I'm superstitious and afraid that I'll harm my work if I do,' he confided to the *Neue Osnabrücker Zeitung* in 1970, shortly before his death. 'I have never discussed my manuscripts with anyone.'[4] His agent and publishers would have no forewarning of when they might expect delivery of a finished manuscript: it would just land on their desks as 'a surprise'.

In a letter around the same time to Baumer who, with Remarque's tacit blessing, was preparing his brief study of him for a German educational series on twentieth-century writers, all he would disclose was that 'I am deep into work on my next book which has already been interrupted several times by illness.'

The book bore the working title *Das gelobte Land* (*The Promised Land*) and would be a continuation of *The Night in Lisbon*, opening the day after that night with the departure of the ship for America, and dealing with the lives of wartime emigrés in New York and Hollywood; it was the first and only novel Remarque set outside Europe.

According to Tilman Westphalen, its origins could be traced back to the anguish of his break-up with Natasha Paley fifteen years earlier and his psycho-analysis sessions with Karen Horney who had recommended that he exorcize the Natasha affair by writing about her[5] – possibly another reason for not wanting Paulette to discover too much about it. He had toyed on and off with the idea in the years since before starting to work exclusively on the book in early 1963.

Remarque and Paulette agreed on a regimen of domesticity for their remaining years together. Winter and early spring would be spent in Rome, living in various hotels, where he found the climate more conducive to his breathing; summer at Porto Ronco where he worked obsessively on *Das gelobte Land* while Paulette travelled to and fro, mainly to New York. The long periods apart left him lonely and pining for her company, as he constantly reminded her in his frequent letters but his forbearance was little short of heroic: he never chastised or remonstrated with her.

They were together in Porto Ronco in June 1965 when disaster struck the Casa Remarque. A ferocious storm precipitated a landslide down the hill behind their home. It came to a halt short of the house itself but obliterated the entire garden and destroyed out-buildings. Remarque was distraught. Strolling or sitting contemplatively in his beloved grounds, never tiring of the view or the flowers, had been one of his most enduring pleasures. He took himself off to Naples for a month while the garden was restored. Paulette, as usual, took herself off to New York.

The following summer of 1966 his health seemed stable enough for her to persuade him to accompany her on her ritual trip to America and with the consent of his doctors they sailed from Genoa in June for a two-month visit.

New York reinvigorated him, as he described in a letter to Hanns-Gerde Rabe:

> New York terrific, and it did me good . . . the most exciting city I know. I have lived too long in the peace of village life on Lake Maggiore, and even Rome, Florence and Venice are merely variations of that life, whereas New York . . . It really is a city without the melancholy and oppression of the past! It is exciting life! It is the future. It is possible that one could grow tired of it and then look forward to cottages and eighteenth-century furniture, but I was only there for two exciting months and that was just right.

He is energized enough to hint that a visit to Osnabrück might be a possibility, perhaps in September, but is careful to hedge the prospect – 'Unfortunately, these attacks have something very sudden about them. Yesterday, still on high, today . . . But let's hope. It would be nice.'

It was not to be. He would never see his home town again, though he was tempted to make the effort in 1968 when the city council officially invited him to attend a ceremony naming part of the Osnabrück ring road the Elfriede Scholz Strasse in memory of his sister, a gesture which touched him deeply.

Honours began to flow his way as he approached his seventieth birthday. In 1967 the West German government announced it was awarding him the Federal Republic's Grand Cross of Merit (*Das Grosse Verdienstkreuz*) 'for service to the community'. Remarque's reaction was not so much flattered as ironic. It was still a source of hurt and anger to him that no post-war German government had seen fit voluntarily to restore his citizenship, and the omission seemed to him to be insensitively compounded in the formal citation:

> The author Erich Maria Remarque, despite the loss of his civil rights at the hands of the National Socialist government, his fate of exile and the tragic events in his family [a reference to Elfriede's execution] has vigorously sought a reconciliation with today's Germany. His attitude has not been without effect on numerous German literary personalities who, like him, chose Switzerland as an exile.

Pleading ill-health, he declined to travel to Bonn for the presentation, receiving it instead at his home from the German ambassador to Switzerland.

'Nowadays prizes are heaped on me,' he commented with a touch of bitterness to Franz Baumer:

> Newspapers don't have enough praises to report about me. Much too much honour. But in 1938 they deprived me of my German citizenship. Now I'm even given the *Grosse Verdienstkreuz* by the President. But of the idea of giving me back my citizenship, there is not a mention! The Foreign Office makes some effort. I should just put in an application, then everything could be cleared up. How have things come to this? I didn't deprive myself of citizenship. Why should I now plead for re-naturalization? No, that I won't do.[6]

He suffered two more strokes in the autumn of 1967, the second confining him to hospital in Locarno for three weeks, but his doctors judged him well enough to winter in Rome. He remained there for six months, alone for most of the time while Paulette was in New York. Each day he wrote a little, and reflected on the past, the days of youth, the simple images of times long gone. 'It's strange how strongly the picture of our home town rises up before me,' he writes to Rabe in Osnabrück. 'Here I have one of swallows flying round the terrace, with a view across the whole of Rome. But they are no longer the same swallows that flew round the cathedral towers when I stood in the cloisters, full of wishes, dreams and hopes. They are not the swallows of youth . . .'

Beside his bed, as he wrote to Karla Hoberg, he kept the picture of old Süsterstrasse she had sent him, remembering the weeks he had lodged in the Hoberg house, the last time he had lived in Osnabrück, while he was working on *The Road Back* . . . 'It was a beautiful time.'

He was back in Porto Ronco in time for his seventieth birthday on 22 June 1968, and more accolades. The German Academy for Language and Literature admitted him to membership and the municipality of Ascona and Porto Ronco appointed him an honorary citizen. Again he pleaded health grounds for curtailing his participation in the ceremonies.

They were genuine enough. 'I am so weak,' he wrote to Rabe, but his spirit remained strong and he persuaded his doctors to let him return to Rome for the winter of 1968/69 and the following October to take Paulette on a brief visit to Venice for a celebratory reunion. She had spent most of the year in New York and immediately after the Venice holiday returned there for Thanksgiving in November. Venice had given him their last happy hours together.

Her prolonged absences were a source of muted disapproval and concern among Remarque's friends, but, more devoted to her than ever, he indulged them uncomplainingly, touchingly grateful for the letters she regularly wrote.

She was back home with him when he had his sixth and final stroke in August 1970. For the next month he clung to life in the Sant'Agathe Clinic in Locarno. Curt Riess, an old friend from the Berlin days when they had been fellow-journalists, recorded a disturbing attempt to contact him in his memoir *Meine berühmte Freunde* (*My Famous Friends*), published in 1987.

> Paulette picked up the telephone. She said, obviously in English, that he was very bad. She said, 'He will die soon,' and then she said, 'Do you want to talk to him?' I couldn't believe it. I couldn't believe that she was in his room and that he had obviously overheard

everything she had said. She could very easily have asked to call me back later, but she had no qualms announcing the death sentence in his presence. He picked up the phone. 'Yes, it's very bad. No you can't help me. No, nobody can help me.' And those were the last words I ever heard from him.[7]

A distraught Dietrich in Paris sent telegrams and flowers to 'dearest Alfred', one of the pet names she had coined for him. 'Time and time again, my heart', she wired, and 'I send you my whole heart.'[8]

Erich Maria Remarque died at the hospital on 25 September 1970, three months after his seventy-second birthday. Paulette was at his bedside.

A few days afterwards, in a letter to a friend, Marlene wrote:

I was alone when Remarque died. But I had known of his illness and, by chance, I tried to telephone him, and he answered. I talked to him, sent him flowers every day, and wires, all to arrive in the mornings because that bitch Goddard only came in the afternoon after her beauty sleep. Maria wrote to him and I also talked to Rudi on the phone and he sent a cable to him which he got during the few days he was lucid, before he died.

He had many strokes, but recovered and even wrote a letter to Maria, showing her how he had learned to write again. But then, life for him without his favourite – wine – was not good any more. He loved to drink a lot – not for the effects but for the taste. Now the bitch has all the riches – Van Goghs, Cézannes. Modiglianis, etc., etc. And the most beautiful carpets – all priceless. Maybe this is why she never allowed him to see me. Maybe she thought he would give me some of her treasures. It could not have been jealousy because she never loved him. I could not go to the funeral last Sunday. If I survive Gabin, it will be the same thing. I could have had it all, the name and the money. But I said No. I couldn't do it to Rudi.[9]

To her daughter, Marlene said: 'Well! It took that terrible woman a few years, but she finally did it. Now she's as rich as Croesus and can rot in her luxury.'

With that, Maria recalled, she 'went into her room to mourn him as the rightful widow she believed herself to be'.

Remarque was buried in the cemetery at Porto Ronco, a short walk up the hillside from the Casa Remarque, with the full rites of the Roman Catholic Church he had not observed since the days of his youth. Though never a demonstrative Catholic, he had renounced the Church in disgust at Pope Pius XI's infamous concordat with the Third Reich in 1933.

Paulette was dressed in a full-length black coat over a white dress, her copper-red hair covered by a loose black scarf draped like a cowl. She wore a minimum of make-up. Erna and her son Klaus, the only surviving members of the Remark family, travelled from Osnabrück, as did Hanns-Gerde Rabe who delivered a eulogy.

Dietrich sent a wreath of white roses.

Epilogue

In April 1971, seven months after Remarque's death, journalists were summoned to a press conference in Munich. The invitation gave scant information about its purpose. All they knew was that it would be presided over by Paulette Goddard, the glamorous Hollywood star, the Widow Remarque.

More than 100 people gathered expectantly. Paulette made a dramatic entrance, flanked by three men. She was, according to one newspaper report, 'bedecked with jewels' and clutching what appeared to be a book bound in red-rose leather which toned exactly with her red-rose dress.[1] Her companions were Remarque's agent, Felix Guggenheim, Willy Droemer, head of the Munich publishing house Droemer Knaur, and its chief editor Dr Nöhbauer. The occasion, they then revealed, was to present to the world – and to Droemer Knaur – the manuscript of Erich Maria Remarque's last novel, *Shadows in Paradise (Schatten im Paradies)*.

The conference quickly degenerated into a mêlée. Dr Nöhbauer attempted, against the general noise, to deliver a few words about the novel, reported the Cologne newspaper *Kölnischer Rundschau*, but 'it seemed that few of the guests had come out of literary motives as for sensation-seeking reasons. Hardly any notice would be taken of the red-bound manuscript, much more of the Hollywood veteran who, with ladylike demeanour, if also undoubtedly irritated, managed the proceedings.'[2]

The gathering was told of the author's 'sacrifice' to complete the novel in the last days of his life, that he had been working on it at home the night before he was admitted to hospital. The impression was deliberately fostered that this was Remarque's final, polished masterwork.

In fact, by his meticulous standards, *Shadows in Paradise* was far from 'completed'. Paulette had taken over responsibility for his literary estate with zeal – and arguably an excess of avarice. The manuscript she was now offering to the world was merely what she, Guggenheim and the publisher considered the most acceptable of several drafts Remarque had written and put aside.

Guggenheim was reported as saying: 'Remarque was polishing this novel until the end. We have found no fewer than six versions, of which the last has been taken.'[3] There is evidence, however, that in Remarque's estimate the novel was nowhere near ready for publication. It had always been his practice to withhold any information about a project while he was still working on it, even from his publishers. He would negotiate contracts before revealing the subject of a book. In the case of *Shadows in Paradise*, Kiepenheuer and Witsch who had published his last five novels had been given no intimation of the final one, still less his American and British publishers. He had not even decided on a title, variously calling it *The Promised Land*, *New York Story*, *New York/Intermezzo*, *The Caravan Passes* and *Meeting of Shadows*. *Shadows in Paradise* had been suggested by his American editor.

Remarque would have been appalled that his 'last testament' should have been published in such a raw form. Many critics were. 'The American reviews were almost unanimously crushing,' Hans Wagener wrote, citing poor action and 'a questionable hero who does not know what his real aim in life is.'[4] This was perhaps unfair because Remarque was reflecting his own experiences as an unwilling emigré in America, stateless, rudderless and facing an uncertain future, frequently without any real aim in life.

There are, Wagener points out, a number of unresolved inconsistencies in the book. 'For example, the hero could not possibly have experienced all the narrated events prior to his arrival in America.

Because of this fact it is safe to assume that Remarque had not finished revising his novel. The publisher should perhaps have edited the manuscript more carefully.' He concedes however that the novel 'is nevertheless of considerable importance, not only because it documents Remarque's later political views, but also because in it Remarque deals with America for the first time.'[5]

German critics were no less scathing, one typical review accusing the novel of 'sliding into triviality' and leaving a 'taint' on Remarque's reputation . . . 'at the end he was only a shadow of his former self'.[6]

With the passing of time a more tolerant perspective becomes possible, and a sense that its contemporary detractors were perhaps unduly harsh. *Shadows in Paradise* is surely Remarque's least subtle novel, its characters veering towards the stereotyped and facile. But it has a confident, if conventional narrative drive and creates an interesting impression of the mutually protective enclave of refugees in war-time New York and how they respond to their unaccustomed freedom – among them Ravic whose fate at the end of *Arch of Triumph* was left undetermined.

The novel reached No. 6 on the German best-seller lists but failed to make the top ten in Britain or America, and interest in it quickly evaporated.

Paulette continued to live at the Casa Remarque, a home for which she felt little affection but considerable financial attachment. Besides, to safeguard her Swiss residency permit she was required to spend six months of the year in the country. Her biographer Julie Gilbert records: 'Apparently, she had urged [Remarque] to sell the house in Switzerland because she disliked it so, but he had refused, and a wedge was driven between them It was the only time she did not get her way with Remarque.'[7] She is also supposed to have confided in one of her employees that her husband had become 'old and smelly' in their last years together, 'and it was just as well that he died when he did because she didn't want to be stuck taking care of him.'[8]

As Dietrich had predicted, she began to liquidate some of the Casa Remarque's treasures, selling thirty of Remarque's French Impressionist paintings at auction for more than three million dollars and disposing of individual items through private dealers. Soon the oriental carpets began appearing at auction houses. She was adept at negotiating film, television and stage deals for Remarque properties. *All Quiet on the Western Front* was remade for American television in 1979, *Arch of Triumph* for British television in 1985 and German television filmed *The Black Obelisk* in 1988, all bringing her healthy royalties. The play *Berlin, 1945* was translated and adapted as *Full Circle* for an off-Broadway production in 1974.

As the years passed she became increasingly eccentric in her behaviour, obsessed with her appearance and alienating many of her erstwhile friends with her arrogance and unpredictability. Her health deteriorated alarmingly, accelerated by excessive drinking and emphysema. For the last five years of her life she was incapable of travel and was confined, ironically, to the Casa Remarque.

She died there on 23 April 1990, two months before her eighty-fifth birthday, and is buried beside her husband just up the hillside above the house she hated, as is her mother Alta. She bequeathed her estate, including Remarque's manuscripts, diaries and letters, to New York University where the Remarque archive is now housed. Her own assets were valued at twenty million dollars.

Jutta Zambona Remarque, who never remarried, died in Monte Carlo in 1975 at the age of seventy-four, her most prized possession, and insurance policy, the original hand-written manuscript of *All Quiet on the Western Front*. After her death it passed to an unknown owner, later to be auctioned anonymously by Sotheby's.

Marlene Dietrich died at her Paris home in 1992, aged ninety. When, five years later, the contents of her New York apartment on Park Avenue were sold by Sotheby's they included two paintings by Corot and a pair of porcelain horses which Remarque had given her.

For more than seventy years *All Quiet on the Western Front* has remained constantly in print throughout the world, a title instantly identifiable whatever the language, even if the name of Erich Maria Remarque has been virtually forgotten in the English-speaking markets. His other books continued to appear in paperback editions into the 1980s but gradually disappeared from publishers' backlists, now to be found in faded copies only on the shelves of second-hand bookshops.

It would have given him a rueful satisfaction to know that it is in Germany that his work and reputation are nowadays held in the highest esteem. There he has been elevated to the pantheon of distinguished German literary figures, every aspect of his output published from his juvenilia, short stories and novels to his diaries, the novels in de luxe as well as paperback editions.

In Osnabrück he shares with his sister Elfriede the distinction of a main thoroughfare that bears his name. A purpose-built Erich Maria Remarque Centre houses the University of Osnabrück's definitive Remarque archive and a permanent exhibition of his life and works. The Erich Maria Remarque Peace Award is presented bi-annually to a candidate from the worlds of literature, journalism or science who has rendered outstanding service in the field of 'inner and outer peace'.

His name and reputation live on worldwide as the author of the most famous anti-war novel of all time. Less known, but in some ways equally important, are the literary records he left of the ordinary German's experience of the Weimar Republic in the aftermath of the First World War and the despair, resourcefulness and flickering hope of the fugitive victims of Nazism for whom he, the life-long emigré who kept a packed suitcase ready to hand in case 'I should suddenly have to take off', had a profound personal empathy.

Appendix:

Remarque's poem of courtship to Luise Rainer, Christmas 1942

Junges Fräulein, ich möcht' fragen
Bin ich nicht der rechter Mann?
Hab' ich nicht die Qualitäten,
Die ein Mädel freuen kann?

Young maiden, I'd like to ask
Am I not the right man?
Have I not the qualities,
That would please a girl?

Ich bin stark und nicht zu hässlich
Nicht zu gross, doch nicht zu klein;
Trinke auch sehr wenig Whiskey,
Hie und da ein bischen Wein.

I am strong and not too ugly
Not too tall, yet not too small;
Also drink very little whiskey
Now and then a little wine.

Respektsperson bin ich für jeden,

Alle lachen meinen Witz;
Manchmal angenehm und reizend,
Oftens Donner, Blut und Blitz.

A person commanding respect I am
    to everyone,
All laugh at my wit;
Sometimes pleasant and charming,
Often thunder, blood and lightning.

Frauen weiss ich wie zu lieben,
Alle suchen meinen Blick,
Wenn sie meine Stärke fühlen,
Kommen immer mehr zurück.

Women I know how to love,
All seek to attract my attention,
When they feel my strength,
Come back still more.

Bin ich wohlgelehrter Junge,
Kenne alles, Alt und Neu,
Die Romane, die ich schreibe
Machen meine Leser treu.

I'm a well-educated young fellow,
Know it all, old and new,
The novels I write
Make my readers loyal.

Darf ich fragen, Gnädig' Fräulein,
Bin ich nicht der Mann für Rainer –
Darf ich meinen Namen sagen? –
Ich heiss
                Herr Sogibteskeiner!

May I ask, dear lady,
Am I not the man for Rainer?
May I give my name? –
I am called
        Mr There-is-no-one-like-him!

Notes and References

Abbreviations: EMR – Erich Maria Remarque
EMR Archive – Erich Maria Remarque Archive, Osnabrück

Preface (pages xv–xvi)

1 Edgar Mowrer, *Germany Puts the Clock Back.*
2 Franz Baumer, *Erich Maria Remarque.*

1. Schooldays in Osnabrück (pages 1–9)

1 Count Harry Kessler, *In the Twenties.*
2 Quoted in C.R. Owen, *Erich Maria Remarque: A Critical Bio-Bibliography.*
3 EMR, interview in the *Observer* (London), 13 October 1929.
4 *Ibid.*
5 EMR, quoted by Rabe, EMR Archive.
6 EMR, the *Observer, op. cit.*
7 Baumer, *op. cit.*
8 EMR, interview in *The Living Age,* December 1930, quoted in Owen, *op. cit.*

2. Action on the Western Front (pages 11–18)

1 Carl Zuckmayer, *A Part of Myself.*
2 Ernst Jünger, article in *The Great War – I Was There,* Part 45, 1939.
3 Stephen E. Ambrose, *Citizen Soldiers.*
4 John Giles, *Flanders Then and Now: The Ypres Salient and Passchendaele.*
5 Ian Kershaw, *Hitler, 1889–1936: Hubris.*
6 Baumer, *op. cit.*

7   *The Times,* 30 June 1917.
8   *Ibid.,* 28 July 1917.
9   *Ibid.,* 1 August 1917.

3. The Peacock and the German Shepherd (pages 19–25)

1   EMR letter to Georg Middendorf, EMR Archive.
2   EMR interview in *The Living Age,* December 1930, quoted in Owen, *op. cit.*
3   Owen, *ibid.*
4   Baumer, *op. cit.*

4. A New Sense of Identity (pages 27–38)

1   Hanns-Gerd Rabe, quoted in Christine Barker and R.W. Last, *Erich Maria Remarque.*
2   Lotte Preuss letter, EMR Briefe und Tagesbuch, EMR Archive.
3   Quoted in Owen, *op. cit.*
4   EMR interview in the *Observer, op. cit.*
5   Rabe, EMR Archive.
6   Rabe, EMR Archive, quoted in Baumer, *op. cit.*
7   Quoted in Baumer, *ibid.*
8   *Osnabrücker Neuen Tagespost,* 13 November 1956.
9   EMR letter to Osnabrück authorities dated 20 November 1922, EMR Archive.
10 Letter to Karl Vogt, EMR Archive.
11 EMR interview with Axel Eggebrecht in *Die literarische Welt,* Berlin, 14 June 1929, quoted in Owen, *op. cit.*
12 Owen, *op. cit.*
13 EMR letter to Edith Doerry, EMR Archive.

5. Berlin and a Turbulent Marriage (pages 39–49)

1   EMR letter to Edith Doerry, EMR Archive.
2   Leni Reifenstahl, *The Sieve of Time : The Memoirs of Leni Riefenstahl.*
3   *Ibid.*
4   Stephen Bach, *Marlene Dietrich : Life and Legend.*
5   Interview with Rabe in *Der Spiegel,* 9 January 1952, quoted in Owen, *op. cit.*

6 EMR interview, *The Observer, op. cit.*

7 Axel Eggebrecht, *Der halbe Weg,* 1975.

8 Maurice Zolotow, *Billy Wilder in Hollywood.*

9 Riefenstahl, *op. cit.*

10 EMR interview with Axel Eggebrecht in *Die literarische Welt,* 14 June 1929, quoted in Baumer, *op. cit.*

11 Tilman Westphalen, Afterword to *Im Westen nichts Neues,* Kiepenheuer & Witsch edition, 1992.

6. All Quiet on the Western Front (pages 51–61)

1 Zolotow, *op. cit.*

2 P. de Mendelssohn, *S. Fischer und sein Verlag,* cited in Barker and Last.

3 *Daily Telegraph,* London, 30 October 1995.

4 Owen, *op. cit.*

5 EMR interview with *Kölnische Zeitung,* 6 November 1929, cited in Owen *op. cit.*

6 EMR interview in *Die Welt,* 31 March 1966, cited in Barker and Last, *op. cit.*

7 EMR interview in the *Observer, op. cit.*

8 *Ibid.*

9 *Ibid.*

10 R.C. Sherriff, *No Leading Lady.*

11 Television interview, *Das Profil,* Berlin, 1963, transcribed in *Ein militanter Pazifist.*

12 EMR interview in the *Observer, op. cit.*

13 *Ibid.*

14 *The Times,* London, 16 September 1929.

15 *The Observer, op. cit.*

16 William L. Shirer, *The Rise and Fall of the Third Reich.*

17 *The Observer, op. cit.*

7. Nazi Sabotage (pages 63–72)

1 EMR letter to Ruth Albu, EMR Archive.

2 Barker and Last, *op. cit.*

3 Obituary of Lew Ayres, *The Times* (London), 1 January 1997.

4 Obituary of Lew Ayres, *Daily Telegraph* (London), 1 January 1997.

5 *Das Auge ist ein Verführer,* unpublished memorandum in the estate of EMR, dated 1958, cited in *Ein militanter Pazifist.*

6 Rolf Georg Reuth, *Goebbels,* and Fred Taylor (ed.), *The Goebbels Diaries 1929–41.*

7 *Das Auge ist ein Verführer, op. cit.*

8 Reuth, *op. cit.*

8. Burning the Books (pages 73–80)

1 EMR letter to General Sir Ian Hamilton, EMR Archive.

2 E. and K. Mann, *Escape to Life,* Boston, 1939, quoted by Barker and Last.

3 Carl Zuckmayer, *A Part of Myself.*

4 *New York Times,* 12 July 1931.

5 EMR interview in *Zürcher Woche,* 30 November 1962, quoted in Barker and Last.

6 Report in *Osnabrücker Zeitung,* 6 April 1932, EMR Archive, quoted in Barker and Last.

7 Barker and Last, *op. cit.*

8 Article in *Volischer Beobachter* reported in *The Times,* 3 March 1933.

9 *Ibid.*

10 *The Times,* 30 March 1933.

11 Alexandra Richie, *Faust's Metropolis* and Klaus P. Fischer, *Nazi Germany: A New History.*

9. New Loves (pages 81–93)

1 Quoted by Barker and Last.

2 Ruth Niehaus, quoted in Baumer.

3 Marlene Dietrich, *Nehmt nur mein Leben …*

4 *Ibid.*

5 Lotte Preuss letter, EMR Archive, cited by Tilman Westphalen, Afterword to *Drei Kameraden,* Kiepenheuer & Witsch edition, 1998.

6 Untitled newspaper article, EMR Archive, cited by Owen.

7 Extract from *All Quiet on the Western Front* in *Volkischer Beobacher,* quoted by A. Kerker, *In Westen nicht Neues: Die Geschichte eines Bestseller,* cited by Owen.

8 Friedrich Holländer, *Von Kopf bis Fuss: Mein Leben mit Text und Musik* (Munich, Kindler, 1967), quoted by Sikov, *On Sunset Boulevard.*

9 Sikov, *Ibid.*
10 Thomas Mann, *Tagebücher,* quoted by Owen.
11 R.C. Sherriff, *No Leading Lady.*
12 Larry Swindell, *Charles Boyer.*
13 Letter from F. Scott Fitzgerald to Joseph Mankiewicz, 20 January 1938, Andrew Turnbull (ed.), *The Letters of F. Scott Fitzgerald.*
14 Otto Friedrich, *City of Nets.*

10. Marlene Dietrich (pages 95–108)

1 Maria Riva, *Marlene Dietrich.*
2 Marlene Dietrich, *Nehmt nur mein Leben ...*
3 Marlene Dietrich, *Marlene Dietrich's ABC.*
4 Marlene Dietrich, *Nehmt nur mein Leben ...*
5 Douglas Fairbanks Jr, *The Salad Days.*
6 EMR interview in *Stern,* 23 June 1968, quoted in Barker and Last.
7 EMR Archive, quoted in Barker and Last.
8 EMR interview in *Zürcher Woche,* 30 November 1962 and *Die Welt,* 1 December 1962, quoted in Owen.
9 Kate Summerscale, *The Queen of Whale Cay.*

11. War and the End of the Affair (pages 109–123)

1 *New York Times,* 24 March 1939.
2 Maria Riva, *op. cit.*
3 *New York Times,* 5 September 1939.
4 Donald Dewey, *James Stewart.*
5 Maria Riva, *op. cit.*
6 Carl Zuckmayer, *op. cit.*
7 David Niven, *Bring on the Empty Horses.*
8 Thomas Mann, *Tagebücher,* 25 July 1940.
9 Paul Henreid, *Ladies' Man: An Autobiography.*
10 Maria Riva, *op. cit.*
11 Clifford Odets, *The Time is Right.*

12. Enemy Alien (pages 125–136)

1 Hugo Vickers, *Cecil Beaton.*

2 *Los Angeles Times,* 25 January 1941, cited by Karen Swenson in *Greta Garbo : A Life Apart.*

3 Maria Riva, *op. cit.*

4 Quoted by Barry Paris in *Garbo: A Biography.*

5 Author's interview with Luise Rainer, 23 June 1999.

6 EMR letter to Hanns-Gerd Rabe, dated 16 August 1966, EMR Archive, quoted by Barker and Last.

7 Quoted by Peter Harry and Pamela Ann Brown in *The MGM Girls.*

8 Author's interview with Luise Rainer, *op. cit.*

13. Treason and Execution (pages 137–150)

1 Victor Klemperer, *To the Bitter End.*

2 Report in *Osnabrücker Presse,* 18 November 1967, cited by Tilman Westphalen, Afterword to *Arc de Triomphe,* Kiepenheuer & Witsch edition, 1996.

3 Cited in Barker and Last, *op. cit.*

4 Marlene Dietrich, *My Life.*

5 Tilman Westphalen, Afterword to *Der Funke Leben,* Kiepenheuer & Witsch edition, 1998.

6 Werner Fuld and Thomas F. Schneider (eds.) *Sag mir, dass Du mich Liebst ...*

7 *Picturegoer,* London, 9 November 1946.

8 Ingrid Bergman, *My Story.*

9 Quoted by Larry Swindell in *Charles Boyer, op. cit.*

10 Quoted by Laurence Leamer in *As Time Goes By: The Life of Ingrid Bergman.*

11 *Ibid.*

12 Memo dated 13 June 1950 in Rudy Behlmer (ed.), *Memo from David O. Selznick.*

14. Switzerland Again (pages 151–160)

1 Fuld and Schneider, *op. cit.*

2 Cited by Hans Wagener, *Understanding Erich Maria Remarque.*

3 *Ibid.*

4 *Ibid.*

5 Churchill letter quoted by Martin Gilbert, *Never Despair: Winston Churchill 1945–65.*

15. Paulette Goddard (pages 161–172)

1 David Robinson, *Chaplin: His Life and Art*.
2 *Ibid*.
3 *Architectural Digest: Academy Award Collectors' Edition*, April 1992.
4 Anita Loos quoted by John Kobal in *People Will Talk*.
5 Behlmer, *op. cit.*
6 Burgess Meredith, *So Far, So Good*.
7 Cited by Jay Parini in *John Steinbeck: A Biography*.
8 Interview in *Neue Osnabrücker Zeitung,* 29 September 1970, quoted by Barker and Last.
9 Quoted by M. Lütgenhorst in *Emigrant zweier Welten*, cited by Barker and Last.

16. A Time to Love (pages 173–183)

1 Jon Halliday, *Sirk on Sirk*.
2 Unpublished essay by Remarque, cited in *Der militanter Pazifist*.
3 Halliday, *op. cit.*
4 Maria Riva, *op. cit.*
5 *Ibid*.

17. A Settled Life (pages 185–194)

1 Author's interview with Luise Rainer, *op. cit.*
2 Cole Porter interview in *Die Welt*, 31 August 1957, cited by Owen.
3 Erik Lee Preminger, *Gypsy and Me*.
4 *Architectural Digest, op. cit.*
5 EMR television interview, *Das Profil,* Berlin, 3 February 1963, transcribed in *Der militanter Pazifist*.
6 M. Lütgenhorst, *op. cit.,* quoted by Baumer.
7 Letters to Rabe, EMR Archive, quoted by Barker and Last and Baumer.
8 Fuld and Schneider, *op. cit.*
9 Shelley Winters, *Shelley II: The Middle of My Century*.

18. A Time to Die (pages 195–206)

1 EMR interview in *Zürcher Woche*, 1968, quoted by Owen.
2 Patricia Roc Reif letter to author, 19 June 2000.

3 Baumer.

4 EMR interview in *Neue Osnabrücker Zeitung*, 31 January 1970, quoted by Barker and Last.

5 Tilman Westphalen, Afterword to *Schatten in Paradis*, Kiepenheuer & Witsch edition, 1995.

6 Baumer.

7 Julie Gilbert, *Opposite Attraction: The Lives of Erich Maria Remarque and Paulette Goddard*.

8 Fuld and Schneider, *op. cit.*

9 Maria Riva, *op. cit.*

Epilogue (pages 207–211)

1 Report in *Kölnischer Rundschau*, 22 April 1971, quoted by Tilman Westphalen, Afterword to *Schatten in Paradis, op. cit.*

2 *Ibid.*

3 *Ibid.*

4 Wagener, *op. cit.*

5 *Ibid.*

6 *Spandauer Volksblatt,* 3 October 1971, quoted by Tilman Westphalen, Afterword to *Schatten in Paradis, op. cit.*

7 Gilbert, *op. cit.*

8 *Ibid.*

Bibliography

Sources

The diaries and letters of Erich Maria Remarque are deposited in the Erich Maria Remarque Collection in the Fales Library of New York University and in the Erich Maria Remarque-Archive at the Erich Maria Remarque-Friedenszentrum in Osnabrück, Germany.

Transcripts, documents and letters relating to the trial and execution of Elfriede Remark Scholz are deposited in the Bundesarchiv (Federal Archive) in Berlin and have been translated by Anna Dowler.

Books Consulted

Ambrose, Stephen E., *Citizen Soldiers*, New York, Simon & Schuster, 1997.

Bach, Steven, *Marlene Dietrich,* London, HarperCollins, 1992.

Barker, Christine R. & Last, R.W., *Erich Maria Remarque*, London, Oswald Wolff, 1979.

Baumer, Franz, *Erich Maria Remarque,* Berlin, Morgenbuch Verlag, 1994.

Beevor, Antony, *Stalingrad*, London, Viking, 1998.

Behlmer, Rudy (ed.), *Memo from David O. Selznick*, London, Macmillan, 1973.

Bergman, Ingrid & Burgess, Alan, *Ingrid Bergman, My Story,* London, Michael Joseph, 1980.

Brecht, Bertolt, *Journals 1934–55*, London, Methuen, 1993.

Brown, Peter Harry & Pamela Ann, *The MGM Girls*, London, Harrap, 1984.

Dewey, Donald, *James Stewart: A Biography*, Atlanta, Turner Publishing Inc. 1996.

Dietrich Marlene, *Nehmt nur mein Leben ...* Munich, C. Bertelsmann Verlag, 1979.

— *My Life*, London, Weidenfeld & Nicolson, 1989.

— *Marlene Dietrich's ABC*, New York, Frederick Ungar, 1984.

Dunaway, David King, *Huxley in Hollywood*, New York, Harper & Row, 1989.

Eggebrecht, Axel, *Der halbe Weg*, Hamburg, Rowohlt, 1975.

Fairbanks Jr, Douglas, *The Salad Days* London, William Collins, 1988.

Firda, Richard A., *All Quiet on the Western Front: Literary Analysis and Cultural Context*, New York, Twayne Publishers, 1993.

Fischer, Klaus P., *Nazi Germany: A New History*, London, Constable & Co., 1995.

Fitzgerald, F. Scott, *The Letters of F. Scott Fitzgerald*, ed. Andrew Turnbull, London, The Bodley Head, 1964.

— *Three Comrades: A Screenplay,* Carbondale and Edwardsville, Southern Illinois University Press, 1978.

Frewin, Leslie, *Dietrich: The Story of a Star*, London, Leslie Frewin, 1967.

Friedrich, Otto, *City of Nets: A Portrait of Hollywood in the 1940s,* London, Headline, 1988.

Fuld, Werner and Schneider, Thomas F. (ed.), *Sag mir, dass Du mir Liebst* (Correspondence between Erich Maria Remarque and Marlene Dietrich), Kiepenheuer & Witsch, Cologne, 2001.

Gilbert, Julie, *Opposite Attraction: The Lives of Erich Maria Remarque and Paulette Goddard*, New York, Pantheon Books, 1995.

Gilbert, Martin, *Nerer Despaire: Winston Churchill 1945–65*, London, Heinemann, 1988.

Giles, John, *Flanders Then and Now: The Ypres Salient and Passchendaele,* London, Battle of Britain Prints International, 1991.

Gill, Anton, *A Dance Between Flames*, London, John Murray, 1993.

Halliday, Jon, *Sirk on Sirk: Interviews with Jon Halliday*, London, Secker & Warburg, 1971.

Hamilton, Ian, *Writers in Hollywood 1915–51*, London, William Heinemann, 1990.

Henreid, Paul, with Fast, Julius, *Ladies' Man: An Autobiography*, New York, St Martin's Press, 1984.

Higham, Charles, *Marlene*, London, Hart-Davis, MacGibbon Ltd, 1978.

Irving, David, *Goebbels: Mastermind of the Third Reich*, London, Focal Point, 1996.

Isherwood, Christopher, *Diaries, Volume One: 1939–60*, London, Methuen, 1996.

Kershaw, Ian, *Hitler, 1889–1936: Hubris*, London, Allen Lane, The Penguin Press, 1998.

Kessler, Count Harry, *In the Twenties*, London, Weidenfeld & Nicolson, 1971.

Klemperer, Victor, *To the Bitter End; The Diaries of Victor Klemperer, 1942–5*, London, Weidenfeld & Nicolson, 1999.

Kobal, John, *People Will Talk*, London, Aurum Press, 1986.

Lassky, Jesse R., *Whatever Happened to Hollywood?*, New York, Funk & Wagnalls, 1975.

Leamer, Laurence, *As Time Goes By: The Life of Ingrid Bergman*, London, Hamish Hamilton, 1986.

Mann, Thomas, *Tagebücher 1940–42*, Frankfurt am Main, S. Fischer Verlag, 1982.

McDonough, Charles, *Berlin*, London, Sinclair-Stevenson, 1997.

Meredith, Burgess, *So Far, So Good: A Memoir*, Boston, Little, Brown & Company, 1994.

Morley, Sheridan, *Marlene Dietrich*, London, Elm Tree Books, 1976.

Mowrer, Edgar, *Germany Puts the Clock Back*, London, Penguin Books, 1933 and 1938.

Niven, David, *Bring on the Empty Horses*, London, Hamish Hamilton, 1990.

Odets, Clifford, *The Time is Right: 1940 Journal*, New York, Grove Press, 1988.

Owen, C.R., *Erich Maria Remarque: A Critical Bio-Bibliography*, Amsterdam, Rodopi, 1984 – privately printed.

Paris, Barry, *Garbo: A Biography*, London, Sidgwick & Jackson, 1995.

Parish, James Robert and Bowers, Ronald L., *The MGM Stock Company*, Shepperton, Ian Allan Ltd, 1973.

Perry, George, *Sunset Boulevard: From Movie to Musical*, London, Pavilion Books, 1993.

Preminger, Erik Lee, *Gypsy and Me*, London, André Deutsch, 1985.

Ragan, David, *Movie Stars of the '30s*, Englewood Cliffs, New Jersey, Prentice-Hall, Inc., 1985.

Remarque, Erich Maria, *All Quiet on the Western Front*, London, Putnam, 1929.

—*The Road Back*, London, Putnam, 1931.

— *Three Comrades*, London, Hutchinson & Co., 1937.

— *Flotsam*, London, Hutchinson & Co., 1941.

— *Arch of Triumph*, London, Hutchinson & Co., 1946.

— *Spark of Life*, London, Hutchinson & Co., 1952.

— *A Time to Love and A Time to Die*, London, Hutchinson & Co., 1954.

— *The Black Obelisk*, London, Hutchinson & Co., 1957.

— *Heaven Has No Favourites*, London, Hutchinson & Co., 1961.

— *The Night in Lisbon*, London, Hutchinson & Co., 1964.

— *Shadows in Paradise*, London, Hutchinson & Co., 1972.

Reuth, Ralf Georg, *Goebbels*, London, Constable & Co., 1993.

Richie, Alexandra, *Faust's Metropolis*, London, HarperCollins, 1998.

Riefenstahl, Leni, *The Sieve of Time: The Memoirs of Leni Riefenstahl*, London, Quartet Books Ltd., 1992.

Riess, Curt, *Joseph Goebbels*, London, Hollis & Carter, 1949.

Riva, Maria, *Marlene Dietrich*, London, Bloomsbury, 1992.

Robinson, David, *Charles Chaplin: His Life and Art*, New York, McGraw-Hill, 1985.

Romani, Cinzia (translated from the Italian by Robert Connolly), *Tainted Goddesses: Female Film Stars of the Third Reich*, New York, Sarpedon, 1992.

Schneider, Thomas (ed.), *Erich Maria Remarque: Ein militanter Pazifist*, Cologne, Verlag Kiepenheuer & Witsch, 1994.

Schrader, Bärbel, *Der Fall Remarque: Im Westen nichts Neues – eine Dokumentation*, Leipzig, Reclam-Verlag, 1992.

Sherriff, R.C., *No Leading Lady*, London, Victor Gollancz, 1968.

Shirer, William L., *The Rise and Fall of the Third Reich*, London, Secker & Warburg, 1959.

Sikov, Ed, *On Sunset Boulevard: The Life and Times of Billy Wilder*, New York, Hyperion, 1998.

Snyder, Louis L., *Encyclopedia of the Third Reich*, New York, McGraw-Hill Inc., 1976.

Spoto, Donald, *Dietrich*, London, Bantam Press, 1992.

Summerscale, Kate, *The Queen of Whale Cay*, London, Fourth Estate, 1997.

Swenson, Karen, *Greta Garbo: A Life Apart*, New York, Scribner, 1997.

Swindell, Larry, *Charles Boyer*, London, Weidenfeld & Nicolson, 1983.

Taylor, Fred (ed.), *The Goebbels Diaries, 1939–41*, London, Hamish Hamilton, 1982.

Vickers, Hugo, *Cecil Beaton*, London, Weidenfeld & Nicolson, 1985.

Wagener, Hans, *Understanding Erich Maria Remarque,* University of South Carolina Press, 1991.

Walker, Alexander, *Dietrich*, London, Thames & Hudson, 1984.

Winters, Shelley, *The Middle of My Century*, New York, Simon & Schuster, 1990.

Zolotow, Maurice, *Billy Wilder in Hollywood*, New York, Proscenium Publications, 1987.

Zuckmayer, Carl, *A Part of Myself*, London, Secker & Warburg, 1970.

Newspapers, Magazines, Periodicals

Architectural Digest: Academy Award Collector's Edition, April 1992
Daily Express
Daily Telegraph
The Great War – I Was There (part-work)
Los Angeles Times
The Nation and Athenaeum
Newsweek
New York Times
The Observer
Picturegoer
Time
The Times

Index

'EMR' indicates Erich Maria Remarque and 'AQWF'
All Quiet on the Western Front.